Opera Biography Series, No. 11

Series Editors
Andrew Farkas
William R. Moran

Lily Pons at the peak of her popularity in the 1940s, proudly displaying the medals she received for her musical artistry and wartime service. (De Bellis Studios, New York. Ludecke-Pons Collection.)

Lily Pons

A CENTENNIAL PORTRAIT

Edited by James A. Drake and Kristin Beall Ludecke

AMADEUS PRESS
Portland, Oregon

To
Dorothy Coley Johnson and Ruth Riley Drake

Copyright © 1999 by James A. Drake and Kristin Beall Ludecke. All rights reserved.

ISBN 1-57467-047-6

Printed in Hong Kong

Published in 1999 by
Amadeus Press, an imprint of Timber Press, Inc.
The Haseltine Building
133 S.W. Second Avenue, Suite 450
Portland, Oregon 97204, U.S.A.

Library of Congress Cataloging-in-Publication Data
    Lily Pons : a centennial portrait / edited by James A. Drake and Kristin Beall Ludecke.
        p.   cm.—(Opera biography series; no. 11)
    Discography: p. ****
    Includes bibliographical references (p. ****) and index.
    ISBN 1-57467-047-6
    1. Pons, Lily, 1898–1976. 2. Sopranos (Singers)—Biography. I. Drake, James A.
II. Ludecke, Kristin Beall. III. Series.
ML420.P8L5   1999
782.1'092—dc21
   [B]   98-30582
                                               CIP
                                             MN

Contents

PART THREE: The Voice

PART FOUR: Radio and Film

PART FIVE: André

PART SIX: Milestones

PART SEVEN: The Last Prima Donna

CONTENTS

Illustrations follow page 80

Foreword

Beverly Sills

$\mathcal{A}$LTHOUGH I WAS only seven years old when my mother first took me to the Metropolitan Opera House, the opera I saw that afternoon, Delibes's *Lakmé*, gave me a lasting glimpse of a real-life opera star—Lily Pons.

When she made her entrance in the first act, she looked like a beautiful porcelain doll. The Brahman temple and the luxuriant garden that surrounded her on the stage accentuated how tiny she was. And her exotic costume—a silken wrap that clung to her hips, a sheer halter-like top, and nothing but her pure white skin in between—put her incredible figure on display. "Mama! Mama!" I exclaimed when she came onstage. "Her belly button is showing!"

In an era when everyone assumed that opera singers had to be rather large, Lily Pons was an exception because of her petite size. But she was also unique for the quality of her voice. My singing teacher, Estelle Liebling, always told me to pay close attention to Lily's head tones, which were truly bell-like. And her coloratura was amazingly accurate. Her staccatos were perfectly sung and always right on pitch.

She was also an extremely generous lady. Because I was so taken with her, I wrote her fan letters. To my surprise, she wrote back through her secretary and invited my mother and me to come backstage at Carnegie Hall, where she was scheduled to sing a concert. We went, and sure enough, she had left our names with the stage manager and we were taken to meet her. She greeted me as if she had really expected me and told me that she was so delighted that I had come. Then she gave me a present: a tiny silk handkerchief with her initials embroidered on it. It is still one of my treasured keepsakes, from a wonderful artist and a very gentle, warm, and gracious lady.

Although the revival of the bel canto era has been credited to Maria Callas, actually Lily Pons was performing *La fille du régiment*, *La sonnambula*, *Lucia di Lammermoor*, and other mainstays of the bel canto repertoire long before the so-called revival. Although she had a totally different voice than Callas's, Sutherland's, or my own (I like to call Lily's a pure coloratura voice), I personally credit her with bringing those bel canto masterpieces before the public.

Today, a young singer looking at the career of Lily Pons will probably be taken with the glamour of her lifestyle—her jewelry, her trendsetting clothes, her movies, the whole look of her. She lived in glamorous times, although the world doesn't live that way any longer. But her voice, thank heaven, will live on through her recordings. Hopefully, a young singer with a coloratura voice and the technique, precision, and discipline that Lily Pons had, will find inspiration in her recordings and the legacy of technique and beauty of sound they preserve.

Preface

James A. Drake and Kristin Beall Ludecke

*I*N THE AUTUMN of 1997, seven months before the centennial of her birth, Lily Pons was selected by the United States Postal Service as one of four legendary singers whose portraits now adorn a special series of U.S. postage stamps—the others being Richard Tucker, Rosa Ponselle, and Lawrence Tibbett. When the Metropolitan Opera and the Postal Service jointly celebrated the first-day issue on 10 September 1997, the family members, descendants, and personal representatives of the honorees gathered at the Metropolitan Opera House to mark the historic occasion.

Despite the presence in opera bibliographies of three commercial biographies of Rosa Ponselle, two of Lawrence Tibbett, and a biography plus a PBS television documentary of Richard Tucker, no book-length treatment of Lily Pons's life and career was available as her centennial approached. Two decades earlier, a biography had been contemplated—during 1976 and 1977, William Seward compiled a detailed outline for such a book in collaboration with Claire Lily Girardot, the soprano's niece—but nothing came of the project, and both collaborators are now deceased.

This volume is intended not only to fill a void in operatic literature, but especially to celebrate the one-hundredth anniversary of Lily Pons's birth. Fortunately, the diligence with which her family, friends, and close associates (especially the late Flora Adler, an Oklahoman who revered the soprano) amassed a documentary record of Lily's career was matched in later years by William Seward, in whose care the scrapbooks, photographs, costumes, and other Lily Pons memorabilia were eventually entrusted.

After Seward's untimely death, the settlement of his estate might have led to the dismemberment of the collection had not Carl and Cheryl Ludecke, the parents of co-editor Kristin Beall Ludecke, purchased the entire collection. Through their substantial efforts, consequently, a record of Lily Pons's life and career has been preserved for future researchers and enthusiasts.

During the preparation of this book, the help of many others was both necessary and invaluable, and we extend our sincere thanks to those who (in alphabetical order) granted interviews, supplied or helped obtain access to photographs, letters, and other documentation, and otherwise gave of their time and expertise as we assembled the contents of this book: Lucine Amara, William Ashbrook, Rose Bampton, Sue Chadwick (Ralph Edwards Productions), Louise Coley, Plácido Domingo, Hazel Eaton, Carl Edwards, Andrew Farkas, Christina (Kiki) Pons Girardot, Roger Gross, Jerome Hines, Lawrence F. Holdridge, Alfred Hubay, Paul Jackson, George Jellinek, Hugh M. Johns, Thomas G. Kaufman, Boris Kostelanetz, Richard Kostelanetz, Lillian Krieger, Michelle Krisel, Lorenzo (Larry) Malfatti, James B. McPherson, Marilyn Mercur, Robert Merrill, Anna Moffo, William R. Moran, Patrice Munsel, Doris O'Connell, Bill Park, John Pennino, Roberta Peters, Jane Ramsey-Carter, Regina Resnik, Bidú Sayão, Beverly Sills, Risë Stevens, Blanche Thebom, Charles Thomas, John T. Trutter, Robert Tuggle, Anna Vester, and Edgar Vincent. Posthumously, we also acknowledge the late Milton Cross, Myron Ehrlich, Claire Lily Girardot, Gustave Haenschen, Helen Jepson, Nina Morgana and her husband, Bruno Zirato, Helen Olheim, Edward Hagelin Pearson, Wilfrid Pelletier, Rosa Ponselle, Max de Schauensee, and especially William Seward.

We also wish to thank Mary Lou Wade and Laura Cisco, of the University of Central Florida staff, for technical assistance during the preparation of the manuscript.

But our greatest debt by any measure, whether as authors or as individuals, is to our respective families—most notably Magali (Mrs. James A.) Drake, and Cheryl and Carl Ludecke—for their extraordinary help and support throughout the writing of this book. Mere thanks, unfortunately, falls far short of expressing the true measure of our gratitude to them.

Introduction

James A. Drake and Kristin Beall Ludecke

ONE HUNDRED YEARS after her birth, Lily Pons has a secure place in modern operatic history. As *The New York Times* and other major newspapers wrote when she died in 1976, Pons transcended opera and entered the popular culture of her time: she was a *prima donna assoluta* in opera, a trendsetting figure in the world of glamour and fashion, and one of the most written-about celebrities of her era—a distinction that relatively few opera singers ever have attained.

No doubt her aggressive publicists (the Constance Hope agency initially, and later the Muriel Francis firm) did much to further her image and fame, but they never had to exaggerate Lily Pons's achievements. Those were extraordinary by any measure. A press kit from Columbia Artists Management summarized Pons's career at the end of World War II:

> From the great opera houses of New York, Paris, London, San Francisco, to the farthest outpost that has a radio, she is the favorite singer of the age. To little Mexican children clinging to the open windows of a Matamoras concert hall, to Chinese laborers edging in on a ring of pilots on a dusty airfield in western Hunan province, to "gallery girls" hanging from the highest seats in some Midwestern arena, the sight of Lily Pons—diminutive, gracious, exquisite—is, like the sound of her voice, one of the rich memories of our lifetime.
>
> From the day of her triumphant debut at the Metropolitan Opera in 1931, as a little French girl then completely unknown, she has pursued a career of endless fascination. She became the star who could draw 360,000 persons to Grant Park in Chicago to hear her, some of them waiting all day long. She became the legendary figure for whom towns, railroad trains, perfumes, hats and even sundaes are named. She became—and for Lily Pons it is her proudest designation— "The Singing Heroine of World War II."
>
> At the war's outbreak, despite the necessity of guarding a priceless voice, the valiant little prima donna turned her back upon footlight glamour and profitable engagements. And for more than 100,000 miles she went around the globe and up and down strange trails to sing for American GIs. A million soldiers

and sailors remember her—from the torrid Persian Gulf where she swathed her head in wet towels between songs, to the penetrating cold of the Belgian front. And B-29 crews now long dispersed will forever tell that she was the first woman performer to visit their remote bases in western China, flying the perilous "Hump" in the Himalayas, chained to a bucket seat.

Among the leading opera houses of the world in which she has appeared are those in Paris, London, Buenos Aires, Rio de Janeiro, Mexico City, San Francisco and Chicago. With her husband, the famous orchestral conductor André Kostelanetz, she has covered five of the world's continents.[1]

That was in 1946. She had already been a Metropolitan Opera superstar for fifteen years, and she would remain a top draw for another twelve. In 1956, she celebrated her silver anniversary at the Met, her high notes intact and her singing still able to rekindle memories of her debut.

Two years later, in 1958, Lily retired from the Metropolitan, and in November of that year she ended her twenty-year marriage to André Kostelanetz, whose long career had intertwined with hers during the world war and whose popularity, like hers, bridged both classical and popular music. Earlier in her career Lily had divorced her first husband, Dutch publisher and sometime-painter August Mesritz, but it had had no impact on her burgeoning fame. Although she was at the end of her career when she divorced Kostelanetz, her popularity again remained unaffected; by then she had added to her dossier (and to an already stratospheric income approaching $1 million annually) a series of lucrative guest appearances on popular television shows hosted by Perry Como, Dinah Shore, Jimmy Durante, and others.

Lily used television to keep herself in the public eye in the 1950s, just as she had used the newspapers and newsreels in the 1930s. When newspapers of that era had noted a resemblance between Pons and Adele Astaire (sister and vaudeville dancing partner of Fred), Lily eagerly posed with Adele for the photographers. Twenty years later, when television commentators took note of a resemblance between Pons and comedienne Imogene Coca, Sid Caesar's partner on the top-rated *Your Show of Shows*, Lily capitalized on the moment by having her publicists wangle an invitation to guest-star on Caesar's show in 1953. In a skit written for Lily by a staff of writers that included Neil Simon, Carl Reiner, and Mel Brooks, among others, she and Imogene Coca played their resemblance to the hilt, dressing as look-alikes in a Broadway skit. Other television appearances confirmed Lily's superstar status: a special installment of *This Is Your Life* in September 1953 and an "at home" interview in 1954 with Edward R. Morrow on his acclaimed CBS series, *Person to Person*. Those were the Eisenhower years, and Lily's close wartime ties to the general-turned-president brought her recurring White House invitations, including two to sing at events at Eisenhower's inaugurations. Such appearances only added to the luster of her celebrity.

By the late 1950s, however, Lily Pons's status as a *prima donna assoluta*, as well as an increasing share of her newspaper coverage, were being dwarfed by the looming presence of Maria Callas. Despite a comparatively limited opera career in the United States, Callas's large, molten, sometimes erratic voice and her smoldering interpretations of otherwise-staid coloratura heroines soon reduced Lily Pons's style of singing to an anachronism. And during the 1960s, Callas's tempestuous affair with Aristotle Onassis and her self-destructive wars with opera managers and the press—and even her mother—seemed to make "Little Lily" (as the Depression-era press had affectionately dubbed Pons) a doll-like remnant of yesterday's news.

Maria Callas would be displaced eventually, too—less by any operatic rivals, arguably, than by Jacqueline Kennedy, who supplanted Callas in Onassis's affections and eventually married him. In opera, meanwhile, Joan Sutherland, *La stupenda*, and Beverly Sills, to whom Pons had been an inspiration during girlhood, furthered the momentum Callas had begun, and in so doing put more distance between the era of Lily Pons and what was now being called the bel canto revival.

At the peak of that revival, Lily Pons decided to launch one of her own: on 31 May 1972, she emerged from retirement to sing a concert in New York City's expansive Philharmonic Hall. André Kostelanetz had encouraged her to do so, and he reunited with her to conduct the orchestra that evening. By the next morning, Lily's trim physique and still-phenomenal voice returned her to the front pages once again. "If those who know her long and well could scarcely believe what they saw," Irving Kolodin wrote in *The Saturday Review*, "they were truly taken aback by what they heard. It was a kind of afterglow, a final flaring up of the barely smoldering vocal flame, a stirring about of the all but exhausted embers."[2] The concert was Lily Pons's calculated way of reminding the public what life had been like before Callas and Sutherland, and the event itself passed quickly into operatic lore.

More than two decades after her death, Lily Pons evokes memories of a glamorous era, and her name still resonates with the public. In these pages her life and career are reconstructed in the words of those who performed with her, those who covered her career in the press, and those whose lives or careers she influenced. Together, they form a mosaic of one of the most popular singers of the twentieth century.

PART ONE

Beginnings

CHAPTER ONE

My Early Life

Lily Pons

In the autumn of 1930, Lily Pons arrived in New York City from her native France. She made her Metropolitan Opera debut in *Lucia di Lammermoor* on the afternoon of Saturday, 3 January 1931. Almost from the start, she became a favorite of the public and press and a *force majeur* in the Metropolitan's Italian repertoire. Her effect on New York society was no less instantaneous: as a columnist for *Independent Woman* wrote in November 1931, from the time Lily arrived in the city it seemed as if midtown Manhattan "had been invaded by a small cyclone."

Printed accounts of Pons's childhood vary, often wildly, depending on the imaginative powers of the source of the information—usually her publicists, though occasionally Lily herself. The events she recounts in these pages, however, are consistent with the documentary record, and they have an immediacy that many printed versions of her childhood and musical beginnings lack. We begin Lily Pons's story in her own words.[1]

W̲E̲ A̲R̲E̲ O̲F̲T̲E̲N̲ T̲O̲L̲D̲ that the habits of adult life are formed during early childhood. If true, then three of my habits—my insistence on punctuality, my love of animals, and my liking for clothes—were shaped very early in my life.

Into life itself, it seems, I managed to arrive early: I was a seven-months' baby when a midwife helped my mother usher me into this world. My mother, whom I have always called "Maman" (as French children do), told me that I was born with thick reddish-brown hair, and with two teeth already in place. I also entered the world with what in French we call a *cale*, or membrane that covers the head at birth; the *cale*, along with my two baby teeth, were considered omens of a healthy and happy life.

Probably because I was so tiny after only seven months in the womb, my parents became concerned that I might be too sickly to live. They took me to the doctor, who looked at my thick hair and my two teeth and said to my mother, "Madame Pons, had this baby waited two months more to be born, she would have come into the world wearing shoes and a skirt!"

My mother's maiden name was Maria Naso. She was born in the south of Italy and she married my father, Auguste Pons, when she was seventeen. Her father—my grandfather, Jean-Baptiste Naso—had been a blacksmith in Italy but had moved his family to Draguignan, near Cannes, when he was still a relatively young man. In and around Cannes he became known for his artistry as a wrought-iron designer.

My parents were living at my grandfather's large farm when I was born in 1905.[2] I spent nearly every day of my childhood happily surrounded, three times a day at the dining table, by fifteen Nasos who were either aunts, uncles, cousins, sisters, or brothers of my mother. My father liked and was liked by all of them because of his adventurous spirit and enthusiasm for anything new.

Automobiles were then a new phenomenon, and the French and Germans were leading its development. My father, a skilled mechanic (one would say he was an engineer in today's parlance), had been bitten by the automobile bug and would often come home in one of the new motor cars that he helped design and test.

One that I especially remember was a bright red wagon with a loud engine that belched smoke and made horrible noises that frightened me. Papa told me that it was a police wagon, and one day it would make horses obsolete. (That did not please me because I didn't want to see anything happen to the horses that my grandfather and the rest of the family kept and used for transportation.) In time, my father became a famous race-car driver, and when I was still a toddler he entered a marathon race from Paris to Peking. He became stranded, however, in Tibet when the automobile broke down. Fortunately, he returned home to us safely.[3]

Papa was fascinated by animals, and to my delight was always bringing me pets. By the time I was five years old I had a guinea pig, a canary and two para-keets, a little white mouse, a piglet, a dog and a cat, and even a frog that I trained to jump like the one in the famous story by Mark Twain. Once an animal lover, always an animal lover—and anyone who knows me will tell you that I am hap-piest when surrounded by the many pets I keep.

My penchant not only for being punctual but, preferably, for arriving early wherever I am expected, might have stemmed from my first attempt at going to school. When I say "first attempt" I don't mean that (as Americans say) I flunked. No, I simply arrived at the school at the age of three years old rather than the cus-tomary age of six or seven.

I had gathered some books together and toted them in a small basket to the nearby school, which adjoined a convent. I went there and knocked on the con-vent door, and when the nuns came to answer it I informed them that I wanted to go to school. When they gently asked if I didn't think I was a bit too young for school, I answered impetuously, "But I'm old enough to go to the bathroom alone, so why can't I go to school alone?" I wasn't persuasive enough, however, and had to wait another three years before I could start my education.

My liking for clothes, especially unique designs, traces back to my school days. For the first few years of my life, until I was about five, Maman always dressed me in simple clothes that invariably were pale blue and white. Later, I learned that she had prayed to the Virgin for a healthy baby girl, and in tribute to the Madonna my mother dressed me in the traditional colors of the Virgin Mary.

After so many blue-and-white dresses I began to rebel, especially when it came time for me to start school. To please me, Maman and Papa had a complete new outfit custom-made for me on my sixth birthday: everything was bright red, including the dress, jacket, gloves, hat, and even the shoes. Those my father had commissioned from a shoemaker friend of his, and they too were bright red—a novelty at the time, especially for a six-year old child, because dyeing leather red was not as easy then as it is nowadays.

I loved those shoes dearly—until some of my schoolmates began teasing me about my "little red feet." Some of them even went so far as to nickname me "partridge feet." That was too much for my young sensibilities—so I came home and threw the shoes into the fireplace! Even though today I have racks full of beautifully designed shoes, I must confess that because of that teasing, footwear is not something I find much interest in.

As for the rest of my clothing, then as now I took a meticulous approach to how I was dressed. Even as a very young girl, I would wash my blouse, my gloves, and my dress stockings. (My father bought me my first pair of silk stockings when I was about ten.) I would get up early in the morning so I could iron everything I intended to wear that day. Although I don't really have to iron anything myself anymore (I still do it occasionally, just to keep my touch), I am just as meticulous about my clothing today as I was during my girlhood.

Birthdays have always been important to me, but one stands out because it shaped my future life. On the morning of my ninth birthday, I was looking forward to the party my parents were to give me that afternoon. With no warning, a water pipe burst in our home and flooded the kitchen and dining room. In all the confusion, my sister Nanette banged her knee and shrieked for help, while our little terrier got tangled in the draperies, tearing them down.

Papa was away and Maman was busy soothing Nanette. That afternoon was to have been my first real birthday party, and I started to cry because I was sure that nothing could be done to clean up the mess in time for my little friends to attend a party. But our maid, Louise—unruffled Louise Mertel, our factotum for years—took charge, and by two o'clock the plumbers had come and gone. By three the floors were neatly waxed, and by four the curtains were in place, the table was set, and my party had started.

At dinnertime the household was back to a smooth routine. Mother asked Louise: "How did you do it? How did you manage? How do you *always* manage to get *everything* done?"

"I wouldn't know, Madame," Louise replied placidly. "I never ponder. I just start."

Those words "just start" turned into a magic wand that opened the way to my American career, to my American citizenship, and many other things dear to my heart.

The first effects were immediate. I was then still a schoolgirl, but I stopped putting off homework. Later, when I was studying the piano, I made a point of practicing the most difficult passages first. Long before I began to pursue a profession in which a lack of precision and alertness could jeopardize one's career, punctuality had become second nature.

Yet, only gradually as I grew up did I understand the full wisdom of Louise's casual reply—that stalling doesn't do our work, that hesitation doesn't solve our problems, that to hold our own in this world we have to roll up our sleeves and "just start," headlong.

My father moved us from Cannes to Paris near the time the World War began. Although he had planned to continue his budding career as a race driver, he was conscripted into the army and was among the first troops that were sent to the front lines. To our horror, he was gassed by the Germans and his lungs were permanently damaged by the effects of the mustard gas. He was to live only three years more, during all of which time he was in and out of hospitals.[4]

After Papa's death, our little family (my two younger sisters, Nanette and

Christine, or "Kiki," were born not long before he entered the army) lacked a steady source of income and it fell to Maman to find a way to support us. She turned one room of our little home into a dressmaking shop, and somehow we got by. Doubtless that is where my love of fashion and attention to well-made clothes stemmed from, because my sisters and I became nearly expert as seamstresses. Mother even made enough of an income to keep me in music lessons, as I was then studying the piano and was judged to have some musical promise. I was a promising enough pianist to be able to enter the Paris Conservatoire when I was thirteen.

One day in the summer of 1918, my mother, who had joined the Red Cross as a nurse, asked me to play at her hospital for the wounded soldiers. My program of light classics went off reasonably well, but as I was taking my bow a voice called out in broken French: "Why don't you sing us a song?"

I had sung a little at school but never before an audience. I hesitated.

"I'll think about it—perhaps some other time—" I stammered. But then an inner voice commanded: "Why 'think about it'? Start!"

I started with a Meridional folk song; the patients applauded. I tried "Madelon"; the acclaim grew. And as I sang I began to realize that no manufactured instrument could establish such personal contact with an audience as this most miraculous instrument of all, the human voice.

But it was drama and acting that had interested me before I discovered the beauty of singing. At fourteen—although I looked about eleven or twelve—I had obtained an audition with the troupe founded by Max D'Erly[5] at the Théâtre des Variétés. Max D'Erly, that great man and excellent producer, gave me a chance and for three years I performed under his direction. I played ingénues most of the time, and now and then I had an opportunity to play light comedic roles.

Throughout my early teens, especially after Papa died and we lost the security of his income, I had said to myself that I would marry a very rich man who would give me a big, beautiful house and a horse to ride in the Bois [de Boulogne]. Perhaps I said it to myself so many times that I fulfilled my own prophecy when I married August Mesritz—my first beau and, as it turned out, my first husband.

I met him at the beach near Cannes, where he was vacationing and I had been visiting my grandfather and my Nasos relatives. He was thirty-nine years old, a widower, and he had a little son, Jean. It was actually the boy who, so to speak, introduced his father to me. I was amusing myself lying in the sand at the beach when I heard a little boy—Jean, it turned out—say aloud, "Papa! Come see the pretty lady with the tiny feet like Mother's!"

Until his father apologized for the little boy's comments—explaining in the meanwhile that his wife, the boy's mother, had died only recently—I had no idea what prompted little Jean's comment. To my great surprise I learned that the boy's mother had been exactly my size (she even wore a size 1-1/2 shoe—my own shoe size!) and, even more amazingly, her name was Lily. I regarded all of those things as more than sheer coincidence, and almost as soon as I came to know August Mesritz, I decided I was going to marry him. I was sixteen when he and I were married in October 1921.[6]

Overnight, my life changed for the better. My new husband, a lawyer who had become very successful as a publisher, provided me not only with the handsome little boy from his earlier marriage, but also a large, well-decorated home with servants to take care of our needs. True to my teenage dream, he even bought me a horse to ride at my leisure!

Although we eventually divorced, I owe August Mesritz a great debt because it was he who encouraged a singing career for me. We had been married about four years by then, and I was spending my much-appreciated leisure time (afforded, thankfully, by his large income) learning to sketch and paint, doing petit point, and pursuing other pleasing avocations. As I still played the piano a great deal, my interest in music was obvious to my husband, and he encouraged me to take some singing lessons. He had heard me sing around the house and saw the pleasure that singing gave me.

When I inquired about singing teachers from some of the friends I had made in the D'Erly troupe, I decided to contact Mme Dyna Beirner-Sellier of the Opéra-Comique. She was in Cannes and I took my first lessons with her. After several of our sessions, I was pleased to hear her tell my husband that my singing voice had more than a little promise. It was then that my husband decided I needed a permanent teacher—and through his contacts we learned of Alberti de Gorostiaga, a Basque with a growing reputation as a teacher in Paris.

As is now well known, Señor Alberti became my teacher and shaped my voice and singing for an operatic career. He was at my side when I made my debut in a provincial theater near Cannes, and he has remained at my side ever since.

CHAPTER TWO

Lily Pons in France

Andrew Farkas

S "We learn with great pleasure of the forthcoming theatrical debut," a Cannes newspaper announced in November 1927, "of our gracious fellow citizen, Miss Lily Pons, who will sing at the end of the month at the Grand-Théâtre of Mulhouse." It was there on 25 November 1927 that the twenty-nine-year-old soprano made her debut in *Lakmé*, soon following it with three other successes in *Die Zauberflöte*, *Hänsel und Gretel*, and *Les contes d'Hoffmann*.

Although acclaimed by critics for her performances with provincial opera companies throughout France, she garnered no offers from the Paris Opéra or the Opéra-Comique; in fact, her first appearance in the French capital would not come until May 1933, when Pierre Monteux engaged her for a concert with the Paris Symphony Orchestra.

Andrew Farkas, biographer of Enrico Caruso, Lawrence Tibbett, Titta Ruffo, and most recently Jussi Björling, traces the development of Lily Pons's career in France, from her first documented appearances until her departure on the *S. S. Ile de France*, bound for New York City and an audition with the Metropolitan Opera Company. Farkas draws upon the French reviews that Marie Pons, Lily's mother, collected from the start of her daughter's career.

*T*HE LABEL "overnight star," overworked though it may be, aptly describes Lily Pons's 1927 operatic debut in her homeland, just as it would nearly four years later when she created a sensation at the Metropolitan Opera in *Lucia di Lammermoor*. There was, of course, a chasmlike difference in the magnitude of the two debuts, just as there was in the reputations of the critics who reviewed them on either side of the Atlantic—differences that surely were not lost on Lily Pons, who had an acute awareness of the marquee value of reviews from big-name critics. Perhaps for that reason, she exhibited little interest in revisiting the reviews of her early performances in France once she became the darling of American audiences. Instead, she tucked away her early press notices in the small leatherbound scrapbooks in which her mother had collected them. Fortunately, the scrapbooks have been preserved and are now accessible, thanks to the collectors who own them.[1]

The first memento Maman Pons appears to have saved from the start of her daughter's career is an undated, unidentified newspaper review of a three-act *fantaisie musicale et burlesque* at the Théâtre des Variétés entitled *Ohé! Cupidon!*, with libretto by Maurice Hannequin and music by Marcel Pollet. At that early point in her development, Lily was gaining stage experience as an ingénue in plays produced by Max D'Erly at the Théâtre des Variétés. In *Ohé! Cupidon!* she did a turn as a comedienne, and her performance earned Lily a special mention for her "very clever mischievousness."

The next entry in the scrapbooks, also undated and unidentified, may well be a newspaper account of her first attempt at singing in public, at a veterans' hospital during World War I.[2] In any event, the clipping is the first musical notice of Lily Pons's career—but, it would seem from the article, as an amateur pianist, not as a singer. Strictly speaking, she was not yet "Lily" Pons, according to the reporter who covered the event at the Bellevue Hospital in Cannes. "Last Tuesday," the clipping reads, "a successful matinee concert took place at this health institution. On the program, Miss Alice Pons, the talented young musician, played *La Tosca* with consummate artistry. . . . A magic act brought to an end this event for the wounded and sick of the hospital, attended by a number of elegant listeners wishing to add their goodwill and devotion."

These two clippings appear to be the only newspaper notices that either of the Ponses, Maman or Lily herself, retained from her pre-operatic career. The next clipping is the November 1927 announcement of her debut at the Grand-Théâtre of Mulhouse in Alsace. The article, which appeared in *L'Éclaireur de Nice* on 8 November, describes her voice as having "remarkable clarity and extension" and predicts that she "will surely receive the success her proven talent deserves."

Along with other Mulhouse dailies, *La France de l'Est* listed on 20–21 November 1927 the forthcoming opera performances, stating that on Friday, 25 November, the first performance of *Lakmé* would take place with "Miss Lili Pons of the Opera San Carlo of Naples." (This spelling of her name would not be replaced with the now-familiar Lily until slightly later in her budding career.) The unexpected reference to a theatrical affiliation between Pons and the San Carlo is a surprise indeed, and it would occasionally find its way into other early notices that Lily received. There was no truth to it, however, as the singer clarified herself in later years: "They announced me as a singer of the San Carlo of Napoli," she wrote, "and I said, 'How can you lie that way?'"[3]

The 26 November 1927 issue of the German-language *Mülhauser Tageblatt* declared the *Lakmé* performance a "complete success." The voice of the tenor who sang the role of Gérald, identified in the review as "Mr. Villabella of the Opéra-Comique," was judged "full of vigor and youthful freshness of rare beauty," while "the voice of Miss Lili Pons is not particularly strong, but it has sublime charm and a most accomplished technique so that her singing made a profound impression. The Bell Song of the second act unleashed in the auditorium such a tempest of applause that she had to encore the second half [of the aria]." The *Express du Midi* of the same date called the performance "a gala, for once deserving that name," resulting in "triumphant ovations" for the principal singers.

In the columns of *L'Alsace* on 27 November, Lily received her first extended review:

> Miss Pons of the Opera of Naples was engaged especially to interpret the role of Lakmé. And the auditorium was enthused by such grace and such skill, the unspeakable ravishment that passes over us—much too seldom, unfortunately—when we can applaud a true star. Miss Pons truly has everything, looks, grace, litheness, voice. What a tender, moving image of the "daughter of the gods" she offered to our enchanted eyes! One could not imagine with more nobility and lightness of expression the chaste and proud Lakmé.

The reference to "our enchanted eyes" might have betrayed an attraction on the reviewer's part for assets other than the Pons voice; if so, it was merely the first of many instances in which a local reviewer would be similarly smitten. Whatever the case, this critic—unnamed, perhaps fearing that his readers might misinterpret the nature of his enthusiasm for the new young singer—put pen to paper and, in prose as purple as the lining of a vintner's barrel, described the Pons voice as follows:

> Blessed be the divine lute-maker who could with such love and skill cut this crystal into the purest and incomparable instrument. Miss Pons uses it as Paga-

nini must have used his violin. . . . One must hear Miss Pons sing the Bell Song. One then knows what singing is, that this is a voice that seems like a clear spring that gushes forth without any apparent effort, whose clear waves cascade with silvery laughter over the thousand obstacles that a discerning composer scatters throughout his score. The legend of the daughter of the pariahs was delivered superbly, and in the third act we had a magnificent high E, pure, clear, like a beautiful crystal.

Young Lily's onstage manners also came in for high compliments: "The graceful artist received in the second act the tribute of an immense basket of flowers, which she plucked to offer, in a gracious gesture, a stem to each of her colleagues surrounding her. This spontaneous act produced a thunder of applause."[4] Spontaneous or not, this extra bit of stage business illustrates that even at the start of her career, Lily had learned how to hold an audience's attention—even after the curtain fell.

The performance's Gérald merited only one sentence in the *L'Alsace* review of 27 November: "Mr. Villabella, the delightful tenor of the Opéra-Comique, came expressly from Paris to sing . . . and made us admire his talent." Miguel Villabella would eventually earn his own share of solid reviews. Six years older than Lily, he was born in 1892 in Bilbao and was now on the brink of a distinguished career. Son of a well-known Spanish baritone, he had first trained for a career in business. While employed in Paris, he was overheard singing by the celebrated Lucien Fugère, who encouraged him to train his voice and also gave him singing lessons. (Villabella also later studied with Jacques Isnardon, the Algiers-born bass who, quite remarkably, began his career as a tenor.)

Villabella's stage debut came in 1918 as Cavaradossi, in Poitiers, and he joined the Opéra-Comique in 1920. His recording career began in 1925. Judging from his records he was an accomplished, stylish singer, with a ravishing, easy top, polished phrasing, and sufficient individuality to distinguish himself from a generous supply of French or French-trained tenors of native and foreign origins. In June 1928 he would become a member of the Grand Opéra of Paris, singing Pinkerton to Fanny Heldy's Madama Butterfly.

At age thirty-six, when he sang Gérald to Pons's Lakmé, Villabella was a worthy partner for the ambitious young soprano. The *Mulhouse Illustré* wrote of him: "Miguel de Villabella, who often performs this role at the Opéra-Comique, came to us preceded by a glorious reputation, and he sustained it brilliantly. This is a tenor with a marvelously sonorous voice, pure timbre, full and youthful, with manly presence (if not with an irresistible physique), and with acting as warm as the voice!"

The *Illustré* did not spare Lily her own share of the accolades when summarizing her performances (four in all) of *Lakmé*:

It was a revelation [to hear] this delightful and light-voiced singer who seems to have inherited the marvelous gifts of her professors: Mr. Alfred Sellier of the Opéra, and certainly those of his wife, Dyna Beirner of the Opéra-Comique. If, in the middle register, the volume sometimes seemed a little thin and demanding some respectful indulgence from the orchestra, by contrast the top is magnificent. One could not dream of more skillful, pure, pearl-like vocalism than Miss Lili Pons let us hear in the Bell Song. The musicianship of this remarkable artist is equaled by the sincerity of her acting. She made Lakmé moving and adorably sensitive, and her success grew from performance to performance.

In her next assignment, Olympia in *Les contes d'Hoffmann*, Pons was the only guest artist in a cast made up entirely of local singers. The spelling of her name in the reviews has now changed to Lily, although "Lili" would still make an appearance from time to time. In the judgment of the reviewer from *La France de l'Est* on 10 December 1927, "Miss Lily Pons consecrated the golden tones of her expressive soprano to the role of Olympia and an aerial limpidity of her vocalises: she offered to excess the most charming aspects of Spalanzani's mechanical doll."

The German-language *Volksblatt* two days later found her Olympia "excellent," and *L'Express*, on 13 December, labeled her voice and characterization "delicious," admiring especially "the pearls rippling in her vocalises." Another German newspaper, *Mülhauser Tageblatt*, wrote on the 12th: "Olympia was this time assigned to Miss L. Pons, whose pleasing appearance made her well suited for the role. She handles the mechanical doll well, and one knows the almost flawless clarity of her light, flexible, and pearly voice even in the highest coloratura reaches from her Lakmé. She was met with great [audience] approval."

As if to top any prior reviews, the 12 December issue of *L'Alsace* cast all caution to the wind. "This young artist is simply ideal," wrote the unnamed music critic. "What purity . . . exudes from her entire being! And the voice! Ah, that voice of divine sweetness that captivates us to such extent that one would gladly have stayed to listen to it for hours. What a formidable success!" Against such a background the brief report in *La Dépêche* on 24 December 1927 seems faint praise indeed: "The doll Olympia could not have had a better interpreter."

The *Journal d'Alsace et de Lorraine* handed the palm to her without hesitation in its 30 December edition.

The main attraction of this performance unquestionably was the presence of Miss Lili Pons, of the Opera San Carlo of Naples, in the role of Olympia. Fragile and slim, the mouth in a slight smile, the glance fixed yet captivating, the gestures jerky yet expressive, one could say it was a veritable doll so full of life that she was able by her charm and grace to set a poet ablaze.

The operatic highlight of the 1927 Christmas season was, perhaps not surprisingly, Humperdinck's *Hänsel und Gretel*. In the female half of the title role, Lily, by now a local favorite, gathered her usual laurels. *La France de l'Est* wrote on 28 December: "Miss Lily Pons's cheerful silvery voice was marvelous, as was her physique and blond tresses and red stockings." The *Mülhauser Volksblatt*, reviewing a performance that took place a few days earlier on 19 December, added, "Madame Lili Pons created an ideal Gretel, that lovely creature, just as the poet had conceived her." Reviewing the same performance, but taking note of one limitation of the youthful Pons voice, the *Republicain* said on 20 December 1927: "Miss Lily Pons was a most girlish Gretel and her fluid, somewhat smallish voice was ideal for this role."

Gretel, however, was not what the local public seemed to want to hear—and see—Lily sing. By popular request, the opera administration felt obliged to schedule additional performances of *Lakmé* for her. When she returned to the role on the evening of 26 December, an article in *La France de l'Est* stated:

> The performance Wednesday evening enjoyed an exceptional explosion [of applause], surely thanks to—I could say "exclusively" to—the presence of Miss Lili Pons, whom we have already admired and applauded as the doll in *Les contes d'Hoffmann*. This delightful and seductive artist imbued the entire role with infinite charm; with her nothing is left to chance; the gestures, the expressions, all translate into a profound study and a very great skill in scenic art. As for the singer, she is beyond all praise. Her voice is pure crystal with an infinitely harmonious and captivating timbre, served by the most irreproachable, most impeccable technique. It is ravishing to hear.

By the beginning of the new year, *Comoedia* pronounced the verdict for this new young singer and in so doing reflected a consensus that every other newspaper and periodical had helped forge. The Mulhouse season, said *Comoedia* in its 8 January 1928 edition, had yielded "a remarkable discovery: that of Miss Lili Pons who, until now unknown in France, triumphed in front of full houses in Mulhouse. Miss Pons, for whom we predict a most beautiful future . . . possesses a voice of extraordinarily clarity, even in the highest reaches, and a remarkable style."

The 29–30 January 1928 issue of *L'Alsace* began its review of *Die Zauberflöte* rejoicing in the return of Pons for her fourth and last role of the season, the Queen of the Night. After devoting several paragraphs to the analysis of Mozart's music, the critic continues: "One saw with pleasure the return of Miss Pons, who has come back to us in full possession of her exceptional gifts and self-assuredness.

The vocal presentation of the Queen of the Night presents great difficulties that she surmounted without any notable effort."

In several local papers it was reported that Lily, among many other artists, sang at the Franco-Russian gala, "La Nuit du Prince Pâle," at the Casino Municipal in Cannes. Because of the number of performers, the reviewers accorded her only brief mention, one making reference to her "crystal pure voice," and another describing her rendering of Saint-Saëns's "Le rossignol et la rose" (The Nightingale and the Rose) as a "delightful nightingale whose voice surely hastens the arrival of spring."

On Saturday, 7 April 1928, *L'Éclaireur de Nice* published a brief notice that "This evening . . . Miss Lily Pons will sing *Lakmé* on the stage of the Casino Municipal. The large number of admirers of the delightful and talented artist will learn of this news with pleasure and will be doubtless ready to assure her the success she deserves." Two days later the same newspaper wrote:

Let's say up front that the debut was a true triumph. The listener was seduced from the first act on by the charm and freshness of a ravishing organ and an incarnation full of poetry and mystery, the personage of the young Hindu woman that perhaps we could not foresee so happily evoked. The public, seduced already in the first act, went completely crazy in the second, as she not only sang the Bell Song most brilliantly, crowning it with a high E that not everyone sings, but she phrased so poetically, so movingly, so caressingly "Dans la forêt près de nous" in an adorable manner, with rare beauty and a truly marvelous phrasing. The third act confirmed the impression that Mme Lily Pons is a born artist.

The columns of *Le Petit Niçois* confirmed this judgment in its 9 April issue:

Delibes's work is certainly not without interest, but one must say without hesitation that the principal attraction of this brilliant evening was provided by the most charming Miss Lily Pons. The public of Cannes wanted especially to prove its sympathy and admiration by paying homage to one of its compatriots of whom they are rightly proud. Miss Pons in fact deserves the most flattering compliments.

Her prior successes at Mulhouse and Strasbourg already projected a certain knowledge of singing, but to debut on our stage with *Lakmé* seemed, let's confess, a gamble. . . . Thus it is with infinite pleasure that we make honorable amends and we direct toward Miss Pons the most sincere encomiums. In the totality of the work she was astonishing in her ability to employ artistically all the attractive qualities of her voice and exquisite musical charm, complemented by a supple and pleasing organ. The Bell Song, a great stumbling block for a singer, was exquisite and marvelously delivered. Miss Pons was obliged to give an encore in the midst of general enthusiasm; the triumphant reception was the just reward well deserved by her great talent.

31

This time the reviewer spread the praise among the other principals in the cast, commending in equal measure (if not in equal length, compared to Pons) the performance's Gérald, Eugèle Graux, and the evening's Nilakantha, Jean Aquistapace.

"One was awaiting impatiently this performance of *Lakmé* at the Casino Municipal," wrote *Le Petit Marseillais* on 9 April. "The hopes centered on Miss Lily Pons were not disappointed. Her interpretation of the role of the Brahman's daughter was most beautiful and forecasts a beautiful career. The voice, with a marvelous timbre, evolves with exquisite suppleness in its entire range, without ever losing its delicious harmony."

September 1928 found Pons increasingly in demand, this time at the La Baule and Deauville theaters, where she sang *Rigoletto, Mireille, Lakmé, La bohème*, and *Il barbiere di Siviglia* in a ten-day period. On 17 September, *Comoedia* summarized the reception accorded her: "Miss Lily Pons [met] with great success as actress and singer at La Baule and Deauville. . . . She will repeat *Lakmé* on 20 September at Vichy." From there she went to Toulouse, where two performances of *Lakmé* earned her some of her best reviews to date. Five of the major periodicals, *La Petite Gironde, Le Télégramme, Le Midi Socialiste, L'Express du Midi*, and *Toulouse Spéctacle*, all reviewed her Lakmé in the most glowing terms, praising the clarity of her voice, her easy high notes (at Toulouse too her high E's made all the newspaper columns), the quality of her acting, her stage presence, and her overall charm.

When *Comoedia* announced on 6 November 1928 that Pons would sing Rosina in *Il barbiere* at the Grand-Théâtre in Lille, *Le Journal* promised its readers in the next day's edition a detailed account of the program for three artists who were scheduled to perform: a young pianist identified as "Claudio Arrau, winner of the International Piano Competition of Geneva," as well as "Lili Pons, star of the theaters of Cannes and Deauville," and the tenor Georges Génin, who had been "acclaimed here fifteen days ago." Keeping its promise, *Le Journal* detailed the program on 7 November. After Arrau and Génin would perform, Pons was to sing an aria from *Die Zauberflöte*, plus "Le rossignol et la rose" from Saint-Saëns's opera *Parysatis*, the Proch Variations, and in the second half of the concert the first-act duet from *Lakmé* with Génin. Other arias were also anticipated.

Five days later, on 12 November, *Le Journal* declared the concert "a triumph," and once again the petite soprano appears to have stolen the show: "Glory to Miss Lili Pons, who sings all the way to a high F and sings with communicative emotion the cantilena of Verdi and Léo Delibes!" Earlier that week, on 8 November, *L'Éclaireur* judged that "Miss Lily Pons after brilliant debuts now shines as a star in the artistic firmament." By then she had garnered accolades for her performances at Lille, Pau, Bordeaux, and Marseille, and she was next scheduled to sing *Lakmé* at the Casino Municipal.

Later that month Pons was again in Lille, where she would sing *Lakmé* at the Grand-Théâtre on 18 November 1928. Her success was noted in the columns of *La Dépêche* on 20 November: "In Sunday's matinee there debuted in *Lakmé* a young singer, Miss Lili Pons, who made an excellent impression. This artist succeeded with nearly consistent skill in her vocal interpretation, and she gave to the sweet heroine a pleasant appearance. She sang the Bell Song with youthful virtuosity, full of self-assurance. It is a promising debut." On Wednesday, 21 November, she returned to Paris to sing at a musicale sponsored by Mrs. E. Berry Wall, held at the American Women's Club. There her partner was the baritone Arthur Endrèze (*né* Krackman, from Chicago), a pupil of Jean de Reszke.

◦∯◦

We first encounter Lily Pons's Mimì in a review of a performance of *La bohème* at Avignon, in a clipping from *Les Tablettes Avignonnaise* dated 7 December 1928:

> Last night [Pons] was an infinitely delicate and soft Mimì, like the muff that envelopes her tiny frozen hands. She sang with a physical anguish, in a moving style. A delicate voice, well suited for this role of feminine fragility. She revealed especially in the third act a supple tone of great purity. She communicated in the entire work an atmosphere of living truth. The audience could not stop their bravas.

She was partnered by Enrico di Mazzei as Rodolfo and Berthe Boyer as Musetta. Added *Le Mistral* on 6 December 1928: "In Miss Lily Pons [di Mazzei] had an ideal partner, because one never saw a more touching Mimì, as well as the singer's somewhat slender voice better adapted to the tender and delicate role." In January 1929 she would sing Rosina in *Barbiere* and Gilda in *Rigoletto*, joined in the latter by di Mazzei as the Duke of Mantua. Her Rosina earned the customary high praises, and her "Caro nome" in *Rigoletto* earned special mention in most of the critics' columns.

On 11 January 1929 Pons and di Mazzei sang a joint concert at the Théâtre Municipal in Bayonne. Both their solo performances and their duets, especially the "È il sol dell' anima" from *Rigoletto*, were acclaimed in the *Courier* on 12 January. But for the first time, a comment about a lack of finish in her singing intrudes into an otherwise laudatory review: "Mme Lily Pons, the young singer with a bright future, has everything necessary to succeed fully in the lighter repertoire. She will shine when she has acquired the style that is still lacking and more flexibility, and will learn how an organ rich in pretty sonorities and a rare extension can also be made to have a clean emission." Unfortunately, the

33

elliptical language the reviewer favored does not shed any light on the nature of the faults he attempts to address. Elsewhere in the review Lily is commended for her "uncommon vocal endurance, singing in the second part in one stretch the Bell Song from *Lakmé*, the Proch Variations, Gilda's aria from *Rigoletto*, and the 'Rossignol' of Saint-Saëns—a piece we especially enjoyed—and after a pause of a few minutes the *Rigoletto* duet."

Tracing her whereabouts through her press clippings, we find Lily next in Pau, where *Comoedia* records (15 January 1929) her "unparalleled success at the Casino Municipal":

> The press echoes it: in the *Indépendant* on the topic of her interpretation of Rosina in *Il barbiere di Siviglia* [the critic] eulogized "the limpidity of her voice, the impeccable correctness of her vocalises, the truly superior interpretation." . . . Mme Lily Pons will return to Pau for a new series [of performances] including [her characterizations of] Mireille, Lakmé, Cherubin, Baucis, and Lucia.

At the end of January, according to *Comoedia*, she was scheduled to appear at the Grand-Théâtre of Bordeaux in *Il barbiere di Siviglia*.

By February 1929, Maman's scrapbook had thickened considerably—a sure indication of an operatic career in rapid ascent. Eight months later, in a review that followed Lily's appearance at a Grenoble theater, a critic identified as "Ko-dack" borrowed liberally from astronomy, aesthetics, and mythology when describing Lily's assets and appeal:

> The perfection of Lily Pons is human, and it is in the poetic sense of the word that her voice is divine. . . . She is a luminous meteor, she shines in the firmament of the stage like a star—I would not say of the first magnitude, because this *mignonne* is willowy—but like an iridescent celestial body whose charm is beyond all common measure of appreciation.
>
> Her natural gifts are infinite. Not the least is her singing technique, the sovereign mastery of her talent that moves, with stupefying ease, in a tessitura that allows her these vocal acrobatics, these freshly colored notes of an even beauty, that range from an impeccable high E to a low E in the Bell Song. But whatever may be the amazing rapture of her high soprano, the caress of the middle register, there is her ideal incarnation of these heroines, the artistic intoxication of youth that bursts forth from her heart now in a blaze of love, now in accents of terror, like an aeolian harp, like the light and burning perfume of the great mimosas in the forest consecrated to Brahma.
>
> I have no memory of greater enchantment than her Bell Song heavy with an indefinable exotic seduction, an indescribable Brahmanesque religiosity. The ovation allowed her the honor of an encore.

A good measure of the sensation Pons had created in the French operatic world can be gauged by the fact that on 19 December 1928, just one year and one month after her debut, she was in a recording studio cutting several sides for French Odeon. The surviving records, made then and in the following year, are mostly sung in French. They show a singer with an appealing young voice of great agility and range, well integrated and finely equalized from a satisfactory low register to the stratospheric high E and F, which made her the object of admiration from the start. Her technical and artistic accomplishments in addition to her interpretive maturity are truly astonishing, especially in the context of the relative brevity of her training.

The four sides of *La bohème* contain the act I finale (minus the off-stage intrusion of the other bohemians), from Mimì's entrance until the end of the act. Pons is a sweet and charming Mimì, not inappropriately more Murger's than Puccini's, and she imbues her part with character and feeling.

In the Italian-language duets "È il sol dell' anima" ("T'amo!") and "Addio, addio" from *Rigoletto*, Pons is a sweet and girlish Gilda. Her partner here, as in the *La bohème* excerpts, is her stage partner Enrico di Mazzei, whose contribution is not on her level. He has a pleasant lyric tenor voice of good quality and range, but somewhat nasal, decidedly beyond what the French language would allow; this becomes quite apparent when he sings in Italian. He is a somewhat passive Rodolfo, but he is able to change character and becomes a much more ardent and seductive Duke of Mantua.

Pons's other Odeon recordings, made in 1929, include the music of several Mozart characters: Blondchen's "Durch Zärtlichkeit," Cherubino's "Voi che sapete," Pamina's "Ach, ich fühl's," and the Queen of the Night's "Der Hölle Rache." The latter is sung with a determined attack, and the difficult staccatos of the coloratura are brilliantly secure. Her "Una voce poco fa" from *Il barbiere di Siviglia* shows more of the *docile* and less of the playful *vipera* side of Rosina. The single verse of Olympia's aria from *Les contes d'Hoffmann*, though well sung, falls short of the showpiece it could have been.

With *Mireille*'s "O légère hirondelle" and Lakmé's three arias, however, Pons is in her element. All are phrased with great sensitivity and delivered beautifully, but the best of the lot, quite predictably, is the Bell Song. Pons's tone is warm and round, the vocal palette rich and sensitively shaded, and she is able to make the difficult coloratura ornamentations a part of the song rather than a mere musical high-wire act. The pure and shimmering notes here truly resemble the tinkling of a silver bell.

These valuable vocal documents show not a mere promise, an aspiring singer with a future, but rather an artist with a presence. Even at this very early stage of her career Lily Pons was clearly an opera singer who could lend artistic distinction to any ensemble by her presence.

By 1930, Lily Pons had sung in most of the provincial opera houses in her native country and had acquired sufficient fame to warrant an occasional recitation of her life story, such as it was. Although she was vague as to her exact age when talking with the press (a vagueness she cultivated early and never abandoned), she spoke of being "in my twenties" but was actually thirty-two. In an unidentified clipping from a Montpellier newspaper, she was described as "still very young." The unnamed writer then recorded what Lily had told him about her background. Gone are any references to a supposed connection with the San Carlo Opera in Naples; nor is there any mention of her first teachers, the Opéra's Alfred Sellier and his wife, Dyna Beirner. In their place we encounter a first mention of Alberti de Gorostiaga:

> Passionate for music and endowed with a very pure organ, our soprano at age thirteen was ranked among the most brilliant pupils of the Paris Conservatoire. The Italian maestro Alberti was one of those who launched her artistic career, and a few years later she was engaged at the Variétés in Paris where at the side of Max D'Erly she created the most brilliant characterizations. Her reputation extends beyond French boundaries, and after her engagements in our native land, Mme Lily Pons will emigrate to North America, Italy, and Spain where she is contracted for the most brilliant engagements.[6]

This first reference to Lily's plans to "emigrate to North America" became the subject of several other interviews that the singer gave during the spring and summer of 1930. Critic Georges Tajusfré, of *La Vérité* in Perpignan, interviewed her for a story entitled "Five Minutes with Miss Lily Pons, Singer." During the time they spent together, Pons apparently disclosed her new association with Giovanni Zenatello and his wife, Maria Gay, and their efforts to obtain a contract for her at the Metropolitan Opera.

> All the big cities of France wanted to showcase her in their season. The Opera of Montpellier signed her for some twenty performances. Nice, Monte Carlo, Bordeaux, Lyon would like to confine her for a long while within their walls. She will interpret everywhere her celebrated unforgettable roles, the girl in *Rigoletto*, in *Lakmé*, and *Lucia di Lammermoor*.
>
> But the talent of Lily Pons cannot suffer the confines of boundaries; to the pleasure of her passionate admirers, she tells me that the manager of the Metropolitan of New York came to hear her and there have been already some serious discussions. Can the international recognition of the brilliant artist take long?

(Of course, Giulio Gatti-Casazza, the manager of the Metropolitan Opera at the time, did not, in fact, "come to hear" Lily sing; she went to the Met to audition for him.)

Subsequent news stories that Maman Pons pasted into her daughter's scrap-books suggest that the rhetorical question raised by Georges Tajusfré in the columns of *La Vérité* was soon answered. An unidentified feature story, probably from Cannes in 1931, reads:

> The charming artist—and our compatriot—Miss Lily Pons, whom we had the pleasure to applaud at the Casino Municipal several months ago, returns to us to spend the summer at the Hotel Victoria.
>
> Miss Lily Pons arrives from the United States where she obtained [an] . . . engagement as a principal soloist at the Metropolitan Opera of New York. If one considers that after twenty years—since Emma Calvé—this is the first time that a French singer became a star of the Metropolitan Opera, one can gauge the approval that has been thus accorded to the magnificent talent of Miss Lily Pons, who has in addition an exceptional organ, elegance, and the distinction of a graceful silhouette such as one has hardly been accustomed to seeing among coloratura sopranos. Miss Lily Pons will debut at the end of this year in New York, in *Lucia di Lammermoor*, and will sing in the course of the fourteen weeks of her engagement her entire repertoire, of which a large portion is French.

"We take special pleasure," the feature ends, "in this magnificent blossoming of the artistic career of the excellent Cannoise artist, to whom we address, with all good wishes, our warmest congratulations." Now was the time for farewells, and *Le Petit Marseillais* closed its tribute with a rueful nod to the inevitable: "We hope that her foreign engagements will permit the charming artist to return to us. She will not regret it."

CHAPTER THREE

Coloraturas at the Metropolitan

Giacomo Lauri-Volpi

Over a career that spanned more than fifty years, tenor Giacomo Lauri-Volpi (1892–1979) earned critical acclaim in nearly every major opera house in Europe and the Americas. During his years at the Metropolitan Opera, 1922–32, he created the role of Calaf in Puccini's *Turandot* and shared *primo tenore* status with Giovanni Martinelli and Beniamino Gigli. In 1955, the erudite tenor (who had trained as a lawyer before beginning his singing career) published *Voci parallele* (Parallel Voices),[1] the fourth of seven books he wrote. In the portions of the book devoted to the coloratura voice, Lauri-Volpi describes and analyzes the voices and techniques of eight great sopranos—Maria Barrientos, Luisa Tetrazzini, Amelita Galli-Curci, Graziella Pareto, Marion Talley, Toti dal Monte, Elvira de Hidalgo, and Lily Pons—all of whom he sang with either in Europe or the Americas. He presents Pons's explosion onto the scene in the light of the series of sopranos who came and went before her. A sub-theme of Lauri-Volpi's analysis is the disparity between the reputations of Barrientos, Pareto, dal Monte, and de Hidalgo in Europe, where they were lauded, and in New York, where they were received indifferently by the same audiences who made superstars, a decade apart, of Galli-Curci and Lily Pons.

$\mathcal{B}$EAUTY OF VOICE and personal beauty do not always coincide, and in the case of the Catalán soprano, Maria Barrientos, it may be said that her elegant bearing and impeccable manners compensated for an aesthetic beauty that she may have lacked. She entered the spotlight just after the splendors of Adelina Patti, and more recently Luisa Tetrazzini, had begun to fade into memory.

Luisa Tetrazzini had a scintillating voice with a brilliant timbre and a range and agility well beyond the norm, and she dominated the major opera houses of the United States and England, where her popularity even rivaled Melba's. Tetrazzini owed much of her success, however, to the concert stage, as her physique did not lend itself to the opera stage. She was the sister of the great lirico-spinto soprano, Eva Tetrazzini, who boasted the more substantial voice and superior aesthetic taste of the two. But Luisa was a coloratura—and coloratura sopranos are the ones whom fortune smiles upon, bestowing upon them wealth and fame.

Maria Barrientos enjoyed a similar reign for approximately two decades in Europe and Latin America. Her voice had an extensive range and was of virtuoso caliber, although it did not possess a distinctive timbre. She was particularly effective in *Lucia di Lammermoor*, *I puritani*, and *Il barbiere di Siviglia*. Her technique was founded upon an exemplary method of breath control and modulation, producing unforgettable effects in the extreme upper range—slender, silvery notes as light as a feather, issuing from a mouth opened to its maximum. Audiences held their breath at hearing these tones, magically suspended in midair like tiny crystalline bubbles liable to burst at any moment into a thousand glittering fragments. Barrientos worked this magic throughout her prime, usually partnered by star tenors like Alessandro Bonci, Giuseppe Anselmi, or Enrico Caruso, or the great baritone Titta Ruffo.

Barrientos was an artist of exceptional distinction onstage, where the naturalness, spontaneity, and intelligence of her acting were best revealed in those roles that lie midway between romantic and modern operatic works. I heard her at the Teatro Reale in Madrid in 1921, where I partnered her in *Puritani* and *Barbiere di Siviglia*, and I also heard her Lucia there. At the Metropolitan Opera, however, she left conflicting impressions. There she was paired with another Catalán, the tenor Hipólito Lázaro, who strove to imitate and surpass Caruso. Together and separately, Lázaro and Barrientos made a pleasing impression upon New York opera-goers, although neither was able to capture the hearts of American audiences. Lázaro suffered by comparisons by the critics and public with the recently deceased Caruso. Barrientos, unfortunately, was unable to compete with Amelita Galli-Curci, whose recent arrival at the Metropolitan had created such a sensation.

LIKE BARRIENTOS, Galli-Curci was not a beautiful woman, yet her voice was incomparable for its beauty and its velvetlike timbre. Her sensitive personality inclined her toward melancholy roles—ones that allowed her to languish her legato style, free of the "drive" that other coloraturas tend to favor. Because of that inclination, hearing Galli-Curci was a spiritual experience rarely found elsewhere. Yet the excessive relaxation that this inclination required of her had an adverse effect at times upon her intonation. Additionally, her avoidance of declamation, of strong verbal expressiveness in her singing, led to a certain ambiguity of tone and a lack of clarity in her articulation of words. Yet these sometime faults depended greatly upon her temperament, her state of mind and nerves when she was onstage.

I was Galli-Curci's partner in her first performance of *Rigoletto* at the Metropolitan, early in January 1923.[2] Later, I sang numerous other performances of that work with her, in addition to *Lucia, Il barbiere di Siviglia,* and *La traviata,* and even her occasional ventures into Massenet's *Manon.* From that very first evening, she gave me the impression of what poets label a "wingèd voice"—a voice wonderfully equalized in its color, albeit a trifle opaque but always extremely suave and soothing and never pale or infantile. Her concluding notes in *Rigoletto* ("Lassù in cielo") were miracles of flutelike sound. She was an expert musician, an excellent pianist, and liked to do her vocalizing accompanied by a flute, which explains her technical security and abandon. After the death of Caruso, we owe to Galli-Curci the continuation of the prestige of the Italian art of singing as enjoyed by Americans. To them, the true bearer of that standard was Amelita Galli-Curci.

Comparing Barrientos and Galli-Curci, it may be said that both were intelligent musicians, skilled technicians, and conscientious performers who disdained cheap effects. Both women were not helped by physical assets. The first, Barrientos, achieved unconditional success in Europe and South America, whereas the second, Galli-Curci, was the object of consistent admiration in the United States. There was a great difference in their temperaments: Barrientos was vibrant and willful, and Galli-Curci was gentle and yielding, which explains the diversity of their approaches to singing. Barrientos exhibited dazzling effects in the upper register, and her singing reflected her vibrant temperament; Galli-Curci graced beloved melodies with melancholy shadows, shaping her phrases intimately, suavely, softly, sustaining a delicate legato in every register of her voice.

The Italian, Galli-Curci, was as successful in *Rigoletto* as was the Spaniard, Barrientos, in *Il barbiere di Siviglia*. To venture a subtle comparison, it cannot be denied that Galli-Curci's shortcomings in intonation were apparent at times, while Barrientos's approach to her art revealed an imbalance between the scope of her abilities and the results she achieved: the demands she made upon her voice detracted from the humanity of her singing. Both women became famous and wealthy, although neither became a countess (as did Patti) nor the wife of some head of state. Yet their wealth and fame never detracted from their sense of refinement and aristocratic grace. They set examples of dignity and nobility for the generation that succeeded them.

THE VOICE of Graziella Pareto represents a link between the true coloratura soprano and a lyric soprano with coloratura ability but without an inclination to virtuoso effects. She was tall in stature, and quiet and somewhat melancholy by nature—qualities that were reflected in her voice and in her contemplative approach to singing. Her tones were slender, clear, well-rounded; the voice was of limited volume but was penetrating and caressing. In such operas as *La travi ata*, *Fra Diavolo*, *L'elisir d'amore*, *Lucia*, *Rigoletto*, and *Il barbiere di Siviglia*, she executed her roles with uncommon skill and a strict adherence to the score. Her singing revealed great aesthetic refinement and taste, and she had a fine sense of rhythm and unusual musicianship. She was particularly successful in von Flotow's *Martha*, a work that perfectly suited her nature, her feelings, and her reserved temperament. Onstage she seemed rather distant and detached, and her audiences were reserved in their reactions to her performing. She was a very complex person, and her psychological complexity was perhaps misunderstood; she never aroused the enthusiasm that other sopranos with lesser gifts and lower artistic standards were able to muster.

The last time I sang with Pareto was at the Teatro Colón in 1927, in a performance of *Rigoletto* with Giuseppe de Luca in the title role. During that performance, I was an eyewitness to a deplorable injustice that the audience inflicted upon her. She had just finished the "Caro nome," which she had sung with faultless intonation and impeccable style. She had endowed the music with a purity of timbre and style that perfectly matched the grace and simplicity of the character Gilda—and all of us were expecting her to receive a well-justified ovation. But *not one pair of hands* applauded. It was as if that lovely voice had been singing in an immense tomb! It is probably safe to assume that Graziella Pareto's premature retirement from the opera stage could be traced to that unfortunate incident at the Teatro Colón. As for the incident itself, there is a lesson in it for all singers: this is the price that artists pay when they do not create a rapport with an audience.

MARION TALLEY was an American meteor in the Metropolitan sky: baby-faced, golden-haired, blue-eyed, a pretty girl with a wonderful smile; this was the "Kansas City Nightingale," the Gilda with whom Giuseppe de Luca and I appeared during the interval separating the departure of Galli-Curci and the arrival of Lily Pons. The Talley voice was less coloratura than lyric, and on the night of her debut she sang with a sort of primordial innocence, while backstage a tele-graph had been installed so that her father could tap out the news of this sensa-tional success, act by act, of a newcomer to the Metropolitan roster. America now had its own coloratura with "the most beautiful voice in the world," just as it had the richest man, the greatest prize fighter, or the finest oranges in the world. The audience went mad while the rosy, chubby little singer was the cen-ter of their admiration; her colleagues on that night of nights were mere puppets.

From that time on, fame and wealth were showered upon this prodigy. One did not know whether to admire the ingenuity of her singing or the willful, headstrong courage with which she inexpertly handled this solid voice. For in this round little girl there was an ill-concealed stubbornness fed by uneasy doubts about just how long all this was going to last. Talley believed in chance, just as she believed in the maxim that "Time is money"; she was in a hurry—and afraid. She wanted lots of appearances and lots of money, and in two years she had sufficient quantities of both; in the meantime she ruined her delicate vocal appa-ratus and undermined her health. Soon the nightingale returned to her native woods, far from the noise, the clamor, the intrigues, the pushy people, the mad whirl of hectic tours. A dazzling meteor had passed over America and had van-ished. Today, it seems that even the memory of this phantom of song has disap-peared, as if she had never lived on this planet.

Between the voices of Graziella Pareto and Marion Talley there is a certain affinity, as both were not coloraturas, properly speaking, but rather lyric voices with coloratura capabilities. Pareto's voice was more ethereal, while Talley's more meaty; the first was more conscientious, and the second the stronger-willed. Pareto had a woman's body and a girl's voice; Talley was the reverse. Both of them appeared during a period of transition: after the departure and before the arrival of stronger, more impressive artistic personalities. Talley was propped up by American nationalism, the pride of a great country—and to this she owed her rapid though transitory fame and fortune. Pareto, on the other hand, achieved a genuine success, her audiences being sincere people of taste. Technique and spirit, in her case, were integrated. With Talley, perpetually in a hurry, the vocal method and artistic conscience of the little girl from Kansas City never found a way or the time to achieve real maturity.

Pareto, after long periods of introspection and analysis, arrived at a proper fusion of her vocal instrument and her mental faculties. Talley, on the contrary, had no time to study herself, no time to evaluate her strengths and weaknesses and profit by comparing them. In the end, her fleeting appearances left no traces in the musical life of her native country—nor, we might say, even in her own life.

TOTI DAL MONTE, the Venetian soprano, had a voice of lyric quality but which she utilized in the coloratura repertoire. Hers was probably the most popular voice in Italy from the mid-1920s through the early 1930s. Her fame dates from

1922–23, after Toscanini revealed her voice at La Scala. Her popularity reached such a high point that she was no longer referred to as "La Dal Monte" but simply as "Toti." She sang with a perfect balance of her technical assets and liabilities, for she had a minute knowledge of her means and limitations, and she respected them. She knew she was not one for "fireworks" or sensational notes above the staff. She knew perfectly well what she wanted to do.

At one of Toscanini's *Rigoletto* rehearsals at La Scala, he asked her to sing the "Caro nome" with a rounder, fuller tone. Dal Monte modestly replied, "Maestro, I will be unable to capture the depths of the aria's expressiveness if I sing it the way you wish." Toscanini said nothing; instead, he opened a cut in the "Lassù in cielo." As a result, the true qualities of dal Monte's voice were revealed not in the "Caro nome" but in the last quarter of the opera, which the public had more or less ignored. Whether it was the beauty of the music or the suavity of her voice that kept the La Scala audiences spellbound in the last act of *Rigoletto* will probably never be known; but it is inarguable that the crowd was almost breathless during the final measures of the opera, and they greeted dal Monte with an avalanche of applause that mingled wonderment with profound admiration.

To anyone who had heard Toti dal Monte in the lyric repertoire, it was evident that she sang *Rigoletto* with a different method of phonation. Unable to master the tessitura that Verdi required, she essentially "invented" her own voice in order to adapt the music to her own powers—and having made a deep study of the character Gilda, she was able to achieve a quality of sound that projected the candor and simplicity of a young girl. Dal Monte had an immense liking for that type of role, so much so that she always seemed ready to say to an audience, as she stepped onstage, "Now you will hear how this piece should be sung"—invariably with a smile on her baby face. With time, dal Monte began to relinquish the coloratura roles, turning to such operas as *Lodoletta* and *Madama Butterfly*—loving (to borrow from Puccini) "small people accustomed to small things."

DURING THE INTERREGNUM between the close of Maria Barrientos's career and the rise of Toti dal Monte's, the dominating figure in the coloratura repertoire was Elvira de Hidalgo. Born in Aragon and full of fire (*sal y pepe* [salt and pepper], as they say in Spain), she sang Rosina in Rossini's opera like almost no other. Her fine figure, the perfection of her piquant tiny face, flashing eyes, and raven hair, plus her fiery delivery, clean-cut diction, and the ring of her crystalline silvery voice filled the stage and enchanted her audiences. I heard her for the first time at the Teatro Costanzi in Rome, in *I puritani* in 1916. Her partner was the Tuscan tenor Dino Borgioli, a poetic Arturo. De Hidalgo was a suave Elvira, but the totality of her personality, her glittering incandescence, her expansive nature were only revealed in totality when she portrayed Rosina. In Bellini's work, by contrast, there were no veiled effects, no starry high notes, no elegiac phrases or languishing turns of melody such as one would have expected.

The burning sun of Andalusia had created de Hidalgo, and she was full of its brilliant glow. What a Carmen she would have made, had she been born a mezzo-soprano! She avenged this impossibility by conceiving a bizarre but fascinating Musetta in *La bohème*: I have never heard so electrifying a "Quand m'en vo" as hers. A sensual and ardent singer, she did not last very long; the last glimmers were heard at an important concert in the Paris Opéra. Later, she was called to Athens to teach singing, and it was there that Maria Callas became one of her pupils.

LILY PONS possessed one of the most slender yet wide-ranging voices perhaps ever heard in an opera house. The impresario Rouché, of the Paris Opéra, turned her down—so, off to America she went. The "Cannes Nightingale" became a fixture in New York City, adopting citizenship in America and singing for approximately three decades on the banks of the Hudson River, and between opera seasons from the Atlantic to the Pacific, from Georgia to California. The Metropolitan Opera, between 1925 and 1930, had been searching tirelessly for a replacement for the fading Amelita Galli-Curci. The comet Marion Talley burned out in a short time, as we have seen, and disappeared without leaving the smallest trail. There were a few performances by Elvira de Hidalgo and dal Monte, but neither the former by her physical proportions, nor the latter by the special sound of her voice, seemed to please the New York audiences. Both singers found the Metropolitan reception cool, so they warbled a few notes and faded away.

Giulio Gatti-Casazza, the Moses of the lyric theater, immersed himself in thought and surveyed the horizon from his own lightning-wreathed Mount Sinai—but in vain. Then out of nowhere there now came the little girl from Cannes seeking an audition. Her Dutch husband had dressed the diminutive lady, all clever and ambitious, in clothes befitting a queen. At the close of her audition, she was smiling happily—and henceforth she dominated the Metropolitan Olympus, letting no possible rival approach her dominion. She appeared first in *Lucia*, then shortly afterward in *Rigoletto*, in both cases with Giuseppe de Luca and myself.

If all goes well on the first night of a new career in America, "a new Pope has been chosen," as an old saying goes. Lily was a success and remained one. In *Lucia*, though her age was something on the order of thirty, she looked like a teenager. It was rumored that she was only eighteen; she was so dainty, petite, and graceful that everyone was willing to believe it. For the first time in history a French coloratura had conquered America, and the novelty of it seemed to please everyone. Lily became their favorite toy, their baby doll, replete with jaguars, Siamese cats, or Tibetan dogs with jeweled leashes accompanying her everywhere, like the descendant of some Grand Lama.

The technique of her voice? A wonder of mathematical calculation. Her stylistic approach? Sober, harmonious, a balanced distribution of a variety of effects.

Her teacher was Alberti de Gorostiaga, a Basque who had been secretary to his countryman, tenor Florencio Constantino. It was Gorostiaga who taught Pons the mysterious secrets of breathing and phonation. He had been observed, during Lily's vocalizing, to come close to her and, for no apparent reason, raise the tip of her nose with his index finger. All the while the imperturbable little Lily would continue to warble her pearly little notes with perfect control and clever metering of breath, both of these abilities combining to remove any obstacles to her ascent to the utmost limits of her pretty and fearless little voice.

CHAPTER FOUR

The Arrival of Lily Pons

Nina Morgana Zirato

Soprano Nina Morgana Zirato (1892–1986) had been at the Metropolitan for nearly a decade when she was introduced to Lily Pons through Giovanni Zenatello and Maria Gay. As a result of that introduction, Morgana's husband, Bruno Zirato, became Pons's first manager. The Ziratos maintained a friendship with Lily Pons that endured for more than forty years.

Morgana was first discovered by Enrico Caruso when she was a teenage coloratura performing in and around Buffalo, New York, where her parents had emigrated from Sicily in the mid-1880s. Caruso auditioned her after a concert he gave in Buffalo, and he recommended her to the renowned Italian soprano, Teresa Arkel, with whom Morgana studied in Italy from 1909 to 1915. Returning to the United States after successful debuts at Alessandria in 1910 and at the Teatro alla Scala in 1915, Morgana was engaged by the Chicago Opera in 1919, and in 1920 she made her Metropolitan Opera debut as Gilda in *Rigoletto*. Before her debut she had toured the U.S. in joint concerts with Caruso from 1917 to 1919. By proxy, the great tenor served as Best Man when Morgana married Bruno Zirato, Caruso's secretary, in 1920.[1]

I FIRST BECAME aware of Lily Pons during the Christmas season in 1928, almost two years before she came to the United States to audition for the Metropolitan. Bruno and I were well acquainted with the writer Frederick Martens, whose wife happened to hear Lily sing at a society luncheon in Paris.[2] Because some years earlier Giulio Gatti-Casazza had retained my husband to serve as a "talent scout" for the Metropolitan, Bruno listened with interest when Fred told him that his wife had come back from Paris with such a favorable impression of this petite young coloratura.

Whether Bruno tried to make contact with Lily at that time, I cannot say; if he did, nothing must have come of it. But early in 1930, Giovanni Zenatello and Maria Gay, whom Bruno and I had known for several years, contacted us and asked Bruno to consider representing Lily as a manager. Bruno said he would be happy to consider their offer, and he arranged with the Zenatellos to meet Lily and hear her sing. Because Maria Gay had made a special point of asking Bruno to be sure that I would be there when Lily sang for him, we invited the Zenatellos to bring Lily to dinner at our home in Chappaqua, near Manhattan. We also invited Emilio Rokzas, my accompanist.

From the moment the Zenatellos introduced us to Lily, Bruno and I were captivated by her. For me in particular, meeting Lily was doubly pleasurable because I too was a coloratura and also because, as one of the Metropolitan's more petite women singers, I found myself at eye level with another soprano—a rare happening for me at five feet tall! Bruno, on the other hand, stood six-feet-three, which made for quite a spectacle as he practically bent himself in half to reach down to clasp Lily's tiny hand.

From the moment we greeted the Zenatellos, they and Bruno and I began conversing in Italian, as we habitually did. It soon became evident, though, that Lily did not have a truly conversational mastery of the language. Much to her delight, I began speaking to her in French, in which I was also fluent. That helped break the ice and allowed more of Lily's sparkling personality to come through that evening. Before dinner, we invited Lily to sing. Of course, she accepted—after all, she knew why she was there. She sang, as I recall, three arias: "Una voce poco fa" from *Il barbiere di Siviglia*, the Bell Song from *Lakmé*, and "Spargi d'amaro pianto" from *Lucia*, with Rokzas accompanying her.

My reactions to her voice and technique are still vivid, almost fifty years later. Her voice was a true *soprano leggiero* (as my generation of Italian singers referred to what we now call the coloratura voice). Especially at that very early stage in her long career, Lily's technique was very well developed and she could sing the most rapid runs, roulades, and staccatos without any slurring of the notes. She attacked every note cleanly, individually, and squarely on pitch.

Although her voice struck me as being rather small, the higher Lily sang the more color, size, and brilliance her tones seemed to have. Her highest tones were amazing! At Maria Gay's suggestion, Lily vocalized from high C to F and then up to the A-flat above high C, all without any visible sign of effort. (I myself used to vocalize to G above high C, but only in the studio. In a performance, where nerves restrict a voice's range, I never attempted anything above an E-flat.) Later in her career, Lily would sing those ultra-high notes in head voice, or falsetto, with her mouth almost entirely closed.[3] But she didn't do that when I first heard her sing; her top tones were very bell-like and of the same timbre as the rest of her upper range.

Despite such a basically beautiful voice and a very fine technique, Lily's singing had some obvious limitations at that beginning point in her career. For instance, she didn't seem to know how to execute a trill the proper way; instead of producing two distinct harmonic tones and alternating them rapidly, she seemed just to exaggerate her vibrato, producing something more like a shake than a genuine trill. A far more serious limitation, though, was her musical interpretation, which was very idiosyncratic at that point. Especially in the *Barbiere* and *Lucia* arias her stylistic approach was not recognizably Italian, and her fioriture and her legato singing didn't sound Italian at all. It was as if she were merely singing the notes and interpreting the music the way she might if it had been written by French rather than Italian composers.

The idiosyncrasies I'm speaking of—how she accentuated certain notes, and the way she tended to emphasize the wrong words and phrases—showed that she had not been schooled in bel canto. These idiosyncrasies were so obvious that over dinner I asked Lily about her training. She spoke of her singing teachers, especially Alberti de Gorostiaga, whose name I had never heard of before then; she said she had prepared her roles with him in France. She also said that she had sung all her roles in French until recently. And she was not just singing coloratura roles in France. She mentioned singing Mimì in *La bohème*, but in French.

When Maria Gay and Giovanni Zenatello contacted Bruno the next day, he told them about our reactions to Lily's interpretive limitations, while of course praising her very fine technique and brilliant upper voice. Maria Gay gave Bruno her personal assurance that she would oversee Lily's future coaching so that she would learn the Italian approach properly. In the meantime, Maria said, she and Zenatello were preparing Lily for her Metropolitan audition, which Gatti-Casazza had arranged a week or two from then.[4]

A few days before the audition, Lily signed a management contract with Bruno so that he could represent her in negotiations in the U.S., Canada, and Latin America.[5] When the audition took place, Gatti-Casazza invited Bruno and me to attend. As with most of Gatti's audition sessions, several other Metropolitan singers had been asked to attend, as well as some of the members of the Metropolitan board of directors—especially Otto Kahn, to whom Gatti was very close. While I don't recall everything Lily sang that afternoon, I remember her singing the Bell Song from *Lakmé*, and I also recall Gatti asking her to sing "Caro nome" at one point.

Mr. Kahn arrived near the end of the audition, probably because of some business appointment. Wanting Mr. Kahn to hear more of her, Gatti asked Lily if she would mind repeating the Bell Song if she wasn't too tired. She said she wasn't tired at all, and she sang not only the Bell Song but most of the Mad Scene from *Lucia* for Mr. Kahn's benefit. Immediately after that, Gatti later told Bruno, Mr. Kahn said to him, "Put this young lady under contract right away. I don't think we want another Galli-Curci situation." Mr. Kahn was remembering how Galli-Curci was first signed by the Chicago Opera, and how Gatti had had to court her and pay her a lot more money to come to the Metropolitan after she had gotten famous in Chicago.[6]

The audition went splendidly, and within a few days Bruno received a call from Gatti to discuss the terms of a contract for Lily. Not long after she signed her Metropolitan contract, she went back to France. As I recall, she didn't return to New York until shortly before the 1930–31 Metropolitan season opened.[7]

Soon after Lily arrived in New York with the Zenatellos, Bruno and I had the pleasure of taking her to see her very first performance at the Metropolitan Opera House: Rosa Ponselle in *Norma*, with Marion Telva as Adalgisa and Giacomo Lauri-Volpi singing Pollione.[8] Lily was completely overwhelmed by Rosa's singing—so much so that she began to worry about how her own rather small voice would carry in such a big opera house. We all reassured her that Rosa Ponselle's voice was not a proper yardstick for anybody else, since no other Italian soprano at the Met had a voice of that size and weight. After the performance Bruno and I introduced Lily to Rosa, and Lily greeted her like an awestruck fan. When Rosa remarked that she had heard good things about Lily's voice, Lily replied demurely, "But a Pons is only half a Ponselle!"

From then until her debut, Lily worked directly with Tullio Serafin, and she also had some coaching from Wilfrid Pelletier.[9] Serafin had arranged for Pelletier to work with her because Pellie (as we called him) knew the French tradition that Lily had come from, and he was also well versed in the bel canto style she was now having to master. No conductor in my time could rival Tullio Serafin in the Italian repertoire. Nor did he have any equal when it came to preparing singers for new roles and new productions. He had a wonderful touch with his artists. Everything he did was with encouragement, patience, and calm. I never knew him to raise his voice or lose his temper with anyone. The only thing that displeased him was if someone was unprepared at a rehearsal. But even then, one disappointed look from that expressive face of his and you could feel about one inch tall.

Lily worked very, very hard under Maestro Serafin, and by the time of her debut she was well prepared. Yet she was not, I have to say, very confident about her debut. In that regard she was very much like Rosa Ponselle. Rosa's nerves were nearly the worst that I have seen in a *prima diva*. I say "nearly" because Lily was a close second. But Lily's nerves affected her differently than Rosa's did. Rosa would get so nervous that at times she needed medication. She would pace up and down the corridor, her eyes would be as big as supper plates, and any little thing might bring about a temper outburst. Lily, on the other hand, would become horribly sick to her stomach before every one of her performances.

Because of Bruno's involvement in her management, and because I sang some of the same roles Lily did, I was around her a great deal. I can still see her doubled over her dressing-room sink, moaning to herself in her French-accented English, "Nevaire! I nevaire sing again! *Ne-vaire!*" Fortunately, though, Lily's nervousness (her "nervosity," as she used to call it) disappeared completely once she got on the stage.

As for Lily's voice, I consider it unique. Neither before nor since have I heard any coloratura voice quite like hers when she was in her prime. I was fortunate to have heard, and in many cases to have known personally, most of the great coloraturas of my time. Both Luisa Tetrazzini and Amelita Galli-Curci were personal friends of Bruno's and mine, and I was also acquainted with Elvira de Hidalgo, Maria Barrientos, Graziella Pareto, Toti dal Monte, and many others who sang the coloratura repertoire.

In 1909, when I went to Milan to study with Teresa Arkel, I heard one of the greatest of all coloraturas, Maria Galvany.[10] After Patti it was Galvany, not Sembrich or Melba (whom I heard when I was young and considered a bore), who was the *soprano leggiero* ideal among the young Italian sopranos of my own generation. Galvany's technique was absolutely stunning! And though Lily's voice was entirely different than Galvany's in timbre and size, the ease with which Lily could sing rapid runs and very fast passages often reminded me of Galvany's electrifying technique.

Tetrazzini's voice, both in terms of size and flexibility, had more to it than any other coloratura voice I can recall hearing in my time. I also heard Emma Calvé when I was very young, but I don't consider her a coloratura any more than Madame Arkel, my teacher, or Lilli Lehmann or Lillian Nordica. They were from a different era, when the great sopranos sang nearly everything from the lyric repertoire to the heaviest Wagnerian roles, and when the soprano voice wasn't fragmented into categories like coloratura, lyric, and lirico-spinto.

The only voice in recent years that I can compare to Tetrazzini's would be Joan Sutherland's, although hers has a veiled quality in the middle range that I don't remember in Tetrazzini's voice. Their approaches and their repertoire were quite different, of course. My impression of Sutherland is that she seems to sing more from the brain than the heart; Luisa, on the other hand, had an emotional and intuitive approach to her repertoire. Sutherland, probably because of the influence of her husband, Richard Bonynge, respects the composer's wishes, whereas Luisa tended to follow her own instincts rather than adhering to the score.

Comparing Tetrazzini and Lily Pons is not possible; they were as dissimilar vocally as they were in physique—and it would have taken about three Lily Ponses to match the weight of Luisa Tetrazzini. (John McCormack once said that doing a love scene with the immense Luisa was like trying to embrace a stack of tires.) Lily's voice, on the other hand, could be compared to Galli-Curci's to some degree, although Galli-Curci's voice was fuller in the lower range and had a more velvety timbre than Lily's. Both had studied to be pianists at first, and they were very good musicians. Unfortunately, Galli-Curci developed a goiter that eventually ruined her technique. But when I met her during our days with the Chicago Opera, her voice was at its peak and her technique was stunning. By the mid-1920s, however, she was already having problems with pitch, especially in any sustained legato passages.

This was something that all of us talked about. Antonio Scotti, another close friend of ours, made a remark about Galli-Curci's pitch problems when he heard one of my recordings. In 1920, I made two test records for the Victor Company under the direction of Mr. Calvin Child.[11] I recorded Chadwick's "He Loves Me," and also "Come per me sereno" from *La sonnambula*, one of my best roles. Unfortunately for me, Mr. Child wouldn't agree to put me on the Red Seal label, so Bruno wouldn't let me accept a contract and nothing came of the recordings.

While we were still having discussions with the Victor Company, Bruno played my *Sonnambula* test record for Scotti after dinner one evening. He asked Scotti to guess who was singing. Scotti listened for a while and said, "Well, it sounds like Galli-Curci, but it can't be her because all the notes are on pitch." That was not a very nice thing to say about Galli-Curci, whom I adored whether or not she sang in tune. But it was a compliment that had been paid to me, so I did the human thing and gladly took it.

I left the Metropolitan when Gatti-Casazza retired in 1935, a little more than four years after Lily Pons had made her Metropolitan Opera debut. During those four years, Lily had transformed herself from the former ingénue who had sung a handful of roles in French provincial opera houses into the biggest star in the Metropolitan's Italian wing and the most popular female opera singer in America. We remained close friends throughout her career. We treated each other with respect and affection. I called Lily "my pet," and in turn she called me her mascot because of the encouragement I was always giving her in order to help her conquer her nervousness.

Bruno and I were among those whom Lily personally invited to attend the gala performance that marked her twenty-five years at the Metropolitan. Of all the occasions I heard Lily sing in the great old house, I consider her silver-anniversary gala a high point in my memory. That night she sang the second act of *Rigoletto*, the "O luce di quest'anima" from *Linda di Chamounix*, "Je suis Titania" from *Mignon*, and the Bell Song from *Lakmé*. But for me the truly special moment came when she sang the Mad Scene from *Lucia*. When she ended the scene with a prolonged high F, I closed my eyes so that I could relish the exquisite sound I was hearing. The tone rang with the same brilliance and sparkle that Bruno and I had heard when Lily first sang for us those many years before.

The last time I saw Lily in person was at the gala that marked the closing of the old Metropolitan Opera House in 1966. That night Rudolf Bing brought many of the singers of my generation together on the old stage for one last time —Giovanni Martinelli, Anna Case, Mario and Ruth [Miller] Chamlee, Edith Mason, Richard Crooks, Elisabeth Rethberg, Bidú Sayão, Lotte Lehmann, and of course Lily.[12] Although she had retired several years before, Lily looked as trim and chic as ever. And she let all of us know that she was very displeased that Mr. Bing hadn't asked her to sing.

Throughout the evening, the singers of my era sat on the stage while the new generation of singers did their performing. After the gala, Lily, Bidú, Lotte Lehmann, Edith Mason, and Elisabeth Rethberg and I compared notes about what we heard. We concurred that most of the singing that night would not have passed muster in our day, and that except for Birgit Nilsson the women's voices seemed to be getting smaller with each generation. We also decided that most of the Americans on the roster wouldn't have made it in Gatti's regime. Eleanor Steber, we said, was hardly in a league with Rosa Ponselle, Giorgio Tozzi was no Ezio Pinza, James McCracken was no Giovanni Martinelli, and Roberta Peters, good as she was, was certainly no Lily Pons. After we made these haughty pronouncements, however, we all laughed when it occurred to us that the great singers of the past had probably said the same things about us!

As the years went on, Bruno and I continued to keep in touch with Lily, and we often dined with Lily and André Kostelanetz. Unfortunately, I didn't get to see the concert she gave with André at Lincoln Center because Bruno was in declining health at that time. When he died a few months later,[13] Lily wrote me a very touching note, reminiscing about that long-ago evening at our home in Chappaqua. I was a long time getting over Bruno's death—we had been married fifty-one years. But especially during that difficult time, Lily's thoughtful notes and telephone calls meant a lot to me.

About two years after Bruno died, I received a call from one of Lily's young admirers, telling me that Lily wanted me to be sure to watch *The Merv Griffin Show* because she would be a guest on the program a few days from then.[14] I saw the show and was delighted to see not only how lovely Lily looked, but also how at ease she seemed when Merv Griffin was interviewing her. She had finally conquered her "nervosity," I decided. Then to my astonishment, Merv Griffin asked Lily if she would sing. I realized afterward that all of this had been carefully rehearsed, but it caught me by surprise because I knew that Lily was at least seventy-five at the time.

Yet sing she did—and she chose "Estrellita," a favorite of mine and a gem that Lily had so often sung as an encore in her concerts. The Spanish title means, literally, "little star," a phrase that just as aptly described Lily Pons. As she sang, there was hardly any hint of age in her voice, and afterward the studio audience gave Lily a standing ovation. Sitting in front of my television, I applauded her too. Almost half a century had come and gone since Lily and I had first met. But that afternoon, I was glad to be her mascot again.

PART TWO

Stardom

CHAPTER FIVE

Lily Pons Cheered at Metropolitan Debut

Lily Pons's rapid ascent to stardom at the Metropolitan may be reconstructed from reviews and articles in music periodicals of that day. Almost without exception, they depict an eager young woman who seems as pleasantly surprised as the critics and opera-going public at her overnight success. Forty years later she would write, "People were standing, screaming, yelling! There were sixteen curtain calls, and still now I can't believe what happened." Novice though she was, however, she had learned in France the value of newspaper publicity and would recall with delight that the morning after her debut, "I was on the front page of all the New York papers." This article, which appeared in the *Musical Courier* a week after her debut,[1] captures the magnitude of her success that Saturday afternoon in January 1931.

*T*HE METROPOLITAN Opera House was all agog for the matinee on this day. A huge crowd early took their seats, and when [conductor Vincenzo] Bellezza stepped on the podium for the *Lucia* overture there was an atmosphere of expectancy electrifying the air. It was the debut of the French coloratura, Lily Pons, about whom there was much curiosity since, very wisely, there had been no trumpets heralding her coming. Already there was admiration for her because, obviously, she wishes to fall or stand by virtue of her real merits.

Before going further, a word of thanks must be extended to Mr. Gatti-Casazza, who continues to give his audiences moments of great thrills, either by the beauty of the Metropolitan performances or by the addition of great voices to the already plentiful roster. This bringing of Madame Pons to America signalizes our introduction to a beautiful coloratura voice, an artist of serious caliber and a very ingratiating personality.

Briefly to relate the happenings of this afternoon it must be said that Madame Pons was received with acclaim immediately after the first act and with a real ovation after the Mad Scene. Cries of "brava" were heard from every part of the auditorium with the added thrill of hearing her compatriots exclaiming "extraordinaire."

As a singer Madame Pons can easily put in her claim with the best coloraturas. The voice is of an exquisite natural beauty, even of register, unusually warm in the lower and limpidly clear in the higher one. And this might be the place to record that Madame Pons sang the Mad Scene in the key of F, something which has not been heard in the Metropolitan since times immemorial.

Furthermore, the voice is fresh and very easily produced in all of its unusual range, and the singer also possesses a remarkable breath control. There were moments when Madame Pons tugged hard at the heart strings with the suavity and warmth of her singing, memorable times being her duet with Gigli in the first act, the famous sextette and parts of the Mad Scene. In the last she also displayed real virtuoso ability because of a certain significant "slancio"; her staccatos are remarkably clean and agile and her chromatics impeccably pure. She knows the art of suave and legato singing and has mastered the very difficult *messa di voce*. From a beautiful *pianissimo* she can with utmost ease swell into a luscious *forte*, and every singer knows that this technical feat is the "bête noir" of all aspirants to vocal greatness.

As a personality Madame Pons is very pleasing; she has assurance, an ingratiating charm and an obviously serious outlook toward her art. On the stage she presents a lovely figure, for she is slender and very vivacious; her acting is convincing and has authority. It must also be said that Madame Pons's costumes were little masterpieces of beauty and good taste.

It was an auspicious debut, and the artist is a valuable addition to a house which can boast of the best available talent.

CHAPTER SIX

"Lakmé" Returns to the Metropolitan with Pons as Star

Oscar Thompson

After the title role in *Lucia* made her an overnight star, Pons assumed four new roles in rapid succession during her first season at the Met: Gilda in *Rigoletto*, Rosina in *Il barbiere di Siviglia*, Olympia in *Les contes d'Hoffmann*, and Philine in *Mignon*. In a review of her first Gilda, the New York *World* reported that "a roar of ecstasy filled the house and upheld an undiminished clamor for ten minutes," the reviewer judging her performance "even more sensational than the success of her debut." Her first appearance as Rosina, on 27 January 1931, was equally well received; *Musical America* recorded that "her numerous assets of looks, voice and acting won the reward of an ovation which surpassed anything witnessed . . . since the debut of Galli-Curci in *Lucia*."

During her second season, 1931–32, Pons took on two additional roles: *La sonnambula*'s Amina and the title role in Delibes's *Lakmé*. The latter was revived especially for her by general manager Giulio Gatti-Casazza, and Pons's portrayal of the Hindu maiden became an immediate sensation. Coupled with the astonishing precision she displayed in the Bell Song, *Lakmé*'s centerpiece aria, her arresting costume—a silk wrap that clung to her hips well below her navel, and a jeweled halter that covered her breasts but little else—guaranteed her a level of media attention that no other soprano could then command. Longtime critic Oscar Thompson reviewed her first performance of *Lakmé* in the pages of *Musical America* in February 1932,[1] a periodical with which Thompson was associated from 1918 until 1943.

*I*N A NEW TURN of the operatic wheel of fortune, spun backward for the sake of the type of singing of an elder day, Léo Delibes's *Lakmé*, book by Gondinet and Gille, was returned to currency at the Metropolitan the night of 19 February. Forty-nine years had elapsed since this work was added to the stock and larder of the French lyric theater; fifteen since its melodies were last sounded within the walls of the New York opera house. Obviously, the revival was undertaken with the thought of providing a suitable role for the popular Lily Pons, and in doing this, to freshen, if the fates would so decree, a rather jaded repertoire.

The revival achieved its purpose with regard to Mme Pons, who was whole-heartedly applauded for her performance of the bravura Bell Song and called before the curtains many times, alone as well as in company with her companion artists, Georges Thill, Giuseppe de Luca, Léon Rothier and others of the cast, augmented by the conductor, Louis Hasselmans, and stage director, Alexander Sanine.

Such success as the work achieved was due to the diminutive soprano's graceful and vocally charming presentation of the titular role and to an elaborate if conventional ballet. Delibes, in his day—the 1870s and 1880s—was the ballet writer par excellence, and he did not fail to include in *Lakmé* an example of his skill in this direction. Inconsequential as the music devised for the dancers was, it enabled Rosina Galli's coryphées to provide another of the quasi-Oriental divertissements that seldom fail to excite the approval of the eye-minded among subscribers.

For the best of Delibes, there are those who feel that *Coppelia* and *Sylvia* are preferable to anything in *Lakmé*; indeed, there are Parisians who will assure you that no later composer has written a ballet superior to them, or to the earlier *La source*. But these are scores for tapering toes and woven spaces, not for larynxes cultivated to make dulcet sounds on the upper tones and to turn with agility scale passages such as may or may not be pertinent to what is taking place upon the stage.

Conceived in the early '80s of the last century, *Lakmé* represents a then current obsession among French artists—poets, painters, novelists, composers—for the East and the Near East. Though its characters are either Hindu or English, they are the product of the French romantic interest in Arabs, Egyptians, Turks, Chinese and Biblical folk that ran to the picturesque more than to any very stern confrontation of the realities. The tale of *Lakmé* is a precursor of that of *Madama Butterfly*, with a Hindu rather than a Japanese locale; but much less affecting, largely because Delibes and his librettists had not the ability to make their characters equally human. The English officers remain chiefly uniforms; the Hindus the lay figures inherited from the grand manner days of Meyerbeer.

The music derives from Gounod and from Auber, who was Delibes's master, and leads naturally enough on to Massenet, who loved and respected Delibes and completed for him one of his later operas. The scoring represents some advance over *Faust* and *Carmen*, but *Lakmé* approximates neither in the inspiration of its melodies or in the vitality of dramatic expression.

The soprano-contralto duet of the first act, Nilakantha's adjuration to Lakmé and her succeeding Bell Song, the "forest murmurs" introduction to the last act (scarcely even diluted Wagner), Lakmé's slumber song and Gérald's awakening "Ah! viens, dans cette paix profonde" are all agreeable examples of the fluency, the taste and the ingratiating neatness of a minor composer's art, but their substance is slight and their dramatic significance almost nil.

The revival was given the benefit of an elaborate stage production in which the ballet and the stage crowds supplied no lack of color. Joseph Novak's scenery was of a conventional order but well executed; a little too suggestive, perhaps, of Cook's or of American Express placards and world tour steamship advertising.

The opportunity to hear Miss Pons in a French role not confined to pyrotechnics obviously was welcomed by many of her admirers. Most of the singing demanded of her was of a lyric order, and she met it with a tone of appealing quality and a nicely poised style. In the brief bravura of the Bell Song she soared brilliantly to the thrice-sounded high E and turned her staccato phrases with charm as well as skill. Her trill was musical and sure. Moreover, her slenderness enabled her to suggest the young Hindu maiden in a manner credible to the eye.

Georges Thill was a handsome figure as Gérald and sang the greater part of his music with good style and appealing tone, though exceptions must be noted with respect to some upper notes that were lacking in support and fullness. Gladys Swarthout united her voice prettily with that of Mme Pons in the first-act duet, and Messrs. de Luca and Rothier brought to the roles of Frédéric and Nilakantha the good qualities to be expected of two such experienced and able artists.

That *Lakmé* will remain long in the repertory, this reviewer can only doubt. Agreeable vehicle that it is for Mme Pons, and popular as the ballet is likely to be, other operas, with or without a ballet, but stocked with more showy bravura are likely to do the young singer greater service in enabling her to maintain and extend her hold upon this public.

CHAPTER SEVEN

Miracles Do Happen, Says Lily Pons

Rose Heylbut

The first detailed interview in which Lily spoke of her early life, her marriage to August Mesritz, and the course of events that brought her to Giulio Gatti-Casazza and the Metropolitan appeared in the October 1931 edition of *The American Magazine*.[1] The author of the article, Rose Heylbut, a freelance writer who specialized in features about music and musicians, would ghostwrite a number of articles published under Lily's name.

O NE JANUARY NIGHT last winter, the great gold curtain of the Metropolitan
Opera House, in New York, parted on a performance of *Lucia di Lammer-moor*. The Lucia of the occasion was an unknown young French girl, making her
American debut. Neither the opera nor the debut gave promise of anything
extraordinary, and the Metropolitan is not easily excited. Its stage is nearly a
city block in length and faces the most critical audience in the world, a cross-sec-tion-of-life audience, composed of people who are used to the best, people who
can pay for the best, and those who simply hunger for beauty.

The lights died down; the conductor walked to his place and began the over-ture. The performance was under way. The house seemed respectful but none
too warm. Fashionable late-comers drew glances away from the stage; here and
there one heard a whisper of "Who's the Lucia? A new one? I wish they'd given
us X instead."

And now the Lucia stepped forward. Instead of a buxom prima donna, the
house saw a small girl, so slight as to be almost fragile, and with burning brown
eyes. A quiver of curiosity tightened up loose ends of interest. Those in the house
who looked at the girl's figure said, "Will she have a voice big enough to be
heard?" Those who looked at her eyes said, "She'll make good!"

Carefully, she followed the action on the stage; fixed those great, ardent eyes
on the conductor; watched for her cue; opened her mouth.

Without effort there floated from between her lips an outpouring of full,
rich, golden tone, which filled the great house to its topmost rafters and pulsed
there thrillingly. Immediately the audience was galvanized. Something almost
tangible flashed from the slim girl on the stage and touched a response in every
heart. There was no more wavering attention; the house was expectant and
tense as the limpid voice rang forth. The act was over at last. The lights went up,
and people could not open their programs fast enough to make sure of the name
of this newcomer. Fingers—jeweled and gnarled—traced the line of dots right
from the word "Lucia." The name of the singer read LILY PONS.

Warm applause greeted Miss Pons for the second act. The house was aroused,
but still curious. It remained for the famous Mad Scene in the third act to confirm
or nullify the evening's promise. The slight Miss Pons came on, at last, in light
robes, her hair disheveled, the look of madness in her eyes, and began poor
Lucy's lament. She sang it, and New York went wild. The performance was
stopped by frenzied applause. That January night wrote operatic history. There
were more than twenty curtain calls. In the wings, world-famed singers clapped
and cheered. Out front, women threw flowers to the stage; men huzza-ed; peo-

ple with wet eyes simply sat still and breathed hard. The performance was over at last; the unknown Lily Pons left the stage a Star.

Seats and standing room were sold out for her subsequent performances. Newspapers and magazines carried her pictures to the farthest reaches of the country. The Metropolitan season was over, finally, and Lily Pons repeated her thrilling successes in Baltimore, Evanston, Chicago, Cincinnati. . . . People began to say, "Who is this Lily Pons? What is there about her?"

Obviously, the first thing to draw attention to a singer is a voice. That, Lily Pons has—a clear, rich, flutelike voice that soars to the F above high C with sweetness and ease, and carries an unexpected warmth in its lower registers. She uses her voice with expert artistry. She is convincing and sincere in her performances.

But Lily Pons has done more than simply sing to the country. She has succeeded in capturing the popular imagination. She has proved to an age that goes on record for being a bit "hard-boiled" that the sheer romance of achievement still exists. As a popular figure, the gifted singer looms less important than the simple girl of twenty-six [sic] who has climbed to the front ranks by means of a little luck and a great deal of hard work and disappointing struggle.

The first thing that pulls one up sharply in talking to Lily Pons is her frank simplicity, her sympathetic, everyday humanness. She is wholly unspoiled by her overwhelming triumph. To meet the honest glance of her brown eyes, to watch her skip about her apartment, to observe the animation of her speech and her graceful French gestures, is to know that no one is half so excited about it all as Lily Pons herself. A spontaneous response rises in one's heart. That spontaneous response, multiplied by thousands, explains the reaction of audiences to this new star, who looks like a schoolgirl.

Lily Pons is entirely unconscious of Self. I met her for the first time about two weeks after her Metropolitan debut. She was ill in bed with *la grippe*. It was a stormy day; the sort of weather that gets on a well person's nerves. In her apartment one could hear the blare of a nearby radio; someone next door was singing endless strings of scales on "Ah"—everyday hotel noises, which can be distinctly disturbing. But Lily Pons was entirely unconcerned by them. She was in bed, in a perfectly plain suit of blue pajamas. A bottle of medicine and a bottle of mineral water stood on a little table beside her.

"The gentleman next door is giving a singing lesson," she said; "he's a teacher. It'll be nicer quiet, of course, but other people have to be considered. And I hope you won't mind if I have to talk in a whisper?"

On the wall hung a Metropolitan Opera House playbill.

"I like to look at my name in print as I lie here," she confided, "and tell myself it's real!"

I asked her point-blank how she explained the extraordinary appeal of her work.

"The real reason is the wonderful kindness of the American audiences. They seem to know just what I mean.

"The people feel that singing means happiness to me. I sing because I love it," she said simply; "I love it more than anything else in the world. When I sing, I am completely content. If I sing well, I feel a definite physical tingling all over my body."

A second answer to the magic of Lily Pons's appeal lies in her natural wholesomeness.

In her twenty-six years [*sic*], she has looked life squarely in the eyes and found it gallantly exciting. She has faced the world, earned her own living, suffered illness that changed the course of her destiny, tasted disappointment. Her life, before last January, ran so close to that of the average girl of her age, that her triumph has a distinctly "Cinderella" quality.

Miss Pons has been singing less than six years; indeed, her singing at all was accidental. She was born in the south of France—in Cannes—of middle-class parents who, though not professionals, had a deep love for music. She tells you that she was a very usual little girl and strictly brought up. Her chief joy was inventing plays—stirring tragedies, by preference!—and acting them out with her dolls and her playmates. A whimsical love for the make-believe marked her from earliest childhood.

The music-loving family was delighted when little Lily showed an aptitude for the piano. At fourteen, she entered the piano department of the Paris Conservatoire. Lily found herself in the midst of a rigorous routine of piano work, theory of music, harmony, and endless hours of practice. And she entered upon it eagerly, seeing ahead of her all the great things she meant to do in her career as a professional pianist. Her dreams were destined for a sorry crash.

The following year she was taken ill with a serious fever—*une meningite*, the doctors called it—and the rigors of the conservatory life had to be abandoned immediately. Lily Pons was taken home in precarious health, to be built up to normal again. During those weeks of convalescence, the fifteen-year-old girl made a gallant fight against scathing disappointment. Her music and her dreams of glory meant more to her than anything else in the world, and she knew she could never go back to them. Her life lapsed into that of an ordinary "home girl." She puttered about the house, fussed over her clothes, and worried her family occasionally as to what she could do next. At the end of three uneasy years, her love for the theater settled her problem for her.

At eighteen, she found an opportunity to play small parts in a very eminent stock company—that of Max D'Erly. She worked hard and was happy. Again a career lay before her; the years ahead would bring her to the front as an actress. Then, at twenty, she married. "My husband did not object to a public career for me," Miss Pons told me, "but he set the condition that it had to be a first-rate career. He felt that in my two years on the stage, I had not made a large enough place for myself to warrant the sacrifice of our home life. So again I went home, to putter about and occupy myself as a French housewife. In all this time, I had never sung a note."

At twenty, Lily Pons had lost one career and willingly renounced a second. "I wasn't unhappy about it," she said. "I was ready to give up anything to please my husband. And, deep down inside, I never lost faith in myself! I knew I could do things! If I couldn't do them publicly, I could devote myself to music and to art in a small way, privately."

Those first months of marriage offered her the novelty of leisure—not a jobless leisure, fraught with worries, but time to do the things she liked. Inevitably, she went back to her piano practice, sheerly for the love of it. Her husband liked to sit by her side as she played, to listen. Once, while sorting some music, she chanced to sing the theme of one of her pieces. Her husband looked up.

"*Bien*," he said; "*tu as une jolie voix* [you have a pretty voice]. Why not take a few lessons? It would be nice, when friends come in, to make a pleasant evening for them."

Together they went to a vocal teacher. Lily Pons sang for him.

"The last master you studied with," he told her gravely, "gave you a splendid foundation. Your voice is properly placed, your breathing is quite correct, and the fundamental mechanics of singing are in good order."

"But," she stammered, "I never took a singing lesson in all my life!"

In great excitement, then, it was borne in upon her that she possessed that rarest of gifts—a natural singing voice.

That was the beginning. She worked earnestly to develop her voice, never thinking it would carry her farther professionally than her piano work and her stage experience had done. With the crash of two careers behind her, she permitted herself fewer dreams! She practiced, as any music student will, but otherwise her life was that of a young housewife with a hobby.

After three years, though, her teacher thought her voice fine enough to warrant an operatic performance. She sang, she was well received, and had "a thoroughly delightful time." When the performance was over, she went back home.

Other engagements followed, but never on the basis of regular membership in an operatic company. For nearly three years she continued in this way, singing occasionally and staying at home the rest of the time.

Then, two years ago, she was "discovered" in Italy [*sic*]. An audition was arranged for her at the Metropolitan Opera House, in New York. This, at last, looked like the beginning of big things! Her first taste of glamour came to her in a hotel in Verona, when she was notified that the great Metropolitan was ready to listen to her!

She had the greatest qualms about coming to New York to sing for that audition.

She entered the great, darkened opera house with a terror of stage fright in her heart. Somewhere out there, in that vast, empty auditorium, sat Gatti-Casazza, the director of the Metropolitan, who has judged some of the world's greatest singers for nearly as many years as Lily Pons has lived. When the accompaniment for her first song sounded in her ears, she wondered how she would ever get her mouth open to sing.

When she left, some hours later, she carried with her a contract that called for a January debut. The January performance was the *Lucia* that made Lily Pons a star.

Lily Pons explodes the theory that an operatic star must be an exotic creature, wrapped in cotton batting and stardust. She looks younger than her twenty-six years because she is slight. Her crisp brown hair is worn short and parted on the right side. Her skin is clear and fine of texture. She uses no make-up offstage. Her unplucked eyebrows form well-marked natural arches above her intelligent eyes.

She has a wide, frank, schoolgirl smile, and she smiles readily.

"My smallness is often a handicap," she told me. "It's good for my roles, of course—all of them depict young girls—but people think that I'm frail. And I'm not, I'm wiry! I can stand anything—and I love to do things!"

Music, of course, ranks first among the things Miss Pons loves to do; but she is not one-sided about her art. She believes that music, to be real music of wide appeal, must reflect everything that goes on about the musician. It must live, with the same sort of life that touches everyone. She enjoys vigorous exercise; she is fond of walking, riding, swimming, tennis, golf. Her husband is interested in bookish pursuits, and they read much together. She likes to learn things—all sorts of things, like politics, economics, cooking, and chess. She reads the American newspapers avidly, and is well posted on international matters.

She loves people. All kinds of people. She was thrilled when the King of Siam visited her backstage after one of her performances; she was no less thrilled, two days before sailing for South America, when her schedule was already overcrowded, to bestow a radio contest award on an unknown young singer. In the rush of those last days before sailing, she let her own business of shopping and packing wait, in order not to disappoint other people who made demands upon her time.

"My fun?" She reflected a moment. "I think that the best fun lies, not so much in things themselves, as in doing them hard—with one's whole heart. That's what counts!"

Young people might draw inspiration from observing Lily Pons between performances, at work. She is Spartan with herself. Her day is scheduled. She rises before eight and, after a very light breakfast, is at work by nine. The morning hours are devoted to practicing—scales, exercise, vocalizing. Toward noon, a coach comes to her, to work over roles, fencing, stage business. She lunches around one o'clock, takes a brief rest, and then is hard at it again, learning new music, languages, and practicing. At any time during the day she is "on call" for intensive rehearsals on the opera-house stage. Her leisure time begins in the late afternoon. Frequently her "leisure" must be given over to professional appointments that have been made for her   visits to the photographer, interviews, or attendance at some club or school function in her official capacity of prima donna of the Metropolitan Opera Company.

Before the great gold curtain parts, she is not a Star, but simply one of an army of ardent young people who give of their best to their life's work.

"I've gotten this far," says Miss Pons, "and I mean to go farther! If hard work and reverent devotion to art help me, I shall go farther! I want to do big things— not to touch them, but to remain with them. My ambitions now concern themselves not with musicianship alone, but with public musicianship. I must keep faith with all those whose kind acclaim raised me from obscurity a year ago."

CHAPTER EIGHT

Lily Pons and Adelina Patti

W. J. Henderson

The veteran New York *Sun* critic W. J. Henderson heard nearly every major opera singer from the 1880s until his death in 1937. Born in Newark, New Jersey, in 1855 and educated at Princeton, he began his career as a music critic for *The New York Times* in 1887 and became the *Sun*'s resident opera critic in 1902.

In a 28 January 1931 review of Pons's Rosina in *Il barbiere di Siviglia*, her third Metropolitan role, Henderson found considerable fault with her and proceeded to catalog the deficits of her singing. After several angry readers wrote letters to the editor questioning Henderson's judgment and contending that Pons's approach to Rossini was in the tradition of the great Patti, the critic answered his objectors with this article for the *Sun*, entitled "Lily Pons and Adelina Patti."[1] This was in February 1931, one month after Lily's debut at the Met.

*A*DELINA PATTI has become a legend. She seems to be regarded as one who lived in a far-off age of fable. Yet she died no longer ago than 27 September 1919. The occasion of this reflection was the death of Andrew Dam, who used to be one of the great men of the hotel business in this town. He passed from the scene last Sunday at the age of 83, and it was justly recorded of him that he had been a patron of opera. It was also set down that he was one of the group which sponsored the first appearance of Mme Patti in this country.

The operatic introduction of Patti in this country was her debut on any stage as an opera singer. It took place on 24 November 1859, at the old Academy of Music down in Fourteenth street, when she was sixteen years of age. The role which she assumed was that of Lucia in Donizetti's familiar work. At that time Andrew Dam was eleven years old. We find it too hard to believe he lent Maurice Strakosch any money toward financing that memorable season.

. . . In the autumn of 1883 . . . the doors of the Metropolitan Opera House [opened] with a performance of *Faust*. Adelina Patti was not in the company. She was singing side by side with Etelka Gerster in Col. James Henry Mapleson's company at the Academy of Music. She had been out of this country for years after her debut, but returned for concerts in 1881. A little later she was entangled in an unfortunate operatic enterprise downtown but finally she became the mainstay of Mapleson's last seasons at the Academy.

It was not until after Mr. [Henry] Abbey's failure at the Metropolitan that she came under his management. Her last operatic appearances in New York were made in 1893, when she came for one of her numerous farewells and sang in a one-act opera called *Gabrielle*, which had been written for her. Nevertheless, there is an army of gay young bucks ready to flood the town with information about Patti and her art whenever her name is mentioned. Nonetheless she has become a legend and her easily accessible history is buried under an imposing structure of fable.

Much authoritative information has been disseminated as to how Mme Patti sang. The present writer has been sternly rebuked by one gentleman who said that Miss Pons had Patti's lyric line. Perhaps that is true; we should be the last to contend to the contrary, being somewhat uncertain what Patti's lyric line was. Others have told us just how the famous diva's voice sounded, though unfortunately they could not reproduce the sounds and the phonograph was not then working the wonders of today. Still others have endeavored by ingenious comparisons of the voices of Gerster, Melba and Sembrich to bring us to a proper realization of the magnificence of the new Patti.

71

Now all this is utterly futile. You cannot tell anyone how a musical tone sounded. He has to hear it if he is to know; and the younger generation, which was not born nearly forty years ago when the gay young bucks referred to above were saturating themselves with knowledge of Patti, can hear Miss Pons, but not the voice of the dead past. Miss Pons will have to sing as if Melba and Patti and all the rest never lived and the flaming youth of today (when it takes time off from its innocent sports long enough to go to the opera) will have to pronounce its own verdict on the charming prima donna just as if there had never been any other.

The elder James Gordon Bennett is credited with laying down a good newspaper rule: "First get your news; then make a domned fuss about it." The experiment of making the fuss first and putting the goods on show afterward, only to have the article declared below the promise, has been tried at the Metropolitan with fatal results. In the case of Miss Pons it was adjudged the part of wisdom to follow the advice of Mr. Bennett. But the fair young soprano has not been benefitted by the plan because everything possible has been done through stentorian ballyhoo to place her in an untenable position. She is not to blame for this. Probably no one else in the whole world is more astonished than this unknown singer from a small-town theater in Europe at the riot raised over her in this naive metropolis. The opera-going public will have itself to thank when it awakens to a realization of the fact that she no longer enraptures it.

After the debut of this young lady *The Sun* said: "The demonstrations made by the disinterested auditors of Saturday afternoon were doubtless evoked by the astonishment and delight of an assembly which found on the Metropolitan stage a new singer who could actually sing."[2] It is no news that in the kingdom of the blind a one-eyed man is king. Miss Pons is not the only real singer in the Metropolitan company, of course; there are others. But there is an astonishing preponderance of bad singing, worn voices, false intonation and general vocal slovenliness. The Wagner list suffers most. About that let there for a moment be silence.

When in such conditions we are made acquainted with a youthful voice fresh and unspoiled, and a delivery in which fluency and smoothness usually preserve melodic lines, we naturally rejoice. And when the owner of the voice belongs to the imperishable breed of florid singers, the select circle of "divas" whose utterances are decorated with all the graces of the most ornate vocal art, we bow in worship; for the dramatic soprano may strut and sob and stagger and die of aromatic pain under her manzanilla tree, but the prima donna, trailing her celestial garments of coloratura and crowned with her glittering diadem of high tones, reigns immortal on the throne of public adulation.

To New York opera-goers, who had for several seasons listened with fading pleasure to a diva grown weary with long well doing [i.e., Galli-Curci], the advent of Miss Pons assumed an importance not entirely justified, and now the young woman is suffering the sudden cooling of the warmth which glowed around her debut. After her Lucia one heard only of her merits; after her Rosina one heard plaintive catalogues of her defects.

The unconsidered references to famous singers of the past, most of whom have not been heard by those making the references, should be taken with large grains of salt. And furthermore, when the reference is made by one who has heard the famous singer, his knowledge of the art of song should be carefully examined. There was a thunder of history when [Rosa] Ponselle sang Violetta and those who stood firmly for the observance of the style of Verdi's music were severely chided for failing to recognize the superior claims of Miss Ponselle's passionate acting.

The answer is simple. Verdi declared that the ideal singer of his Violetta was Adelina Patti. The great soprano displayed in all her impersonations about as much passion as one of the ladies on the frieze of the Parthenon. Comedy she had indeed; her Rosina was enchanting. Only the beloved Sembrich ever rivaled her in that role. But when Mme Patti sang Aida, which she ventured once or twice, the tortured slave of the Nile became a perfect lady. And once upon a time—such a lamentable time—she sang Carmen, right in the Metropolitan Opera House. This writer said of that impersonation that Carmen was a cat, but Patti made her a kitten.

She was the ideal Violetta of Verdi because she attended strictly to her business of singing the music into which the immortal master had translated the soul of the courtesan glorified by love. All the successful singers of the part have reached their ends by pure singing, not by pantomimic demonstrations, gasps or coughs.

Reverting to Rosina, the question may be asked, what made Patti irresistible in the part? Two things: first the elegance, the élan and swallowlike grace and swiftness of her delivery of the music; and second, the captivating daintiness and charm of her comedy. As the distinguished baritone Ffrangcon-Davies once said to this writer, "Patti was a witch." There was never any doubt in the mind; when Patti sang Rosina, she was simply adorable. And Rossini's gay and volatile music seemed to be the natural and spontaneous utterance of her own spirit.

We do not wish to make too ponderous a theme of Miss Pons; but here is a charming and (in the beginning, at any rate) modest young woman whose promise has been treated as the full fruition of a rich talent. The truth is that she has much, very much, to learn. "Ars longa; vita brevis." Artists are made, not born. The singer may be born with the voice of a decade, but she has to learn how to use it, and after that to find the way to penetrate the meanings of masterpieces and publish them to auditors.

Violin prodigies like Ricci and Menuhin are born with a special gift for the violin, but they have to learn how to play upon the instrument and afterward to interpret great compositions. Little boys do not come into the world with some magic power which enables them to grasp the form and content of the Beethoven concerto. They have to toil up the long slopes of Parnassus before they reach the top. Year by year the relation of the various parts of such a work to the whole is made clearer and clearer by study till one day the infant phenomenon, grown to the stature of a young master, sends out the strains of the masterwork into the crowded auditorium with the voice of authority.

Miss Pons has precious gifts. Someday she may be a great singer. She is not one yet. Applause is hurled at her in masses, but how long will that last if she stands still? The public is indifferent to all things save its own pleasure. It is fatally ready to shout: *"La reine est mort; vive la reine."*

CHAPTER NINE

A Lady Who Can Scrimshaw a Melody

P. K. Thomajan

Although Lily herself seems to have taken the negative comments in stride, W. J. Henderson's review of her first Metropolitan Rosina generated sufficient controversy for other columnists to take up her defense. P. K. Thomajan did so in the pages of *Literary Digest*, in an article entitled "A Lady Who Can Scrimshaw a Melody."[1] Thomajan borrowed his title from the writings of Henderson, who had an expertise in sailing and navigation as well as in music; in his review, Henderson had made a reference to the public's peculiar fascination with birdlike sopranos who "can scrimshaw a melody more elaborately than a sailor can carve a whale's tooth."

For her part, Lily found a positive side to Henderson's remarks, as she often would when confronting something negative and discomforting. In a letter addressed to Henderson on 9 February 1931, she wrote: "To read the comments of such a distinguished and authoritative gentleman as yourself, who has favored me by including my name in print next to that of the great Adelina Patti, is assuredly an honor that I do not deserve." She closed the letter (which she had written in French) with an artfully phrased thank-you that must have softened the flinty Henderson: "Be assured, kind sir, that your little lady who knows that she has much to learn, appreciates your advice and will do her best to heed it."[2]

W ILL *COUSINE* Pons simply repeat the history of Marion Talley?

The frank and simple little French girl from the Riviera, with dark, sparkling eyes, has awakened the slumbering echoes of Talley first nights at the Metropolitan, and wiseacres are saying [Lily] is just another nine days' wonder.

"Miss Pons has to face the fate of all newcomers," writes Mr. Henderson of the New York *Sun*. "History shows us that one singer after another is made the subject of uproarious acclamation at the Metropolitan, only to be treated after a season or two with heartless indifference."

This, though, is an indictment of the musical public rather than the singer, and the curious fact is that the victim is usually a singer like Marion Talley or Lily Pons. Mr. Henderson proceeds:

"No other type of singer ever excites such hysterical utterances of ecstasy as the lady who can scrimshaw a melody more elaborately than a sailor can carve a whale's tooth.

"The death knell of florid song has been sounded many times, and its perfect absurdity as a form of song speech in lyric drama demonstrated with irrefutable logic.

"Nevertheless the vox populi screams itself hoarse whenever a Jenny Lind, an Ilma di Murska, or a Melba swims up from the eastern horizon.

"Miss Pons is not any of these.

"She is just a slender young woman to whom nature gave a very pretty voice, not 'phenomenal,' with a serviceable range from C to F in alt. Miss Pons sang the 'Spargi d'amaro pianto' in *Lucia* in F, not in E-flat, as it stands in published scores, and finished at the top with a genuine vocal tone, not a squeal. She ended 'Caro nome' in *Rigoletto* with a high E. All of which has not the slightest musical or dramatic importance, but ravishes the ear of a human public always hungry for tonal specialties."

Mr. Henderson is sorry for the young lady: "We hope she will be retained as a regular member of the company. But she will have to meet the inevitable diminuendo. They all do."

He thinks she is "in danger of being killed by ridiculous publicity—and the frantic demonstrations of a clacque which has become an intolerable bore to every disinterested opera-goer, and which has almost stopped applause from the general public."

Who is this Lily Pons?

"She is the smallest and thinnest singer you have seen since Maggie Teyte." And she has lovely brown hair.

Some of her sponsors advertised her as having "sung in all the great opera houses of Europe." And the New York *World* rebuked them in saying that "the truth was a better story," for she has appeared in none of the great houses.

Maria Gay and her husband Zenatello, singers of other days, heard her at Montpellier in France. The rest Louis Sherwin tells us in the New York *Evening Post* [15 January 1931]:

"It was through Zenatello that Gatti heard of the phenomenal French coloratura, and offered her an audition if she would come to New York.

"So her first trip to the United States was made last February—just to sing three arias in private. She did the Mad Scene from *Lucia*, the 'Caro nome,' and that good old war-horse, the Bell Song from *Lakmé*. When she had finished, Mr. Gatti turned and rumbled a few words in the ear of Maestro Serafin, who nodded in reply.

"'Are you too tired to sing again?' he asked her.

"'But, no; not at all,' she answered.

"So there was a hasty telephone call to the office of Kuhn, Loeb & Company, and inside of half an hour Otto Kahn walked into the Metropolitan. Once again la Pons sang her three arias, and Mr. Kahn said to Mr. Gatti:

"'Don't let her get away from us.'

"Within twenty-four hours she had signed three contracts—one for five years with the Metropolitan, another to make phonograph records, and another with Coppicus for two years of concerts, after which she had nothing to do but go back home and to work.

"'I worked the entire summer,' she says, 'and how I worked!'

"'But the roles were already familiar, weren't they?'

"'In French, certainly. But I had to learn them all over again in Italian. And I am still doing it. I am working on *The Barber* now.'

"During the brief conversation there is a constant *va-et-vient* [come-and-go] through the apartment. Telephones ring, and you hear appeals for interviews and appointments being rejected. Invitations pour in, for the town is full of people who would gladly exploit the new lion. Madame Pons herself is unruffled, and Zenatello sits beaming peacefully and silently.

"'I cannot go anywhere,' she explains. 'When I do not sing, I go to bed at nine o'clock, and sleep nine hours. Otherwise I could not do all I have to do.

"'It is a bewildering country, this. The rehearsals and the visitors and the interviewers and the photographers. Meanwhile, one has to work. Figure to yourself that I have had three rehearsals already today, and now I must have another.'

"Her manner is frank, simple, and direct. She has a ready smile and keen, vivid eyes. She gives the impression of being a genuine and charming person. At the Metropolitan everybody swears by her. Except probably the other *prime donne*."

Lily Pons is quite an unusual creature. To speak with her is a pleasure; everything about her is sincerity, animation and simplicity. To look at her slim little figure with the great, sparkling brown eyes and radiant smile is to recognize a personality of grace and vitality. One would hardly think her more than eighteen years of age, and, indeed, she is very young still. One cannot imagine that in her short life she could have found the time to prepare herself for the high place she occupies in the lyric world by reason of her natural gifts, hard work and study, now counting twenty French and Italian operas in her repertoire.

"I always have been in a hurry," she answered laughingly, after the writer had remarked upon her meteoric career. "I was born a seven-months' baby, and a few weeks afterward cut my first tooth. At thirteen I entered the Conservatoire de Paris to study for the piano, and graduated at fifteen. Then the legitimate stage appealed to me and while not yet seventeen I played ingénue parts in the famous Théâtre des Variétés in Paris under the direction of the great French actor, Max D'Erly. But the theater without music could not hold my interest as a life work. One day in Italy I heard the great Claudia Muzio in *Traviata*. She made an enormous impression upon me, and coming home I opened my piano and tried my voice, saying to myself, 'Anch'io son cantatrice' (I too am a singer).

"I did not waste time. Next day, I found a teacher. I knew that I possessed a voice but had no idea how far I could go as a singer. I studied seriously in France and Italy, feeling I had a new aim in life and had at last found myself. Three years ago I made my debut as Lakmé at the Municipal Opera of Mulhouse. 'Fortunate nations have no story' goes a French proverb; nor, in my opinion, do fortunate singers. I sang the coloratura repertoire in several of the most important opera houses of France and Belgium, studied hard between performances, and that is about all I can tell you about my career."

When pressed to tell about her past successes, Lily Pons answered with decision, "No, I will only say that what the world calls success is to me only a great stimulant, urging one on to do larger and better things every time. When I hear the sincere warm applause of my audience, I always feel very grateful, and coming home, I often run over the score of the last performance in a spirit of self-criticism and, perhaps, in these moments an artist does the most constructive work."

"You surely seem to love your profession," this writer added.

"Yes," she said slowly, "I love everything about it. My greatest happiness, of course, is the singing itself. I do not know if my career will always bring me success but there is one thing I pray for with all my heart: that I may sing as long as my ears and voice are good and that I may always have the good fortune to be able to appear in productions where every detail is as carefully prepared as at the Metropolitan Opera House."

"How do you learn your parts?" she was asked.

"First of all, I must know them musically, with painful precision. That is easy enough. Then I have to seek for the greatest beauty of every note, every passage, every phrase. I always am thinking about those things, even in the street or in the train, trying to find out if I cannot give a finer nuance or a deeper expression. This [demands] steady work and sometimes months and months pass before I am satisfied with an aria. But then when, by practicing over and over all these technical difficulties, something seems to crystallize in my subconscious mind, as Freud would say, at last I am able to sing as if everything came from my own heart. Then for me all other things disappear, there is no conductor, nor public— I sing for the mere joy of singing and sometimes the applause wakes me up as out of a dream. These are the best moments of an artist's life."

"But how do you manage the dramatic part of it?"

"This goes hand in hand with the musical study, not only of my own part but also of the whole work. I read my text carefully. The music gives the main indications for the character I have to incarnate. An actor can hesitate if he will play a certain scene with passion or melancholy, with irony or fury; a singer cannot, the music gives the cue.

"To assure myself of the correct interpretation of any part, I study everything I can find about the opera and the original drama or novel it is taken from. So for *Rigoletto*, I studied that old *Le Roi s'amuse* of Victor Hugo; for *Il barbiere di Siviglia* and *Le nozze di Figaro* I took up Beaumarchais's comedies and read his private letters about his own conception of the characters. Some of these letters are very polemical. For instance, about the character of Cherubino, that critics of the eighteenth century judged to be immoral, Beaumarchais in his private letters gives the most useful information. But one has to be careful. The Lucia of Walter Scott is quite another person than Donizetti's idealized bride and, of course, I must interpret Donizetti's."

"And what about your costumes?"

"They must answer to my own conception of the character I have to play. Therefore, I usually design them myself. Having grown up in a milieu of painters and sculptors, I became an amateur of plastic art. In my Paris home I possess quite a collection of documents about costumes, styles and ornaments. If ever you go to Paris and I am there, I will show you some of them. I have a most interesting collection of reproductions of Hindu art and Hindu costumes of all times. I started it when I had to make my debut in *Lakmé* and it revealed many pretty things to me, not only about costumes, but also about attitudes and gestures. My dresses for Rosina in *Il barbiere* are taken from Spanish pictures; the first one is from a Llanos which is in a private collection—I only changed the colors. The second one is from Goya himself. I believe they are rather unusual, but of the purest Spanish style.

"It is one of the most amusing and relaxing things for me to design and study the costumes appropriate for each part. But then I have to pay for the pleasure, for nothing is more tiresome than to pass a whole day at the dressmaker's trying them on and afterward posing for the camera."

"What do you like beside your profession?"

"Everything that appeals to a woman. I like art, nice frocks, motor cars. I have a special love for animals and they like me. I am fond of traveling. I like a good dinner, and even—but do not tell it to anybody—a glass of our good French wine. I like life because it has been kind to me, and I can tell you that at this hour of the night, I like to sleep!"

A Photographic Portfolio

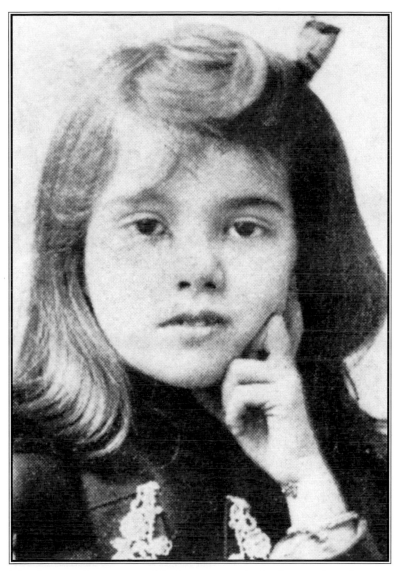

Lily Pons at four years old, the age at which she saw her first opera. Prophetically, the opera was *Lucia di Lammermoor.*
PHOTOGRAPHER UNIDENTIFIED. LUDECKE-PONS COLLECTION.

Lily with her mother, Marie Pons, in 1940.
PHOTOGRAPHER UNIDENTIFIED.
LUDECKE-PONS COLLECTION.

Lily Pons and her first husband, August Mesritz,
in 1931. PHOTOGRAPHER UNIDENTIFIED. LUDECKE-PONS
COLLECTION.

Pons in 1929, displaying the large diamond ring that Mesritz gave her on the occasion of their engagement. CLAYTON PHOTO STUDIOS, BUENOS AIRES. LUDECKE-PONS COLLECTION.

Lily Pons during her budding singing career in her native France in the late 1920s. STUDIO LORELLE, PARIS. LUDECKE-PONS COLLECTION.

A portrait of Pons in the role of Rosina from *Il barbiere di Siviglia* during the 1928 season at the Grand-Théâtre in Lille, France. STUDIO LORELLE, PARIS. LUDECKE-PONS COLLECTION.

Lily Pons in 1931, on the verge of her American career. ROSÉ STUDIO, PARIS. LUDECKE-PONS COLLECTION.

Pons and Amelita Galli-Curci in 1936. The *coloratura assoluta* of the Metropolitan
Opera during the 1920s, Galli-Curci retired in January 1930, creating a void in the
Met's coloratura ranks that paved the way for Pons's debut the following season.
PHOTOGRAPHER UNIDENTIFIED. COURTESY OF BILL PARK.

With Giulio Gatti-Casazza, general manager of the Metropolitan Opera, and tenor
Beniamino Gigli, who sang opposite Pons in her Met debut in *Lucia di Lammermoor.*
WIDE WORLD PHOTOS. COURTESY OF THE METROPOLITAN OPERA ARCHIVES.

Four days after her *Lucia* debut, Pons created another sensation at the Metropolitan when she sang her first Gilda in *Rigoletto*. METROPOLITAN MUSICAL BUREAU, NEW YORK. COURTESY OF THE METROPOLITAN OPERA ARCHIVES.

Rosina in *Il barbiere di Siviglia* was Pons's third Metropolitan role, coming less than a month after her Met debut. CARLO EDWARDS STUDIOS, NEW YORK. COURTESY OF THE METROPOLITAN OPERA ARCHIVES.

As Rosina, Metropolitan Opera Company, 1930–31 season. METROPOLITAN MUSICAL
BUREAU, NEW YORK. LUDECKE-PONS COLLECTION.

Pons first sang the role of Olympia, the
mechanical doll in *Les contes d'Hoffmann*,
on 14 February 1931. The role was her
fourth at the Met in a mere six weeks.
METROPOLITAN MUSICAL BUREAU, NEW YORK.
COURTESY OF BILL PARK.

Philine in Thomas's *Mignon*, Pons's fifth
Metropolitan role, entered her repertoire
on 6 April 1931. CARLO EDWARDS STUDIOS,
NEW YORK. COURTESY OF BILL PARK.

LILY PONS
COLORATURA SOPRANO
METROPOLITAN OPERA C°

As Cherubino in *Le nozze di Figaro*, a role Pons sang in Europe and South America, but never in North America. STUDIO LORELLE, PARIS. LUDECKE-PONS COLLECTION.

Pons's greatest triumph was as the title heroine of Delibes's *Lakmé*. In addition to her vocal assets, Pons created a sensation by her trim figure, which allowed her to don an array of revealing (for the time) costumes. MAURICE SEYMOUR STUDIOS, CHICAGO. LUDECKE-PONS COLLECTION.

Of the several costuming variations Pons tried in *Lakmé,* this was by far the most revealing. In the Met dressing room, March 1932. PHOTOGRAPHER UNIDENTIFIED. COURTESY OF BILL PARK.

Program from a 1935 Met performance of *Lakmé.* LUDECKE-PONS COLLECTION.

Pons displays yet another variation of her *Lakmé* costumes as she greets French ambassador Henri Bonnet after a touring performance in Cleveland on 11 November 1946. Due to a permanent scar resulting from an appendectomy she underwent in 1934, Lily could no longer wear the hip-hugging silken wraps she had favored in the early 1930s. PHOTOGRAPHER UNIDENTIFIED. LUDECKE-PONS COLLECTION.

General John J. Pershing, commander of the Allied forces during World War I, greets Lily in her dressing room following a 1932 performance of *Lakmé*. METROPOLITAN MUSICAL BUREAU, NEW YORK. COURTESY OF THE METROPOLITAN OPERA ARCHIVES.

Entertaining a group of students in her dressing room after a matinee performance of *Lakmé* sponsored by the Metropolitan Opera Guild. Seated at far left is a young student named Bernard Schwartz, who would later make his mark in Hollywood as Tony Curtis.
METROPOLITAN MUSICAL BUREAU, NEW YORK. LUDECKE-PONS COLLECTION.

Amina in Bellini's *La sonnambula* became Pons's seventh Metropolitan role on 16 March 1932. CARLO EDWARDS STUDIOS, NEW YORK. COURTESY OF THE METROPOLITAN OPERA ARCHIVES.

Pons as Amina, with conductor Tullio Serafin, in February 1933. Throughout her early years at the Metropolitan, Pons benefitted from the mentoring of Serafin, who over the course of his long career also served as mentor for Rosa Ponselle and Maria Callas.

METROPOLITAN MUSICAL BUREAU, NEW YORK. COURTESY OF THE METROPOLITAN OPERA ARCHIVES.

Mezzo-soprano Gladys Swarthout (right) sang the role of Pierotto, the orphan boy in Donizetti's *Linda di Chamounix,* when Pons undertook the title role in the opera's Metropolitan premiere on 1 March 1934. METROPOLITAN MUSICAL BUREAU, NEW YORK. COURTESY OF THE METROPOLITAN OPERA ARCHIVES.

INTERNATIONALLY FAMOUS COLORATURA
of the
METROPOLITAN OPERA COMPANY

LILY PONS

Concerts
-1936

Baldwin Piano   Photo "PIAZ" PARIS

113 WEST 57TH ST., NEW YORK
OF COLUMBIA BROADCASTING SYSTEM

By the 1935–36 season, Lily Pons was a leading artist for the Metropolitan Musical Bureau, predecessor of Columbia Artists Management, which booked her concerts for the duration of her long career. LUDECKE-PONS COLLECTION.

Pons introduced her ninth Metropolitan role, the Queen of Shemakha in Rimsky-Korsakov's *Le coq d'or*, in February 1937. METROPOLITAN MUSICAL BUREAU. LUDECKE-PONS COLLECTION.

As the Queen of Shemakha, Pons accomplished the rare feat of both singing and dancing the role. Here she rehearses the dance sequences with Ezio Pinza, who portrayed King Dodon in the 1937 revival of *Le coq d'or*. PHOTOGRAPHER UNIDENTIFIED. COURTESY OF ANDREW FARKAS.

The United States's entry into World War II lent an undeniable poignancy to Pons's portrayal of Marie, the plucky *vivandière* in Donizetti's *La fille du régiment*, which the Metropolitan Opera revived for her during the 1940–41 season. METROPOLITAN MUSICAL BUREAU, NEW YORK. LUDECKE-PONS COLLECTION.

Pons as Marie in the final act of *La fille du régiment*, her tenth and final role at the Metropolitan

As the irrepressible *vivandière* for a wartime revival of *La fille du régiment* in San Francisco, November 1942. PRESS ASSOCIATION, INC. LUDECKE-PONS COLLECTION.

In financial duress during the Depression, the Metropolitan Opera staged a series of benefits, including the elaborate lampoon called *Opera-Tunities* on 31 March 1935. Playing upon the contrasting physiques of the petite Pons and the gargantuan Lauritz Melchior, one scene featured them as circus acrobats and, through the magic of unseen wires and hoists, had Pons appear to lift the 300-pound tenor with one hand. WIDE WORLD PHOTOS. COURTESY OF THE METROPOLITAN OPERA ARCHIVES.

At a subsequent Metropolitan Opera benefit in 1937, Pons and Melchior delighted the audience with a cross-dressing sketch. METROPOLITAN MUSICAL BUREAU, NEW YORK. COURTESY OF THE METROPOLITAN OPERA ARCHIVES.

RCA Victrola
(RADIO-PHONOGRAPH)

..*"IT FAITHFULLY AND PERFECTLY REPRODUCES MY VICTOR RECORDS"*

Lily Pons

Having signed a recording contract for RCA Victor's prestigious Red Seal label in the same week she was awarded her first Metropolitan Opera contract in 1930, Pons would remain a top RCA attraction throughout the decade. RADIO CORPORATION OF AMERICA. LUDECKE-PONS COLLECTION.

RCA Victor was quick to exploit its newest coloratura after her singing—and costuming— in *Lakmé* made headlines. STUDIO LORELLE, PARIS. LUDECKE-PONS COLLECTION.

By January 1935, owing chiefly to her growing relationship with conductor André Kostelanetz, Pons had achieved star status on radio. ARTWORK BY EARL CHRISTY. LUDECKE-PONS COLLECTION.

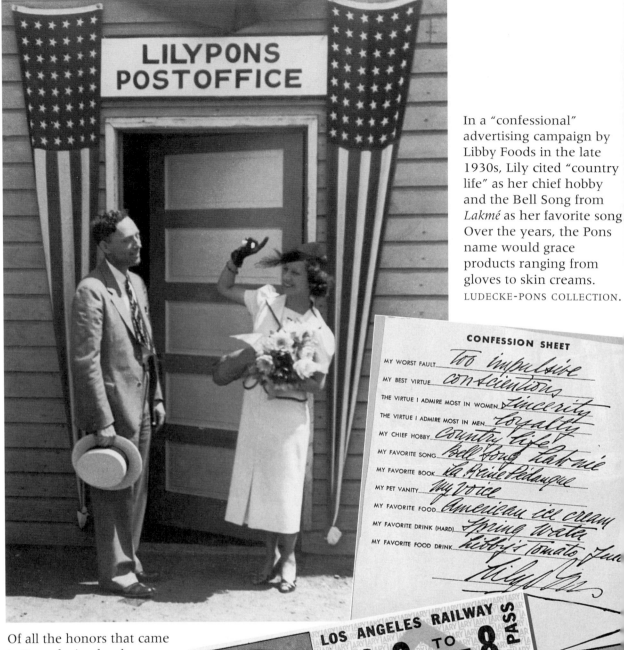

In a "confessional" advertising campaign by Libby Foods in the late 1930s, Lily cited "country life" as her chief hobby and the Bell Song from *Lakmé* as her favorite song Over the years, the Pons name would grace products ranging from gloves to skin creams. LUDECKE-PONS COLLECTION.

CONFESSION SHEET

MY WORST FAULT *Too impulsive*
MY BEST VIRTUE *conscientious*
THE VIRTUE I ADMIRE MOST IN WOMEN *sincerity*
THE VIRTUE I ADMIRE MOST IN MEN *loyalty*
MY CHIEF HOBBY *Country life*
MY FAVORITE SONG *Bell Song Lakmé*
MY FAVORITE BOOK *La Reine Pédauque*
MY PET VANITY *My Voice*
MY FAVORITE FOOD *American ice cream*
MY FAVORITE DRINK (HARD) *Spring water*
MY FAVORITE FOOD DRINK *Libby's tomato Juice*

Of all the honors that came to Pons during her long career, she had the singular distinction of having a town named for her. In June 1936 Lily was photographed with the local postmaster, Clarence C. C. Thomas, at the door of the newly named post office of Lilypons, Maryland. PHOTOGRAPHER UNIDENTIFIED. COURTESY OF CHARLES THOMAS.

A Los Angeles Railway pass promoting Pons's appearance at the Hollywood Bowl in August 1936. LUDECKE-PONS COLLECTION.

In the early 1950s, the soprano's popularity spawned a collection of Lily Pons dolls, each costumed for a specific role—including two she never sang, Carmen and Nedda in *Pagliacci*. LUDECKE-PONS COLLECTION.

In the mid-1930s, RKO studios brought Alberti de Gorostiaga (far right), Pons's voice teacher, to Hollywood to work with Lily during the recording of the soundtrack for her first film, *I Dream Too Much*. PHOTOGRAPHER UNIDENTIFIED. LUDECKE-PONS COLLECTION.

Pons in her first film, *I Dream Too Much*, 1935, opposite the up-and-coming Henry Fonda.

Henry Fonda as Jonathan Street, a struggling American composer, and Pons as Annette Monard, his singer-wife, in *I Dream Too Much*. RKO RADIO PICTURES. LUDECKE-PONS COLLECTION.

A carnival scene provided the setting for Pons's "The Jockey on the Carousel," the most enduring of four songs written for *I Dream Too Much* by composer Jerome Kern and lyricist Dorothy Fields. RKO RADIO PICTURES. LUDECKE-PONS COLLECTION.

Pons prepares to sing "I Got Love," another Jerome Kern–Dorothy Fields collaboration from *I Dream Too Much*. RKO RADIO PICTURES. LUDECKE-PONS COLLECTION.

Pons, as Annette Monard, is transformed into a glamorous opera star in *I Dream Too Much*. Although surrounded by unbilled extras in this scene, Pons underwent a similar transformation at seven o'clock every morning on the RKO lot. RKO RADIO PICTURES. LUDECKE-PONS COLLECTION.

A dressing-room confrontation between Jonathan Street (Henry Fonda), Annette Monard (Lily Pons), and impresario Paul Darcy (Osgood Perkins) in *I Dream Too Much*.

As the filming of *I Dream Too Much* neared completion in September 1935, Pons sat for the obligatory publicity photographs. A collector of pets since childhood, she insisted on having an assortment of dogs, birds, and other pets travel with her during prolonged stays. JOHN ENGSTEAD STUDIOS, HOLLYWOOD. LUDECKE-PONS COLLECTION.

A flower in her hair and a lace fan in her hand, Lily poses for a publicity portrait for the release of *I Dream Too Much*. PHOTOGRAPHER UNIDENTIFIED. LUDECKE-PONS COLLECTION.

Aviator-turned-producer Howard Hughes (center) and New York raconteur Lucius Beebe were among the guests at a Hollywood party Pons gave during the filming of *I Dream Too Much*. PHOTOGRAPHER UNIDENTIFIED. LUDECKE-PONS COLLECTION.

A still from Lily Pons's second film, *That Girl from Paris*. RKO RADIO PICTURES. LUDECKE-PONS COLLECTION.

In *That Girl from Paris,* Pons was cast opposite Gene Raymond and a platinum-blond contract player at RKO named Lucille Ball. RKO RADIO PICTURES. LUDECKE-PONS COLLECTION.

Veteran film comedian Jack Oakie (right) smiles as Gene Raymond is about to become Pons's captive groom in *That Girl from Paris*. RKO RADIO PICTURES. LUDECKE-PONS COLLECTION.

The musical score of *That Girl from Paris* contained little operatic music, but it did offer Pons in a much-abbreviated version of "Una voce poco fa" from *Il barbiere di Siviglia*.
RKO RADIO PICTURES. LUDECKE-PONS COLLECTION.

The principals at RKO Pictures tried to fashion a look for Pons as a potential Hollywood star. This version suggests a Katharine Hepburn look, circa 1936. RKO RADIO PICTURES. LUDECKE-PONS COLLECTION.

Most of the studio publicity photos for *That Girl from Paris* depicted Pons in costumes and poses familiar—if more revealing, in this case—to her opera fans. RKO RADIO PICTURES. LUDECKE-PONS COLLECTION.

In the meager plot of 1937's *Hitting a New High*, Pons was cast as Suzette, a nightclub singer in search of a wealthy patron. RKO RADIO PICTURES. LUDECKE-PONS COLLECTION.

Jack Oakie (left) was cast in *Hitting a New High* as Corny Davis, a press agent who devises a scheme to attract the attention of wealthy hunter Lucius B. Blynne (played by Edward Everett Horton, center) by transforming Suzette into a jungle-dwelling "bird girl" answering to the name Oogahunga. RKO RADIO PICTURES. LUDECKE-PONS COLLECTION.

Pons at the RKO sound studios, in August 1937, reviewing the musical score for *Hitting a New High*. RKO RADIO PICTURES. LUDECKE-PONS COLLECTION.

While concertizing in Hollywood in the late 1930s, Pons paid a visit to Jack Oakie on the RKO lot. After two films together, Pons had developed a lasting fondness for the irrepressible comedian. At right is actress Linda Darnell. RKO RADIO PICTURES. LUDECKE-PONS COLLECTION.

André Kostelanetz in 1935, the year after his popular radio program, *The Chesterfield Hour*, premiered on the CBS network. G. MAILLARD KESSLÈRE, NEW YORK. LUDECKE-PONS COLLECTION.

Pons rehearsing with Kostelanetz at her Connecticut farm, 1936.
PHOTOGRAPHER UNIDENTIFIED. LUDECKE-PONS COLLECTION.

During preparations for *That Girl from Paris*, Pons and Kostelanetz made numerous coast-to-coast flights together. In 1936 André gave Lily a portable piano, custom-made to fit aboard airplanes. PHOTOGRAPHER UNIDENTIFIED. LUDECKE-PONS COLLECTION.

André and Lily on their wedding day, 2 June 1938, in Silvermine, Connecticut. Lily designed the temporary altar and floral backdrop for the intimate ceremony. NEW YORK *DAILY NEWS*. LUDECKE-PONS COLLECTION.

Pons and Kostelanetz prepare to leave for an extended honeymoon in South America. Fashion designer Valentina (far left), mezzo-soprano Gladys Swarthout (directly behind Lily), and the distinguished French basso Léon Rothier (far right) were among the well-wishers attending the intimate reception. MICHAEL CAPUTO STUDIOS, NEW YORK. LUDECKE-PONS COLLECTION.

In Connecticut in late July 1938, Lily poses for magazine photographers in her favorite gardening attire: a Midwestern straw hat, short-sleeve blouse, and culottes (left) and in Oriental garb (right). ACME NEWS PHOTOGRAPHS. LUDECKE-PONS COLLECTION.

The newlyweds, in a 1938 publicity photo.
DE BELLIS STUDIO, NEW YORK. LUDECKE-PONS COLLECTION.

A spray of lilies crowns the cake André gave Lily for her forty-fourth birthday on 13 April 1942—though the soprano claimed it was her thirty-seventh. Her niece, Claire Lily Girardot, looks on as Lily prepares to cut the cake. PHOTOGRAPHER UNIDENTIFIED. LUDECKE-PONS COLLECTION.

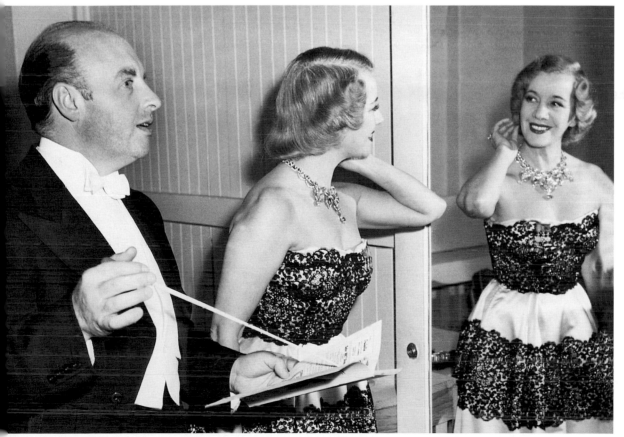

Though the color of her hair may have changed, Pons's sense of glamour as well as her successful collaborations with Kostelanetz continued into the postwar years.
PHOTOGRAPHER UNIDENTIFIED. LUDECKE-PONS COLLECTION.

Ten Gracie Square, the Pons-Kostelanetz penthouse home in Manhattan, reflected both their tastes. The conductor was especially fond of the spiral staircase at the entranceway. BEN GREENHAUS, NEW YORK. LUDECKE-PONS COLLECTION.

André's spacious study at Ten Gracie Square. BEN GREENHAUS, NEW YORK. LUDECKE-PONS COLLECTION.

Lily's dressing room at Ten Gracie Square. BEN GREENHAUS, NEW YORK. LUDECKE-PONS COLLECTION.

COLOR FOR A COLORATURA

MAYBE IT'S SOOTHING—MAYBE
IT'S JUST A FAD. ANYWAY,
LILY PONS SLEEPS IN
A BLACK BED WITH
GREEN SHEETS.

The Pons-Kostelanetz bedroom at Ten Gracie Square. André's preference for muted pastels ultimately gave way to Lily's love of bold, contrasting colors—including (inset) a black bed with emerald-green sheets and bedspread. BEN GREENHAUS, NEW YORK. ; ILLUSTRATION FROM THE SPRINGFIELD [ILLINOIS] STATE JOURNAL. LUDECKE-PONS COLLECTION.

Pons and Kostelanetz relaxing on the patio of her Connecticut home. ACME NEWS PHOTOGRAPHS. LUDECKE-PONS COLLECTION.

With France at war with Germany and Italy, Lily began supporting war-relief causes well before the United States entered World War II. At a September 1940 ceremony in New York's Central Park, the U.S. Army's 71st Regiment officially designated her "a Daughter of the Regiment." Col. Grant Layng accompanies Lily in a salute.

INTERNATIONAL NEWS PHOTOS. LUDECKE-PONS COLLECTION.

Arriving at Grand Central Station in New York after USO appearances in Florida, March 1943. Wartime restrictions reduced Pons's luggage to bare essentials, compared to the twenty or more trunks that she usually traveled with during the 1930s. COSMO-CILEO COMPANY. LUDECKE-PONS COLLECTION.

Signing autographs at the George A. White Servicemen's Center in New York City, October 1943. HAL WHITE, JR. LUDECKE-PONS COLLECTION.

Pons and Kostelanetz receive a paper-cup toast from the Canadian Merchant Marines after a benefit concert with the Toronto Philharmonic Orchestra in 1943. PHOTOGRAPHER UNIDENTIFIED. LUDECKE-PONS COLLECTION.

Flanked by a U.S. Coast Guard contingent, Lily sings "The Star-Spangled Banner" at a Musicians Emergency Fund benefit, 1944. NEW YORK *DAILY NEWS*. LUDECKE-PONS COLLECTION.

With the French tricolor as a backdrop, Lily autographs a brass shell casing for the French battleship *Richelieu,* January 1944. J. WALTER THOMPSON PRESS BUREAU, NEW YORK. LUDECKE-PONS COLLECTION.

Launching the China Relief campaign, 1944. LARRY GORDON STUDIOS, NEW YORK.
LUDECKE-PONS COLLECTION.

Lily and André surround conductor Sergei Koussevitsky at a gathering of supporters for a Russian Relief tour in March 1944. Composer Aaron Copland is seated second from the left. PHOTOGRAPHER UNIDENTIFIED. LUDECKE-PONS COLLECTION.

Packing for the Russian Relief tour, Lily displays her USO uniform. RUSSELL BIRDWELL AND ASSOCIATES/METROPOLITAN PHOTO SERVICE. LUDECKE-PONS COLLECTION.

Before leaving for their first USO tour in May 1944, noncombatant Captains Lily Pons and André Kostelanetz posed for a studio portrait in their wartime uniforms. DE BELLIS STUDIOS, NEW YORK. LUDECKE-PONS COLLECTION.

Frank Versaci (left) and pianist Carolyn Gray (right), shown here with André and Lily at the Fifth Army Headquarters in Italy in July 1944, were among the professional musicians who traveled with the Pons-Kostelanetz USO unit. U.S. ARMY SIGNAL CORPS. LUDECKE-PONS COLLECTION.

Acknowledging applause at a USO appearance, with flautist Frank Versaci accompanying. U.S. ARMY SIGNAL CORPS. LUDECKE-PONS COLLECTION.

Lily and André at the Great Pyramids at Giza while on their USO tour in the Persian Gulf in the spring of 1944. ACME NEWS PHOTOGRAPHS. LUDECKE-PONS COLLECTION.

Taking a bow after a concert in the Persian Gulf, where she had to cope with desert temperatures as high as 120°F. U.S. ARMY SIGNAL CORPS. LUDECKE-PONS COLLECTION.

Lily waiting backstage in Calcutta,
December 1944. Seated with her
is a young baritone from the U.S.
Army, Lorenzo (Larry) Malfatti.
PHOTOGRAPHER UNIDENTIFIED.
COURTESY OF LORENZO MALFATTI.

Invitation to a
wartime black-tie reception
for Pons and Kostelanetz in
Palestine, July 1944.
LUDECKE-PONS COLLECTION.

MAJOR GENERAL B. F. GILES
Commanding General
of the
TED STATES ARMY FORCES IN THE MIDDLE EAST
requests the pleasure of

reception to meet Miss LILY PONS and Mr. ANDRE
KOSTELANETZ, at the Office of War Information,
1 Midan Kasr El Doubara, following their performance on the
evening of Saturday, July 8th, 1944.

Black Tie

R. S. V. P.
TELEPHONE: 46359
EXTENSION : 8 or 29

Signing an autograph for Private George Smith, one of many GIs recovering from
wounds at a field hospital in Burma, December 1944. U.S. ARMY SIGNAL CORPS. LUDECKE-
PONS COLLECTION.

Kostelanetz and Pons with New York mayor Fiorello H. LaGuardia, in 1944. Before his political career, LaGuardia served as personal attorney to Beniamino Gigli and other Metropolitan Opera artists. MICHAEL CAPUTO STUDIOS, NEW YORK. LUDECKE-PONS COLLECTION.

With First Lady Eleanor Roosevelt at a war-relief benefit in Norwalk, Connecticut, 1945.
M. H. MANUGIAN STUDIOS. LUDECKE-PONS COLLECTION.

The Acting Consul General
of the Union of Soviet Socialist Republics
and
Mrs. Mikhailov
request the honor of the company of

Mr. and Mrs. André Kostelanetz

at a reception
in celebration of the
Complete Victory over Nazi Germany
on
Friday, the Eighteenth of May
from five until seven o'clock
at the Consulate
Seven East Sixty-first Street

R.S.V.P.   Please bring this invitation with you

Invitation to a celebration at the Soviet Consulate
in New York City commemorating V-E Day, May
1945. LUDECKE-PONS COLLECTION.

In December 1945 Grace Moore hosted a planning session at her Manhattan apartment for the Musicians for Franco-American Friendship. Left to right: Robert Casadesus, John Brownlee, Lawrence Tibbett, Lily, Mme Henri Bonnet (wife of the French ambassador), Grace Moore, Martial Singher, Jennie Tourel, Lily Djanel, and Emil Cooper.

IRWIN DRIBBEN STUDIOS, NEW YORK. LUDECKE-PONS COLLECTION.

RÉUNION
DES THÉATRES LYRIQUES NATIONAUX

ADMINISTRATEUR
M. MAURICE LEHMANN

THÉATRE NATIONAL DE L'
OPÉRA-COMIQUE
DIRECTEUR
M. ALBERT WOLFF

1.200*

LAKMÉ

OPÉRA-COMIQUE EN 3 ACTES
PAROLES DE E. GONDINET ET PH. GILLE
MUSIQUE DE
LÉO DELIBES

AVEC LE CONCOURS DE

LILY PONS

MERCREDI 10 AVRIL 1946

Publicity photo after an open-air concert in Monte Carlo in April 1946, which attracted an estimated 10,000 attendees. Kostelanetz conducted this benefit concert for the French Second Armored Division. ERPÉ STUDIOS, NICE. LUDECKE-PONS COLLECTION.

Title page from the program for a performance of *Lakmé* in Monte Carlo, 10 April 1946.

Cast list for Pons's Covent Garden debut, in *Il barbiere di Siviglia.* Her three appearances there in May 1935 were the only opera performances Lily ever sang in London. LUDECKE-PONS COLLECTION.

ROYAL OPERA
: : COVENT GARDEN : :
Lessees: Royal Opera House Company, Ltd.
Managing Director: Geoffrey Toye

London & Provincial Opera Society, Ltd., Season

THIS EVENING'S PERFORMANCE
Thursday, May 23rd, 1935, at 8.15

In Italian

IL BARBIERE DI SIVIGLIA

By ROSSINI
debut

Rosina . . . . LILY PONS
Bertha . . . . . . EBE TICOZZI
Conte d'Almaviva . . HEDDLE NASH
Figaro . . . GIOVANNI INGHILLERI
Don Basilio . . . . . EZIO PINZA
Fiorello . . . ARISTIDE BARACCHI
Dr. Bartolo . . . CARLO SCATTOLA
Sergente . . . . . FRANK SALE

Conductor . . . VINCENZO BELLEZZA

Princess Alice, sister-in-law of Britain's Queen Mary, pays tribute to Pons for her
contributions to British and Canadian war-relief efforts, 1946. WIDE WORLD PHOTOS.
LUDECKE-PONS COLLECTION.

In a ceremony at the Palais Elysées in May 1947, Vincent Auriol, president of the Republic of France, presents Pons with the rosette of the Legion of Honor in recognition of her support of the Allied war effort. INTERNATIONAL NEWS PHOTOS. LUDECKE-PONS COLLECTION.

Pons and Kostelanetz's wartime activities only increased their celebrity status in peacetime, as they set attendance records in major cities across the U.S. On 20 July 1945, Milwaukee's "Music Under the Stars" concert drew an estimated 30,000 people.

In the 1946–47 season, Pons drew record crowds for a concert at the Teatro Colón in Buenos Aires. PHOTOGRAPHER UNIDENTIFIED. LUDECKE-PONS COLLECTION.

Lily poses atop a globe to symbolize her world travels. By the late 1940s, her appearances in operas, concerts, and the USO tours had spanned five continents.
KARSH, OTTAWA. LUDECKE-PONS COLLECTION.

Pons in concert, Chicago, 1938–39 season. Her dress, which closely resembled her costume as Rosina in *Il barbiere di Siviglia,* was what publicist Humphrey Doulens called "one of those 'planned coincidences' that Lily would use to publicize something she was doing." In this case, the "coincidence" was her first Chicago appearance as Rosina, at the Chicago City Opera that same season. DE BELLIS STUDIOS, NEW YORK. LUDECKE-PONS COLLECTION.

"Many opera parties have been inspired by *Lucia,* in which Lily Pons will be starring at the Opera House this evening," the San Francisco *News* reported on 25 October 1939 before Pons was to sing the title role there. METROPOLITAN MUSICAL BUREAU. LUDECKE-PONS COLLECTION.

Program from a 1942 Metropolitan Opera
performance of *Lucia di Lammermoor.*
LUDECKE-PONS COLLECTION.

In a Saturday matinee performance on 28
November 1942, the Met presented a refurbished
production of *Lucia di Lammermoor* with Lily in the
title role. Manhattan couturière Valentina designed
Lily's costumes for the production. DE BELLIS
STUDIOS, NEW YORK. COURTESY OF ANDREW FARKAS.

Pons as Lucia, San Francisco Opera production, 1944. DE BELLIS STUDIOS, NEW YORK.
LUDECKE-PONS COLLECTION.

Lakmé continued to attract audiences wherever Pons performed the role. In 1940 she sang Lakmé at the Chicago Civic Opera House. DE BELLIS STUDIOS, NEW YORK. LUDECKE-PONS COLLECTION.

In July 1945 in Mexico City, Pons sang *Rigoletto* under the baton of Gaetano Merola (center) at the Opera Nacionál. The cast included (left to right) Mario Berini as the Duke, Concha de los Santos as Maddalena, Pons as Gilda, and Francesco Valentino as Rigoletto. To Valentino's right is stage director Armando Agnini. FOTO MONTERREY. LUDECKE-PONS COLLECTION.

As Gilda in *Rigoletto* during the Metropolitan Opera's 1947–48 season. A Christmas Day 1947 performance featured a cast reminiscent of a past golden age: Pons as Gilda, Jussi Björling as the Duke of Mantua, and Leonard Warren in the title role. BENDER PHOTOGRAPHY. LUDECKE-PONS COLLECTION.

Twenty seasons into her American career, Pons took a calculated risk by undertaking a new role: Violetta in Verdi's *La traviata*. Although she had been asked to consider preparing the role during her first season at the Metropolitan, she did not sing it until October 1951 with the San Francisco Opera. ROMAINE STUDIOS. LUDECKE-PONS COLLECTION.

San Francisco impresario Gaetano Merola (center) conducted Pons's performances of *La traviata* in Los Angeles. Veteran director Armando Agnini (right) staged the production.
SKELTON STUDIOS, SAN FRANCISCO. LUDECKE-PONS COLLECTION.

For Violetta, as for her other roles, Pons spared no expense in costuming. But this time Lily chose Eugene Berman, rather than the usual Valentina, to be her designer. MOULIN STUDIOS, SAN FRANCISCO. LUDECKE-PONS COLLECTION.

THE FRESNO MUSICAL CLUB
PRESENTS
San Francisco Opera Company
IN
LA TRAVIATA
BY VERDI
✦
LILY PONS — JAN PEERCE
FRANK VALENTINO

GAETANO MEROLA, GENERAL DIRECTOR
HOWARD K. SKINNER, GENERAL MANAGER

MONDAY, OCTOBER 20, 1952
8:30 P. M.
✦
FRESNO MEMORIAL AUDITORIUM
FRESNO, CALIFORNIA

Front cover of the program for a performance of *La traviata* in Fresno, California, October 1952. Pie[ro] Cimara conducted the performance. LUDECKE-PONS COLLECTION.

Pons in rehearsal for the ballroom scene in act one of *La traviata*. PAUL C. TRACY, SAN FRANCISCO. LUDECKE-PONS COLLECTION.

Society matron and veteran party-giver Elsa Maxwell, costumed here as P. T. Barnum, escorts not one but two Jenny Linds to a postwar Manhattan soiree: Gloria Swanson (left) and Lily Pons. ACME NEWS PHOTOGRAPHS. LUDECKE-PONS COLLECTION.

In her concert appearances Lily occasionally featured her operatic costumes—in this instance, from the second act of Thomas's *Mignon*. PHOTOGRAPHER UNIDENTIFIED. COURTESY OF BILL PARK.

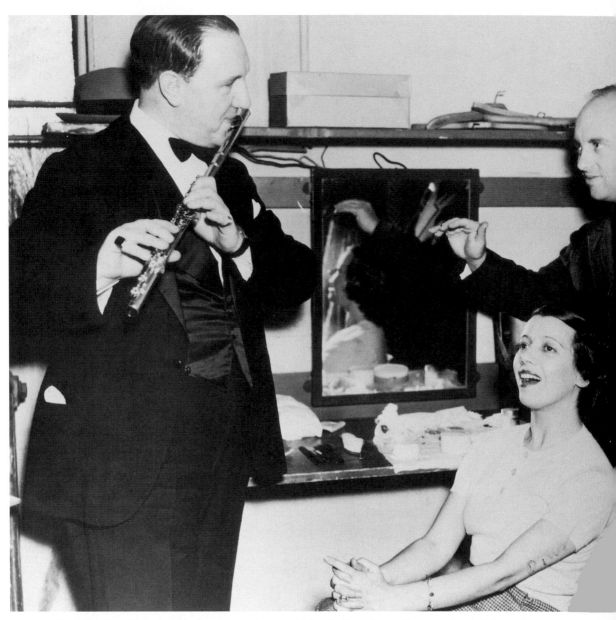

Bandleader Benny Goodman exchanged his clarinet for a flute as André Kostelanetz conducted an impromptu cadenza with Pons in her dressing room, 1937. PHOTOGRAPHER UNIDENTIFIED. COURTESY OF THE METROPOLITAN OPERA ARCHIVES.

In 1943 Pons shared billing with the legendary violinist Fritz Kreisler (left) and conductor Eugene Ormandy at a concert for the University of Michigan's Musical Society in Ann Arbor.
CHARLES A. SINK, UNIVERSITY OF MICHIGAN.
LUDECKE-PONS COLLECTION.

Lily's January 1934 appearance at the University of Michigan was the second of seven occasions on which she would perform for the University's Musical Society between 1931 and 1958.
LUDECKE-PONS COLLECTION.

In the spring of 1946 Pons paid a visit in France to Henri Matisse, whom she numbered among her friends and whose works she avidly collected. PHOTOGRAPHER UNIDENTIFIED. LUDECKE-PONS COLLECTION.

With playwright Noel Coward in London, June 1946. In November 1936, Pons played the heroine, Mélanie, in a radio broadcast of Coward's 1934 musical play, *Conversation Piece,* and again on a recording for Columbia Records. PHOTOGRAPHER UNIDENTIFIED. LUDECKE-PONS COLLECTION.

During a postwar concert tour, Lily called upon Cornelia Otis Skinner in her dressing room at the Harris Theater in Chicago, where the actress was appearing in the Somerset Maugham–Guy Bolton comedy, *Theatre*. PHOTOGRAPHER UNIDENTIFIED. LUDECKE-PONS COLLECTION.

When Lily entered the ranks of the Metropolitan Opera, her diminutive size invited comparisons with the petite English soprano Maggie Teyte, with whom she was photographed in 1947. PHOTOGRAPHER UNIDENTIFIED. LUDECKE-PONS COLLECTION.

In Mexico City to sing *Rigoletto* in August 1946, Pons is greeted backstage by General Dwight D. Eisenhower. A self-described fan, Ike displayed a boyish charm whenever he was with Lily. FOTO MONTERREY. LUDECKE-PONS COLLECTION.

By special invitation, Pons performed at President Eisenhower's Inaugural Ball on 20 January 1953. Here she acknowledges the audience's applause after singing "Caro nome" from *Rigoletto*. WIDE WORLD PHOTOS. LUDECKE-PONS COLLECTION.

The inaugural festivities for Eisenhower's second term, January 1957 (from far left): bandleader Fred Waring, tenor Lauritz Melchior, Elivera Doud, the First Lady's mother, Tony Martin, Jeanette MacDonald, First Lady Mamie Eisenhower, James Melton, President Eisenhower, Pons, and dancer (later Senator) George Murphy. WIDE WORLD PHOTOS. LUDECKE-PONS COLLECTION.

In honor of

The President of the United States and Mrs. Eisenhower

and

The Vice President of the United States and Mrs. Nixon

The Inaugural Committee
requests the pleasure of the company of

Miss Lily Pons

at the

Inaugural Ball

Monday evening the twenty-first of January
One thousand nine hundred and fifty-seven

at nine o'clock

Washington, District of Columbia

Inaugural Committee
Robert V. Fleming, Chairman

Inaugural Ball Committee
Carl L. Shipley, Chairman

William H. Press, Executive Vice Chairman   *George E. C. Hayes, Vice Chairman*
Edward Burling, Jr. Vice Chairman   *Garfield I. Kass, Vice Chairman*
Newell W. Ellison, Vice Chairman   *Mrs. I. Gordon Moore, Vice Chairman*

Invitation to the Inaugural Ball for Eisenhower's second term, 21 January 1957.
LUDECKE-PONS COLLECTION.

The Inaugural Committee

requests the honor of the presence of

Miss Lily Pons

to attend and participate in the Inauguration of

Dwight David Eisenhower

as President of the United States of America

and

Richard Milhous Nixon

as Vice President of the United States of A———

on Tuesday,

one thousand n———

in the t———

Please reply to
The Inaugural Committee
1420 Pennsylvania Avenue
Washington 4, D. C.

The President and Mrs. Johnson

request the pleasure of the company of

Miss Pons

at a reception to be held at

The White House

on Thursday evening, November 21, 1968

at six o'clock

Invitation to the inauguration
ceremonies for the first Eisenhower-
Nixon term, 20 January 1953.
LUDECKE-PONS COLLECTION.

Invitation from President and
Mrs. Lyndon B. Johnson to a White
House reception, 21 November 1968.
LUDECKE-PONS COLLECTION.

A publicity photograph for Pons's appearances with the Chicago Opera Company, November–December 1940. Her dress is a Pauline Trigère design. DE BELLIS STUDIOS, NEW YORK. LUDECKE-PONS COLLECTION.

Promotional photograph for Lily's North American concerts, 1944–45 season. DE BELLIS STUDIOS, NEW YORK. LUDECKE-PONS COLLECTION.

In a Valentina creation, during one of Lily's occasional "blond periods," 1949. FARKAS STUDIO-ROEDEL. LUDECKE-PONS COLLECTION.

"In millinery," *The Washington Post* reported in March 1942, "Miss Pons favors extreme hats . . . that attract attention and give the illusion of height." DE BELLIS STUDIOS, NEW YORK. LUDECKE-PONS COLLECTION.

With floral bouquet and flower-bedecked sable hat and stole, 1942. The ensemble, a Valentina design, also appears in the official portrait of Pons on display at the Metropolitan Opera House in New York. DE BELLIS STUDIOS, NEW YORK. LUDECKE-PONS COLLECTION.

Pons occasionally tried her hand at original designs—in this instance, a hat described in a March 1951 press release as "a 'beau tickler' creation with feathers covering the face in place of a veil." According to the release, the design "was inspired by the same face-covering look of Miss Pons's two Tibetan poodles." ACME NEWS PICTURES. LUDECKE-PONS COLLECTION.

A modified version of the "beau tickler," designed by Suzanne Talbot, Paris, 1951.
HARCOURT STUDIOS, PARIS. LUDECKE-PONS COLLECTION.

Lily's fondness for unusual hats included this beret-style creation. When Pons sent a copy of this 1950 publicity print to longtime friends Nina Morgana and Bruno Zirato, the tart-tongued Morgana telephoned her and exclaimed, "Lily, my dear, that hat must go at once! It makes you look like one of Mr. Disney's mice!" DE BELLIS STUDIOS, NEW YORK. LUDECKE-PONS COLLECTION.

As this publicity portrait reveals, Pons's finely shaped hands were expressive assets, both onstage and off. In the late 1940s, the Elizabeth Arden cosmetics firm acquired the rights to a sculptor's recreation of Lily's hands, which the company used in a national advertising campaign. DE BELLIS STUDIOS, NEW YORK. LUDECKE-PONS COLLECTION.

In October 1950, Pons exhibited a lighter side at the San Francisco Opera Ball and Fol de Rol, doing a convincing cancan to a Carol Channing recording. Doodles & Spider, a popular San Francisco nightclub team, partnered her in this fundraising sketch. MOULIN STUDIOS, SAN FRANCISCO. LUDECKE-PONS COLLECTION.

Comedian Danny Kaye greeting Lily after a rehearsal for the Fol de Rol. PHOTOGRAPHER UNIDENTIFIED. LUDECKE-PONS COLLECTION.

With Dinah Shore, reviewing the script for a radio appearance in the mid-1940s.

Rehearsing for a radio appearance with Edgar Bergen and Charlie McCarthy, November 1946. ROBERT PERKINS STUDIOS. LUDECKE-PONS COLLECTION.

During the 1950s, Pons increased her popularity through appearances on such radio programs as *The Standard Hour*. Here she poses at the microphone before a September 1951 broadcast. MOULIN STUDIOS, SAN FRANCISCO. LUDECKE-PONS COLLECTION.

NATIONAL BROADCASTING COMPANY. INC.

Shrine Auditorium
665 W. Jefferson Blvd.

| Sun. Oct. 28 See Reverse Side | STANDARD OIL CO. of CALIFORNIA Presents *"THE STANDARD HOUR"* SAN FRANCISCO OPERA ORCHESTRA GAETANO MEROLA, General Director LILY PONS, Soprano NICOLA ROSSI-LEMENI, Basso ★ CHILDREN UNDER 14 WILL NOT BE ADMITTED ★ | STUDIO · Shrine Auditorium Doors Close 8:15 P.M. |

THE STANDARD HOUR

LILY PONS, Soprano
NICOLA ROSSI-LEMENI, Basso
TANO MEROLA, Conductor

Faust: Act IV: Mephisto's
. Suppe   Serenade · . . . Gounod
Dance   Boris Godunov: March of
Meyerbeer   the False Dmitri; I Have
I: Attained the Highest Power
amo . Verdi   Mussorgsky
. Faure   Program subject to possible change

unday 8:30 p.m. KFI

STANDARD OIL COMPANY OF CALIFORNIA

Tenor Eugene Conley was Lily's partner for a September 1950 *The Standard Hour* broadcast. MOULIN STUDIOS, SAN FRANCISCO. LUDECKE-PONS COLLECTION.

Advertisement and admission ticket the studio audience for a broadcast of *The Standard Hou* with Pons and basso Nicola Rossi-Lemeni, San Francis 28 October 1951. LUDECKE-PONS COLLECTION.

SCENE FIFTEEN ... TALK AND MEDLEY ...
COMO ... PONS ... SHORE ... LEE ...
DERRINGER
(COMO COMES ON AFTER MISS PONS' SONG.
HE'S IN ONE AND SHE COMES INTO ONE.
HE ENTERS APPLAUDING)
      COMO:
Lily that was just beautiful.
What a marvelous voice.
      PONS:
Thank you very much, Perry. Where
are the two high stools we sit on
to sing our duet?
      COMO:
Would you like some tea, Lily?
      PONS:
Where are the two high stools.
      COMO:
Oh, well I've had a kind of a
problem about that this week. You
see Dinah is on the show too, and
she expected to sing the duets
with me.

"Spontaneous" dialogue from *The Perry Como Show,* on which Pons and Dinah Shore guest-starred in 1956. Written by a staff headed by Goodman Ace (of radio's popular *Easy Aces*) and telecast live each week, the hour-long Como program required split-second timing on the part of the crooner-host and his celebrity guests. A typical script ran nearly seventy typewritten pages. LUDECKE-PONS COLLECTION.

Relaxing with host Perry Como during a rehearsal for the Thanksgiving 1956 telecast of his popular variety hour. PHOTOGRAPHER UNIDENTIFIED. LUDECKE PONS COLLECTION.

LILY PONS

Coloratura Soprano

METROPOLITAN OPERA ASSOCIATION

Frank La Forge, Composer - Pianist, at the Piano

Henry Bové, *Flautist,* and The Renaissance Quintet

Programme

I.

Air de Momus, from "Phoebus et Pan"	BACH
Quell ruscelletto	PARADIES
La Fauvette avec ses petits, from "Zemire et Azor" . .	GRETRY
Alma mia, from "Floridante"	HANDEL
Lusinghe piu care, from "Alessandro" . . .	HANDEL
Air de Blondine, from "Enlevement au Serail" . . .	MOZART

II.

Echo Song	BISHOP-LA FORGE

(With flute obligato)

(Groups I and II with accompaniment of ancient instruments by The Renaissance Quintet)

INTERMISSION

III.

Il pleure dans mon coeur	
Mandoline	
Green	DEBUSSY
Fantoches	

IV.

Après un rêve	FAURÉ
Villanelle des petits canards	CHABRIER
The Nightingale	ALABIEFF-LA FORGE
Poupée valsante	POLDINI-LA FORGE

V.

Mad Scene from "Hamlet"	THOMAS

(With flute obligato)

BALDWIN PIANO

TICKETS: Orchestra $2.75 and $2.20; Dress Circle $1.65; Balcony $1.10;
Boxes, each seat, $2.75 and $2.20; at Carnegie Hall Box Office

Management: METROPOLITAN MUSICAL BUREAU, Inc.
Division: Columbia Concerts Corporation of Columbia Broadcasting System
113 West 57th Street, New York City

Program for a Carnegie Hall recital, 27 January 1951. LUDECKE-PONS COLLECTION.

Met general manager Rudolf Bing presents Pons with silver mementos at the gala honoring her twenty-fifth anniversary at the Metropolitan Opera, 1956. INTERNATIONAL NEWS PHOTOS. COURTESY OF ANDREW FARKAS.

METROPOLITAN OPERA

SEASON 1955-1956

Tuesday Evening, January 3, 1956, at 8:15

Special Non-Subscription Performance

LILY PONS GALA

On the occasion of the Twenty-fifth Anniversary
of her first appearance at the Metropolitan

RIGOLETTO, Act II

Libretto by F. M. Piave
Music by Giuseppe Verdi

Conductor: Fausto Cleva   Staged by Herbert Graf

Sets and Costumes by Eugene Berman

The Duke .... Jan Peerce
Rigoletto .... Robert Merrill
Gilda, his daughter .... Lily Pons
Sparafucile .... Giorgio Tozzi
Giovanna, Gilda's nurse .... Thelma Votipka
Marullo .... Clifford Harvuot
Borsa .... Gabor Carelli
Count Ceprano .... Calvin Marsh

Scene: Rigoletto's home
Musical Preparation: Corrado Muccini

INTERMISSION

LUCIA DI LAMMERMOOR, Mad Scene

Libretto by Salvatore Cammarano
Music by Gaetano Donizetti

Conductor: Pietro Cimara   Staged by Desire Defrere

Designed by Richard Rychtarik in 1942
Ballet costumes designed by Ruth Morley

Lucia .... Lily Pons
Raimondo .... Nicola Moscona

Scene: A hall in Lammermoor Castle

Program continued on the next page

IN THE EVENT OF AN AIR RAID ALARM REMAIN IN YOUR SEATS AND OBEY THE INSTRUC-
TIONS OF THE MANAGEMENT.—ROBERT E. CONDON, DIRECTOR OF CIVIL DEFENSE.

INTERMISSION

"O luce di quest'anima," Linda di Chamounix .... Gaetano Donizetti
"Je suis Titania," Mignon .... Ambroise Thomas
"Chant du Rossignol," Le Rossignol .... Igor Stravinsky
"Bell Song," Lakme .... Leo Delibes

Conductor: Max Rudolf

KNABE PIANO USED EXCLUSIVELY
LOUIS SHERRY BAR AND RESTAURANT ON GRAND TIER FLOOR
CURTAIN DINNERS SERVED TWO HOURS BEFORE PERFORMANCE TIME
THE USE OF CAMERAS IN THIS THEATRE IS NOT ALLOWED

Metropolitan Opera Program is published by Opera Magazines, Inc.,
108 Wooster Street, New York 12, N. Y.

Program for Metropolitan Opera gala honoring Lily Pons on her twenty-fifth
anniversary, 3 January 1956. LUDECKE-PONS COLLECTION.

Lily sang the final *Lucia* of her long career in the 1961–62 season in Fort Worth, Texas. Fittingly, her last performance was opposite a young Plácido Domingo, three decades after she debuted in the role at the Met with the great tenor of a previous generation, Beniamino Gigli. PHOTOGRAPHER UNIDENTIFIED. COURTESY OF PLÁCIDO DOMINGO.

Lily post-retirement, in her Riviera home in 1971, still accompanied by pets.
TRAVERSO PHOTOGRAPHIE, CANNES. LUDECKE-PONS COLLECTION.

With Brazilian soprano Bidú Sayão in the spring of 1972, the same week as Lily's post-retirement concert at Lincoln Center's Philharmonic Hall. PHOTOGRAPH BY WILLIAM SEWARD. COURTESY OF BIDÚ SAYÃO.

Lily Pons in 1957, taking a well-deserved bow near the end of a career that would span more than forty years. WIDE WORLD PHOTOS. LUDECKE-PONS COLLECTION.

PART THREE

The Voice

CHAPTER TEN

Fame Overnight!

Lily Pons

Between 1931 and 1946, many articles were published in music periodicals analyzing Lily Pons's vocal technique. The majority of these appeared in *The Etude*, which frequently commissioned detailed interviews with leading singers and instrumentalists, querying them on topics ranging from their methods of practice to their lifestyles and hobbies.

One of the earliest first-person features published under Lily Pons's name is this article that appeared in the June 1931 edition of *The Etude*.[1] Although the thoughts, experiences, and viewpoints are no doubt her own, the feature was written by R. H. Wollstein, a frequent *Etude* contributor.

$\mathcal{F}$AME OVERNIGHT! I wonder whether people realize just what that magic
term means, whether the observer ever projects his thoughts into the years
of indefatigable work, and effort, and perseverance back to that one glamorous
night which works the metamorphosis from singer to star. To be frank, I must
believe that fame can come overnight; my own most generous, and to me most
surprising, welcome at the Metropolitan Opera in New York proves it. But, upon
closer analysis, it is only the bestowal of public acclaim which comes from one
day to the next. The preparation for that one night which "turns the trick" is a
matter of years. In my own case, I may say that that one night was in preparation
all my life.

Even granting this, I consider myself singularly fortunate for I have, through
no merit of my own, been endowed with certain gifts. I am grateful for these and
I try to develop them by tireless effort, the only way to develop one's self artistically. "Fame overnight" is extremely glamorous and delightful; but it can be
brought to its climax only by the hardest and most intensive work.

All my life I have been both "music struck" and "stage struck," although I never
had a singing lesson until five years ago and then quite casually. As a child I
"played theater" with my little friends. Organizing dramas and taking part in
them meant more to me than dolls and toys. When I early showed a love for
music and began studying the piano and the science of music along with it, I
found a new avenue of expression which made my small life quite complete. I
am thankful today for that early training when, not dreaming of the possibility
of a public career, the serious little music student I used to be pored over her theory and harmony, learning musical values for their own sake. I do not think
that too much stress can be laid on a thorough musical foundation for singers.

My studies progressed satisfactorily, and, at fourteen,[3] I was entered as a
piano student in the Paris Conservatoire. I hoped, in those days, to make the
piano my profession, and worked hard with that goal in view. I should admit, I
dare say, that all my life I have been determined to "arrive." Long before I dared
dream of the success which has been so kindly accorded me, I fixed my eyes on
the topmost rung of the ladder and devoted every ounce of energy toward getting there. I have had to sacrifice most of the fun of a young girl's life to this
ambition, but I love my work and my music so dearly that I can scarcely call it a
sacrifice.

While I was at the Conservatoire a serious illness [meningitis] overtook me; and since I have always been small and slight of build, my family judged me frail as well—a great mistake!—and took me home, to drop work and to rest. It seemed as though my great ambitions were to come to nothing; but deep inside me I never gave up. As soon as I was able, I practiced again and received my old love for theatricals. In all this time, I had never given singing a thought except to hum about the house as any person must who loves music.

When I was able to do things again, my love for the theater gained the ascendant, and I got a tiny place, to play tiny parts, in the company of the eminent Max D'Erly. There I first tasted the delights of contact with an audience. I never gave up my piano practicing, but felt that if there was a career ahead of me at all, it lay in the theater. Then I married.

My husband had not the slightest objection to a public career for me, provided I could make it a distinguished career! Since there was nothing the least distinguished in playing small bits in a theatrical company, I came home. So a second time I contented myself with living happily at home, and singing and playing for my own amusement. My husband took pleasure in hearing me sing; he said I had a pretty voice, and asked me, at last, whether I shouldn't like to have singing lessons, just for the fun of it. I accepted his offer with joy. Anything pertaining to music and music study was the delight of my life. And then, along with my first singing lesson, there came a surprise.

My [teacher] heard me sing and asked me with whom I had last studied, complimenting me upon my method. My voice, he said, was well placed and my breathing quite correct. He seemed amazed when I told him I had never had a singing lesson, that I could boast my first vocal instruction only after he had taught me something.

"But you sing naturally," he exclaimed. "*Bien sûr*," I replied, "it is natural for me to sing. I always sing. Even when I do things about the house. I love it."

"But I do not speak of natural likes or dislikes," he cried. "I speak of a natural voice!"

From him and for the first time, I learned that my case was not typical of that of the ordinary singer. I learned the significance of technicalities like voice placement, range, diaphragm breathing and correct head tones, and discovered that, by the mysterious workings of a kind Fate, all these things had been given me without my having to struggle for them. To perfect them, to develop them, to maintain them—for that I work. But to acquire them in the first place needed no effort from me.

At the time of that memorable first singing lesson, I was twenty-one years old [*sic*]—five and a half years ago. I thought that was by no means a late age to begin singing. Girls I knew had commenced their vocal studies at seventeen and eighteen. But they, I told myself, had voices; they were headed for careers; for them it was different. For me, a year or two more or less could be of no moment. I was singing only because I loved it and because my husband enjoyed hearing me.

Because of these unconscious gifts, though, I found myself as advanced after half a dozen lessons as the girls who had been studying for years. That was gratifying. Having got that far, I worked harder than ever. Then, when my master had gradually tested out the full extent of my range, he grew thoughtful.

I sing high F-sharp with ease. My highest tone is the A-flat above it. As there is no music written to that, though, I have no occasion to use it. Massenet wrote the highest note ever known to be sung, in a cadenza for Sibyl Sanderson; it is high G, I believe. But even if I do not sing my half of a tone above that, it is of the greatest use to me in developing notes below. Working down, mentally, from that high A-flat, I produce high F-sharp and high G with the ease of attack, the roundness and resonance of high C. Today I sing *Lucia* in its original key of F-sharp—a full tone higher than the E which is the highest it has ever been sung before. I do not mind speaking of this, because it is all perfectly natural for me. I did not know my range was unusual until my master told me so, and then, as I say, he became thoughtful.

"You should pursue your studies seriously," he said. "There is a career before you."

Naturally I was enchanted and hastened to discuss it with my husband. He made me the same terms as before. If I wished a career, very good; but he would permit only a career of distinction—nothing second-rate or half-way.

If I had worked diligently before, I may say I slaved now. Work, development and a glimpse of the goal ahead filled every moment of my life. No balls, no late parties, no noisy fun, no frolics which would tax the strength or interfere with a strict regularity of life. *Never* a cocktail nor a cigarette. I strained every fibre to prove myself. I practiced all my master gave me and, when I felt that my voice needed especial building up, I invented vocal exercises of my own. In time, I went to Italy, to work at the great art of bel canto. I left the piano, except to accompany myself, and turned to the vocal library, arriving, at last, at the study of roles. My preparation, intensive as it was, lasted only three years. When I was twenty-four [*sic*], I made my operatic debut at Mülhausen with a success which encouraged me and which won my husband's consent to my making music my career.

A curious circumstance of my preliminary work is that I never worked at my medium register. I centered all my attention on developing my upper range (I shall talk of exercises and methods later) and found that the middle voice developed along with it. When my pure coloratura was in presentable form, I had a nicely developed medium range ready for me to work with.

I have never shared in the routine of small opera-company work for which European training is famous. I have never been a member of any company before coming to the Metropolitan. My operatic experience has been confined to one, three, five performances at Mülhausen, Marseille, Liège, Milan and other cities of France and Italy, which have fine companies and charming tradition. I have never sung in Paris.[2] My first company membership is with the greatest company of all! I had gratifying successes during my three years of operatic work in Europe, but, when the call came to go to the Metropolitan, I was dazzled! Of course that had been my dream, but when it came at last—it seemed too magical to be real.

First and foremost, though, it meant work again. I immediately gave up all my summer's engagements and declined offers to sing in Chile, in Spain, and in Germany, in order to retire once more to Italy and begin anew the routine of intensive work and study. All the roles which I had been singing in French had to be worked over in Italian, with the precision and care of new parts. And of course my work in exercises, vocalises, and stage *tournure* went on. And then came the night when I appeared at the Metropolitan and tasted the glad experience of a fame which was kindly awarded overnight but which had been in preparation since the days of the serious little harmony student who played at theatricals instead of dolls.

The exercises I use are calculated to meet my own needs. I doubt that they represent any "school" of singing. Many of them I have conceived myself; many I have arrived at by the method of trial and discard. I firmly believe that each singer's studies should be adapted to suit his individual needs, regardless of whether or not they represent a system or a school which can be applied to the instruction of other students. Thus it is perfectly possible that the work which is best for my requirements might not be so well suited to another voice. It is well to discuss these individual technicalities with a reliable teacher. I am certain, though, that my methods cannot possibly harm anyone. I am glad to outline them for the readers of *The Etude*.

I practice only for short periods at a time. Too much use at any one time tends to rob the coloratura voice of much of its freshness. My day's practice is made up of four or five periods from fifteen to twenty minutes each. I practice directly after I rise, again around eleven, again around one, and then perhaps once or twice more during the afternoon. This method breaks into my day, of course, but I prefer to follow the system which is best for my voice.

I sing all my exercises mezza voce; never do I practice them in full voice. Again, the nature of the coloratura soprano is such that a constant and prolonged giving forth of too much voice robs it of its color and luster. My operatic roles are the only work which I sing in full voice.

Before going into detail as to my methods of procedure, let me say that the singer's chief work is not done with the throat at all, but with the brains! I can get along with fewer hours of practice, perhaps, because I study and challenge every tone. Each note I produce is mentally full-composed and constructed before I draw breath for it. Hours upon hours of throat work are unavailing unless the wits are alert and challenging to everything that goes on. The singer must also have a quick, exact ear. It is only after the brain and the ear have paved the way for the notes which are to come that throat work can do any good.

I practice without notes. There are no set exercises which I follow. I work at what I happen to need. Often enough I invent vocalises of my own, based on the intricacies of some cadenza, or simply following scales and standard exercises, but stressing something which is of especial use to me. I am always careful to watch for any point in my voice or technic which seems to need attention. I find, for my own needs, that this method is more intelligent and is productive of better results than singing the same set exercises every day.

Every morning at nine I begin the day with perhaps five or ten minutes of scale work. I begin all my exercises on the G above middle C—I never go below that—and work my way up to my full range, singing first five notes and then octaves. I sing all my scales on the single syllable *non*. This nasal syllable pushes the voice forward and "arches" it into a fine roundness, which is neither nasal nor harsh. This scale work warms the voice for the exercises which follow.

I sing all my other exercises and vocalises on the one syllable of short *o*. I do not use *a* (ah) and I expressly avoid *e* (ee) in practicing. The *e* sounds have the tendency to throw the voice back. I enunciate them clearly, of course, in all passages where they occur in the text, but, for the voice building exercises, I prefer to use only those sounds which give the best tone production.

Next come scales sung first in sharp staccato and, directly after, in a smooth, round legato. And then the trills. I begin with the simplest trill, progressing from one note to the next, working my way to clear trills of the interval of a third and even of a fourth, always carefully maintaining the pure trill character. This is excellent for the perfection of coloratura color and technique. Since this exercise requires a high, round, well-placed tone, I know that when the multiple trills go well, all is well with my voice.

Another excellent exercise is to attack a high note easily, without a suspicion of forcing, and to hold it through all degrees of volume, beginning with a *pianissimo*, swelling to a *forte*, and shading down again to a *pianissimo*, all with relaxation.

I sing many scales and vocalises with closed lips, or humming. This exercise is very helpful to me. Still, I counsel students to consult their masters before adopting it. It is one of the exercises I invented myself. It is calculated to bring the voice forward to a fine head tone, of full nasal resonance. But such a tone will result *only if the voice is well placed*. If there are any defects in voice placement, this exercise may tend to throw the voice back and cause harm. I use it as a check-up on myself. I hum a scale and suddenly, while I am singing, I close my nasal chambers by pinching my nostrils shut. If the tone stops short the moment the nostrils are closed, it is a proper head tone. I release my fingers and the hummed tone continues; I pinch them together again and the tone stops. If the tone were to continue when I closed my nostrils, it would mean that it was not being produced in the head. And a throat tone is not desirable for the coloratura. Never do I use a chest tone. Never do I press upon the diaphragm for the (mistaken) purpose of giving a tone force. This is a grave error; instead of making the tone more powerful, such forcing robs it of both color and volume. In the coloratura soprano, of all voices, freshness, luster, and nuances of light and color are essential.

So much for actual exercises. I sing vocalises and proceed to the songs or arias or roles on which I am at work. My coach comes to me and I rehearse every day—some days more than once! In preparing for my Metropolitan performances, I rehearse as much as three times a day.

Rehearsals in full voice, with action and stage business, are invaluable, because the opera means much more than singing alone. An intelligent operatic performance requires the most diversified preparation. Taking adequate vocal equipment quite for granted, there is the stage business which needs as much care as in any dramatic role without singing. There are the languages. There is the characterization of the part to be mastered. There is the historical or mythological accuracy of the time and place in which the role is set. A singer who would give her best to her public cannot afford to be haphazard in any of these. She must play her part, feel it, understand it, dress it, and infuse into her audience the very atmosphere surrounding the person she portrays—all in addition to the singing itself.

Personally, I take great pleasure in studying the history and manners of the various epochs which form the background of my roles. A knowledge of the history of the times helps one to feel and to portray the role with greater sympathy and intelligence. And accuracy in costuming is an important factor in creating atmosphere. I take the greatest delight in my stage wardrobe and design all my costumes myself. Often it requires months of research among old plates and volumes to assemble the correct details for the gowns and accessories of a part. But the work is extremely interesting, and it is my pride to feel that, when I appear before my public, I am able to give it an authentic picture of how Cherubino, Gilda, Lucia and Lakmé looked. Pleasant as these tasks are, they are none the less tasks, and demand a great expenditure of time, thought and energy. They, too, help form the necessary, if invisible, background of "fame overnight."

CHAPTER ELEVEN

The Girl Who Wants to Sing

Lily Pons

Throughout her long career, Lily Pons was frequently asked by budding sopranos how to go about building a career. In this article, which appeared in *The Etude* in 1933 in her first-person voice, but which was actually the work of feature-writer Juliette Laine, Pons addresses the questions most commonly asked by young women wanting to pursue operatic careers.[1]

*T*O BE BORN with a pretty voice is not especially remarkable, and to learn to sing fairly well is not at all difficult, but to achieve the heights of a musical career requires far more than a good natural voice and a willingness to learn. Success in music demands an indomitable spirit, as well as voice and intelligence. Therefore, if I had a daughter who wanted to become a singer I would watch her very carefully, even as a little girl, to make sure that she possessed the requisite courage, strength of character and tenacity as well as talent.

The singer's general education, beginning in earliest childhood, should be conducted upon the broadest, most approved lines. Anything that will develop and broaden her mind will be of much value in her subsequent career especially in these modern times when the operatic repertoire makes a so much greater demand upon the singer's mentality than did the roles of our grandmother's day. In those days it was quite satisfactory to the audience if the singer stood on one spot in the center of the stage and tranquilly warbled the woes of *Lucia*, *Linda* or *La traviata*. Vocal virtuosity was all that mattered; histrionics were pleasantly ignored. But the present-day singer must have intellect as well as voice if she is to cope with such widely different works as *Madama Butterfly*, *Aida*, *Carmen*, *Bohème*, and so forth. Such roles require at least a smattering of knowledge of the customs, traditions and thought of different countries and epochs, if they are to be convincingly presented. However, such knowledge can be obtained long before the actual music education is begun.

The would-be singer should be given lessons on some instrument, preferably piano, as soon as she is old enough to read music. In my own country it is not at all unusual to begin such lessons at the age of six or seven. My own piano lessons began when I was barely five and were continued until I graduated from the Paris Conservatoire, at the age of thirteen. Of course, the girl who intends to become a singer need not develop a degree of technical ability equal to that of the professional pianist, as I did, but she should have the ability to play her own accompaniments.

In addition to a knowledge of the pianoforte she should be taught music history and appreciation. She should know how to listen to music and how to understand and judge a musical composition whether it be a popular song or a symphonic poem. Above all, she should learn sight-reading, so that she may be able to read a printed melody as readily as she would a book. This, too, can be acquired before the actual training of her voice is begun.

Singing lessons should not be undertaken before the student is sixteen or seventeen years of age. Oh, I know we are frequently hearing of remarkable young singers who are only fifteen or so, and I grant you that many of them do sing amazingly well at that early age. But they usually pay a high price for such precocity. You watch those children and see how many of them ever get any further. Not one! The voice of a girl of that age is an incredibly delicate and fragile instrument, and, if used too soon or incorrectly, is destroyed for all time. It is what you Americans call a "flash in the pan."

The voice must be trained slowly and very, very carefully. I attribute the power and quality of my own voice largely to the fact that I was not allowed to use it at too early an age. You know, no one thought I would be a singer. I was trained to be a concert pianist and never sang at all, in those early years. Then, during the war, when we were all trying to do what we could, I used to go once a week to play to the soldiers. They liked my playing, but invariably I was asked to sing. I did so just to please them, and though they liked it, no one ever thought my voice unusual in any way. It was not until I was married, a few years later, that my husband noticed my singing and suggested that I find a teacher. The rest you know.

To return to the student, I would advise her to hear all the great artists in person as often as possible. To the girl living in the smaller cities and towns this is not always possible; however, it is possible for her to hear them by way of the radio and the phonograph. I consider a good collection of phonograph records—those made by the big artists—an almost indispensable part of any student's equipment. All of the important arias, duets, and so forth, have been recorded, and from these one may learn valuable lessons in style, phrasing and interpretation.

Every student should acquire one or two foreign languages. If he or she can master three or four, so much the better. I was born in France, but my mother was Italian; so I heard both languages daily, all during my childhood. If a girl aspires to the concert stage instead of that of opera, she will find the need of more than one language imperative. All concert programs require from two to five languages, as audiences prefer to hear such works in their original language instead of in translation.

I do not care to discuss the various "methods" of voice-training, as there does not seem to be any infallibly right way. Many times singers have traveled by what seem wholly different roads to reach the same end. However, it is an indisputable fact that very few singers have made long or signally successful careers unless they have had a thorough foundation in coloratura. Such music requires absolute purity of tone and technical dexterity, and turns a veritable searchlight upon the voice, allowing no blemish or flaw to pass unnoticed.

In order to master all these subjects the girl with a voice must be willing to give almost her entire time and thought to her training. Moreover, the regularity of her practice and study hours is of utmost importance. One cannot work hard for ten days and then loaf for a week. System, rigid discipline of one's self, sacrifice of the social side of one's life, all these things are imperative if one is to achieve an appreciable success as a professional musician.

The girl who hopes to enter opera should do what she can to acquire a measure of stage experience, if possible, before her actual debut. Even little amateur theatricals or little community theaters can be very helpful in providing an opportunity of this sort. I myself felt like a veteran actress when I made my operatic debut because I had already filled a lengthy engagement at the Théâtre des Variétés, in Paris. I played the parts of young girls—what you call ingénue roles, light comedy and drama—so I was already accustomed to footlights and audiences when my "big opportunity" came. I assure you the experience was of immense value to me.

It seems to me that far too many students overrate the value of the natural voice and underestimate the importance of these other things. In the mad rush of modern life we do not take sufficient time fully to develop our gifts. The average student expects to make a successful debut after one year's training. Moreover, the moment she does so, she stops studying. Almost every young soprano is misled by the belief that Melba only studied nine months before she made her debut; yet the statement is only a half-truth and so very dangerous. We are told that Melba studied only nine months with Mme Marchesi, and so far the statement is true. But everyone seems to forget that this "Queen of Song" had studied a long time in her own country, before ever coming to France. You see? That sort of thing is romantic and what modern young people call "thrilling," but it leads easily to erroneous and harmful conclusions.

Moreover, we are all prone to attach too much importance to personality instead of artistry. So often we hear people say, "No, her voice isn't so very remarkable, but she is so beautiful!," or they say, "She has so much charm," or, "She always wears such beautiful costumes!" When a student-singer hears such remarks she (or he) remembers them and decides to emulate the external qualities of that person. For, she figures, if she can succeed with so little voice, why not I? She does not realize that big allowances are made for established artists but that until she is established she will find it far more important to develop her artistry than her personality. Personally, I have never seen one of these "voiceless" wonders. On the contrary, I have always found that the Chaliapins and Farrars whose histrionics and personalities were so outstanding were likewise blessed with fine voices. After all, how is one to project one's art or one's "interpretation" if one's voice or technique is inadequate? Will striking costumes atone for an inaudible middle register, or a lovely smile for a tremulous high C?

No indeed! No voice can be developed overnight, not even if it is of naturally fine quality. Any singer who imagines that he is the one exception is sowing only disappointment and frustration. It just "cannot be done."

So many people marvel at my frail physique and my ability to withstand the rigors of the frequent long journeys that my work entails. They marvel, too, that my voice should be so strong, coming from so slight a body. They fancy that I have evolved some magic secret of health, some complicated diet, or perhaps a set of physical exercises known only to myself. But none of these things is true. I eat what I please, and as much as I please—excepting nuts and chocolate—and I exercise very little. That my voice is full and strong and my health perfect I attribute to just one thing, and that one thing is no secret. It is simply a matter of deep breathing.

⸙

Because of the importance of breath control, every singer is taught the principles of correct breathing at the very beginning of his vocal training; and so, for the rest of his life, he adheres to these fundamental principles and reaps the benefits thereof. However, it is not only the professional singer but, in fact, everyone who values his health (especially the musician, who, because of the sedentary nature of his work, does not exercise enough) who should devote a few minutes each day to the cultivation of the habit of deep breathing.

Although it is the easiest thing in the world to breathe correctly, very few of us do so, unless we've been taught. The proper and only truly beneficial method of breathing is from the diaphragm, with no forcing of the chest muscles at all. In fact, the chest should be ignored entirely, and the throat should be used merely as an air passage. All the work must be done by the powerful diaphragm muscle.

⸙

To begin, one should stand very straight, but not tense or taut. There must be no rigidity of shoulders or backbone. Now, placing the fingertips upon the diaphragm, just below where the chest bone ends, exhale the breath as completely as possible, so that the lungs are almost entirely emptied of air. Then, slowly and very gradually inhale, letting the breath go right past the upper chest and down into the very bottom of the lungs. When this is done correctly you should feel the air filling the upper part of the lungs and chest last of all. But bear in mind, please, that during this inhalation the throat and chest must be completely relaxed. Then, after holding the breath a few seconds, exhale slowly, through slightly opened lips.

It is simple, but oh, how effective! Later, as one grows proficient in this technique of the breath, one should make the length of time that the breath is held gradually longer. Also one can vary the exercise by inhaling as before, but, instead of exhaling slowly, one can expel the entire breath in one sudden exhalation through the widely opened mouth. This is a particularly refreshing exercise and one that children invariably enjoy.

Whether you hope to become a singer or not, I cannot too greatly stress the value of these exercises as health-builders. Moreover, they can be practiced anywhere, on a moment's notice, and do not require apparatus of any sort, as do so many other kinds. Even business people who are confined in offices all day can take advantage of them by practicing them while walking through the street on their way to and from their work, instead of waiting for a leisure hour.

Anyone doubting the direct influence of breath efficiency upon brain efficiency should try the following experiment sometime: after reading for a while in a closed, unventilated room, the mind wandering and unable to concentrate, lay down your book for a moment and go directly out of doors or to an open window. There take from ten to twenty deep breaths of air, fully expanding the lungs each time. Then go back to your book, and see what a mental transformation has taken place. The mind is now all attention, thought is quickly directed and controlled, and the brain is wide awake and active. This is because such breathing purifies the blood and sends it tingling through the blood vessels of the brain, where it washes and refreshes the cells with its life-giving properties. A "well ventilated brain" is as essential as a well ventilated house.

No breathing exercise should ever be practiced directly after a meal. Nor should any other kind of exercise. It is always best to wait at least one hour. Preferably such exercises should be done on arising in the morning and upon retiring at night. Furthermore, no exercise should be practiced too strenuously at first. In this, as in everything else, regularity is of prime importance. A little, performed regularly and carefully, is far more useful than a great deal on one day, somewhat less on the next, and nothing at all on the next! Ah yes, a mere five minutes each day—or preferably twice each day—will work wonders. And it is so interesting to work wonders, especially on ourselves, isn't it?

CHAPTER TWELVE

Profitable Vocal Study: A Conference with Lily Pons

Rose Heylbut

For this article, originally published in *The Etude* in the autumn of 1943,[1] twelve years into Pons's American career, writer Rose Heylbut interviewed the singer to discern what changes in her vocal technique, her preparation for new roles, and her overall philosophy of life had taken place during the intervening years. Interestingly, in the interview Lily seems to diminish the role Alberti de Gorostiaga played in the refinement of her technique.

*I*T IS NEARLY a dozen years since Lily Pons sang her first performance at the Metropolitan Opera as an unknown and unheralded newcomer, and became overnight the sensation of the musical world. At the time it occurred, Miss Pons's triumph made stirring, spectacular news. What is infinitely more important, however, is the fact that the diminutive artist has not only maintained the high level of achievement she set that day; she has steadily raised it. Today, Lily Pons is no mere "sensation"; she ranks as one of the most musical and artistic vocalists of all time. Her debut proved that there is still room for a beginner to assert herself; her career proves that through sensitive and consummate musicianship only can a sensational reputation be continued.

Miss Pons, it will be recalled, began her musical studies as a pianist at the Paris Conservatoire, working at theory, harmony, solfège, and composition in addition to her instrumental work. Her phenomenal voice was discovered purely by accident. Eager for further musical development, she went to a vocal teacher. After hearing her sing, he asked her how long she had studied and with what master, because her voice placement, her emission, and her technic were perfectly developed. In amazement, Miss Pons replied that she had never had a singing lesson in her life, and had never sung except for the fun of it—after which it was the teacher's turn to register amazement. Miss Pons has always remained the chief guardian of her remarkable natural voice and her equally remarkable natural production. After a brief but thorough period of vocal study, she accepted a few engagements, chiefly as a means of discovering whether she could possibly be as good as she was led to suppose. As a result of a half-dozen performances in France, she was invited to the Metropolitan—and Lily Pons was established. In the following conference, Miss Pons outlines for readers of *The Etude* her theories on developing the voice and on keeping it in good condition.

The first counsel I offer to ambitious young singers is *not* to try to become a prima donna in a year. We live in a rapid age, an age of rapid methods and rapid achievements. This may be wonderful in some fields, but it is useless in art. Nothing of artistic integrity can be built quickly. I am never more shocked than when I hear of some young girl of fifteen who begins vocal study with the hope of being "ready" for the stage at seventeen. Of course, it is quite impossible that she could be "ready." She may make a commercial sensation, perhaps, but after a few years her vocal career will be done. No girl is ready, either mentally or physically, to begin serious vocal work before the age of seventeen at the earliest. I began to use my voice at twenty-one. And not only should a girl take time in beginning her studies; she should progress slowly, gradually, along every step of the way.

The best way to make haste slowly is to devote the early years of study to general musicianship. She should acquire a solid musical background before she attempts florid vocalises. And the best introduction to general musicianship is the serious study of an instrument. Naturally, I incline toward the piano, which is the instrument of my own "first choice" and which is also the most helpful in a mastery of polyphonic music. But whether our young singer works at the piano, the violin, the violoncello, or the flute, she should master her instrument as gradually and as completely as if there were no other musical outlet awaiting her.

As to the vocal work itself, the young voice should never be used longer than one hour at a time, if that long. The average young singer generally falls victim to the common temptation of working diligently at prescribed studies—and then trying her abilities at songs and arias "on the side" for her private edification. This should never be done, privately, secretly, or any other way. Only the schooled voice is able to sustain long and difficult arias; the developing vocal organ may be seriously impaired by attempting them. And not only for the sake of the voice alone do I suggest this counsel. Serious pieces should be studied only under competent guidance in order to avoid the danger of learning them incorrectly, and later, of having to unlearn and relearn them. Whatever one does, musically, one should try to learn it correctly the first time. This fixes it securely both in the voice and in the mind, and precludes the possibility of later correction, too much of which destroys self-confidence. This has always been my own habit, and I can say that the only work I need to do on a part I have learned is one of review and refreshment.

As to "methods" of developing the young voice, I can only describe my own, which came perfectly naturally to me and which I have never varied. This "method" is to center attention on the breath. I think of my breath as a firm column of air, supported by the abdominal muscles, upon which the tone is balanced as a light ball might be balanced on a firm column of water. The tone does not rest, it moves. I am careful that my breath is entirely natural. Its support should cause no visible motion anywhere in the body. We have all seen singers who move their chests and shoulders when they draw breath, and others whose abdomens push in and out noticeably. Either motion is wrong. The function of the abdominal muscles is one of firm (not tense) support, and they should not be seen to move. The expansion that is necessary for adequate breath support must lie in the region around the diaphragm. I remember that when the Metropolitan first revived *Lakmé* for me, I told Mr. Gatti, then Director of the company, that I should like to sing the part dressed in the authentic costume of a native Hindu girl, which calls for no draperies over the abdomen. At first Mr. Gatti shook his head. "You will get into difficulties," he presaged gloomily; "your breathing will be noticeable and the effect will be marred." I told him that he need feel no uneasiness on that score, since my breathing is never visible. I dressed the part as I had planned, with no adaptations whatever of the authentic costume—and Mr. Gatti was convinced that it is quite possible to carry a full performance on a purely diaphragmatic breath. As to motions in the upper body, that kind of breathing is even worse! The head, neck, throat, and shoulders should be absolutely free and relaxed.

Since breathing, to me, is the absolute foundation of singing, I naturally advocate the use of breathing exercises for the development of lung capacity and diaphragmatic control. One of my most useful exercises of this kind is the skip of two thirds, up and down, sung on *ee*, with the final tone held (on *ee*) for the duration of two measures; then three, then four, and so on, as breath capacity increases. The holding of the final note must never be forced; when it is let go there must still be a reserve of unexpelled breath. And while the exercise is being sung, great care should be taken that the abdomen is firmly held in without rigidity or tension, yet, at the same time, without motion. This single exercise, I find, gives firmness to the tone, develops breath capacity, and arches the voice forward into the masque, where it belongs.

Much of the singer's preparation has to do with unmusical precautions. The first of these should be careful attention to general health and to vocal health. The serious singer should never smoke, drink alcoholic beverages, or make use of irritating spices in the diet. I find pepper an irritant and avoid it—although I dearly love the flavor it imparts to foods. I avoid eating nuts, too. As the singer's career progresses, she will find it necessary to sacrifice more and more of the amenities of ordinary life to her art. When I first sang here and was rewarded with such a wonderful reception, I found myself invited to innumerable parties —which I attended. Usually these parties took place immediately after a performance, when I was already tired out. The rooms were crowded, tobacco smoke filled the air, there was the buzz of conversation and clattering dishes, and quantities of rich (and very tempting!) food. Soon I found that I invariably took cold, or caught a germ of one kind or another, after the parties. The result is that I have abandoned completely all that is meant by the term "social life." I go to no parties at all. When my performances are over, I retire at once to rest—and keep on resting for twenty-four hours. I see my close friends in little groups of three or four, but never is there any smoke, loud talk, or over-rich food. To be quite frank, all this is no hardship to me, since I much prefer simple pleasures to the allurements of "society." My home, my garden, my pets, my books, my music—those are the sources of my best fun, and they never disappoint me.

My singing routine today is, naturally, different from what it was when I was still gaining control of my voice. My task now is to keep my voice flexible and in good health condition. Through a system of mirrors which my doctor has devised, I am able to see my own vocal cords whenever I choose. They are like very short, firm elastic bands, and they are very white. That is a healthy sign, because the least strain on the vocal cords becomes quickly visible in the redness of inflammation. My serious study, these days, is confined to my free periods in the spring and later summer. It is then that I do my coaching and the learning of next season's extensive repertoire of roles and programs. I work two hours in the morning and two in the afternoon at such times, not to exercise my voice, but to train my memory on the new material so that it becomes photographically exact. During my singing season, I work only once a day at "practicing." An hour before a performance, I go over the entire program in mezza voce (half voice), making sure that every effect sounds exactly the same as it will, later, in full voice. It is an excellent test of surety and technical skill to get the same effects (of dynamics, color, phrasing, emphasis) in half voice that are desired in full voice.

At all times, the voice should flow forth naturally and freely. It should never, under any circumstances, be forced. Forcing the voice for greater power defeats its own end, since the forced voice does not project freely and sounds tight and "small." Forcing the voice by trying to sing when one has the slightest indication of a cold, or when one feels ill in any way, is harmful to the entire organ. When I first came to the Metropolitan, I was often required to sing with a cold—and the result was that an ordinary inflammation, that should normally have been entirely cured inside of four days, hung on for weeks. Thus I have learned my lesson! My voice, today, never tires. It is the kind of voice that grows warmer and more "shiny" with use. When I recorded my Mozart album with Bruno Walter, we began the recording at two in the afternoon—and ended it at six, as fresh as when we began. The reason for the freshness after four hours of singing is that my voice has never been forced beyond its natural power.

CHAPTER THIRTEEN

Glamour, Glitter, and Grit

Lily Pons

In addition to the various articles about Lily Pons that appeared in music periodicals throughout the 1930s and 1940s, the Constance Hope agency released publicity materials that presented, in her own words, Pons's reflections on voice and artistry. This piece from the Hope agency dates from 1946.[1]

*T*HE VOICE is a very delicate instrument. Unlike a piano or a violin, it is inseparable from us, and its health is our own. If you have ever seen a photograph or drawing of the vocal cords, it will seem incredible that so small a mechanism can produce sounds that fill a hall as large as the Metropolitan Opera House without additional amplification. Properly trained, the human voice is unmatched by any instrument for beauty and expressiveness. Improperly trained, no instrument deteriorates so rapidly.

The premature eclipse of very gifted singers is often the result of improper or inadequate training. Even with a well-trained voice, however, a singer will sometimes miss the mark. Voice study should not be begun until the age of sixteen or seventeen. Before that, one should thoroughly master another instrument, preferably the piano, and cultivate as many other interests as possible. Too early specialization in any field is bad. A singer who has not learned how to discipline his musical impulses, however beautiful the voice, will often find himself rejected in favor of one whose tones may be less ravishing but whose musicianship can be relied upon. Moreover, an art that is above all the celebration of life will not carry conviction in a singer whose experience suggests adolescence.

It takes years to train the voice. It takes a much longer time to mature as an artist. It is the same with writing. The mere fact that you have memorized the dictionary or mastered a grammar is no proof of your ability to make your readers feel the subject you are attempting to portray. Intelligent effort under competent guidance will develop the technique of singing. But the art of singing is a much more elusive thing, requiring the intelligent control of one's expressive sensibilities, and, above all, patience.

Artists are sometimes so anxious to hear the applause in their ears before they have put music into yours, that they are sometimes ill-prepared to face the problems ahead. And they are many. The competition is keen, the physical demands are arduous, the inroads against one's private life must be guarded against. In other words, there is grind as well as glamour. But unless you give everything to your singing, you will have little to give your audiences. To develop the voice to its full potentialities, a singer must first submit to a self-discipline that will eventually permit him the utmost freedom and resourcefulness as an artist. This is true in every art, but even more so in one as intimate as singing. Health is of first importance, since everything else depends upon it. This entails proper diet, early hours, and regular physical exercise. In addition, there is the basic regimen of a singer—vocalizing, constant and intelligent study of interpretation, repertoire, dramatics, and languages. Beyond this, broad cultural interests and stimulating social activities are essential, for it is in our personal growth and our responses to other people and arts that we find the unique individuality which marks the true artist.

To look upon singing as merely a means of self-glorification is to misunderstand the nature of vocal artistry, which is to play sensitively and persuasively upon the emotions of the audience, without doing violence to the composer's intentions. The singer is a medium through which the audience enters a world of intensely intimate expressiveness. He is their voice. His deepest artistry will therefore be best expressed when they are least aware of the interpreter. To conceal art is the supreme achievement of all art. Whatever stands in the way of its realization is a distraction.

A profound sense of responsibility to one's audience is required of any singer who wants to stay at the top of his form for many years. He must have a sense of dedication that will enable him to surpass his own best efforts even after he has "arrived," and a sincere responsiveness to the people for whom he sings. (An artist never sings *to* his audience.)

Great artists cannot thrive without great audiences—live audiences. Radio, television, and recordings, marvelous as they are, can never replace the thrilling immediacy of the concert hall. More than any other musical performer, I think, the singer needs you in order to give his best. By the same token, you must hear the singer in person to enjoy his highest art, because you alone inspire the magic that lifts a song from the merely enjoyable to the unforgettable.

I have always felt deeply indebted to my audience for whatever beauty I could bring into their lives. Without them I could not have done my best. There would have been no incentive. Their devotion deserves something more than respect, a little less than love. Perhaps affection is the right word. Wherever I sing—in the red and gold splendor of the Metropolitan, a plain white hall in the Midwest, a palm-ringed beach on a lonely Pacific island—I spare no effort to ensure the best performance of which I am capable.

A case in point is my one-woman campaign against draperies and curtains. However beautiful, they are acoustically intolerable, and wherever I sing I insist that they be removed. Though my stubbornness may present problems to the management, I know the results are approved by the audience. On stage, I also see to it that flats or screens are erected in front of the rear curtains. At a recent concert in the South, where no flats or screens were available, the local YMCA loaned us eight ping-pong tables, which we used for this purpose after removing the legs. A few plants relieved their starkness. I remember another hall where the management assured me that the draperies had been acoustically treated. Skeptical, I agreed to decide after my first number. Before the second, they were removed.

I am also a stickler for lighting. I do not like an auditorium so dark that I cannot see the faces of the audience clearly. I like to pick out various people in the audience to sing to. It helps to project a song. Because traveling spots and footlights are not standard equipment in every hall, I carry my own with me. This may strike some people as fussy perfectionism. My feeling is that people attend a concert to see as well as hear. It is therefore a matter of courtesy as well as pride to appear to best advantage.

A constant threat to every singer is the danger of contracting a cold. Before singing in any hall I inspect the premises for drafts. Another wise precaution is to place a table between the artist and those who come backstage after a concert. While I love people and, like all performers, am grateful for my fans, colds and coughs are our greatest occupational hazard, and self preservation is the first law of singing.

As one of the first artists to patronize motels regularly on tour, I am able to ensure privacy not always possible in a hotel, where stray conventioneers or friendly townspeople might knock on my door at any time and plead, "Give us a tune, Lily." With the best will in the world, I am usually forced to decline graciously. In fact, the warm hospitality a singer encounters on the road is one of those pleasant indulgences he must ration carefully. Too many Bacchian feasts and entertainments not only play havoc with his diet, but rob him of much-needed rest. A device I have sometimes employed to discourage an importunate host is to accept his dinner invitation on the condition that the menu is of my choosing—for example, steak châteaubriand, a rare and exotic salad dressing, an almost unobtainable wine. It usually works.

Another malady singers are prone to is nervousness, or as I call it, "nervosity." I have never met a singer who did not suffer from it, and am resigned to its punctual onset some hours before each performance. I have several ways of coping with it. On the road, for example, I prepare my own meals in pots and pans brought along for just such emergencies. There is nothing like applying oneself to the mysterious complexities of a menu to overcome the insidious terrors of nervous anticipation. Between meals, you are apt to find me laughing my head off with whatever jokester happens to be around, or bending over an ironing board with various items of my wardrobe, even doilies and curtains from my room.

And speaking of wardrobes, apart from my own special fondness for clothes, and without subscribing to the notion that "clothes make the singer," tasteful and imaginative grooming do enhance a performance. An audience in formal dress also adds a festive air that can be very stimulating to a singer. A well-dressed woman is a kind of grace note, on whichever side of the footlights she happens to be. For my operatic roles, I have made a number of innovations in costumes of my own design which I felt to be most suitable to the role and to my own particular interpretation.

In fact, I have spared no effort to master every aspect of a role in order to make my portrayal as convincing as possible from every point of view. In *La fille du régiment*, for example, I did not pretend to beat the snare drum, as every coloratura before me had done. I actually learned how to play it by practicing on the train between concerts, to the amusement of my accompanist, manager, and (I'm sure) my fellow passengers. And in *Le coq d'or* I sang and danced the role of the Queen, which until then had always been mimed. Efforts to add dramatic realism to conventional opera performances are appreciated by modern audiences, conditioned by Hollywood and Broadway to expect dramatic and visual as well as vocal excitement.

I am not one of those people who think it beneath the dignity of an opera singer to appear in a Broadway show, on television, or in nightclubs. In the first place, no singer can live solely on his operatic earnings. And, provided the voice is not abused and the performance is in good taste, the added experience in new fields, in some ways more demanding, is all to the good.

One of the most important considerations for any artist is the maintenance of good relations with his employers and colleagues. A reputation built on solid achievement, dependability, and cooperation is a far more valuable asset to a career than one that thrives on sensationalism. Any singer who ignores or abuses those on whom his career depends, does so at his own peril. It is much easier to get to the top than to stay there—*non*?

Oui.

PART FOUR

Radio and Film

CHAPTER FOURTEEN

Lily Pons and the Metropolitan Opera Broadcasts

Paul Jackson

For most of America, hearing the voice of Lily Pons in a live performance was made possible by the advent of the Saturday afternoon Metropolitan Opera broadcasts. In this chapter, Paul Jackson reviews several of Pons's on-the-air performances in her most famous roles: Lucia, Lakmé, Marie in *La fille du régiment*, Gilda, and Rosina.

Jackson is author of *Saturday Afternoons at the Old Met* and *Sign-off for the Old Met*, from which these reviews have been excerpted and abridged.[1] His introductory comments were written for this centenary tribute.

*I*F NOT QUITE JOINED at the hip, the Metropolitan Opera broadcasts and Lily Pons's international career enjoyed a close union from their infancy. The petite diva had the good fortune to arrive at the house just a year before general manager Giulio Gatti-Casazza warily embraced radio as a proper outlet for opera. The conjunction was apt, for the prima donna's enduring career was kept aloft to a great extent by the welcome caress of the media. Her singing, especially during her early years, had assets sufficient to justify a spectacular career launch, but films and radio initially solidified and then magnified the popularity that was hers for more than three decades on the American scene.

The radio audience made her acquaintance as Rosina on the sixth broadcast of the inaugural season when acts two and three of *Il barbiere di Siviglia* were aired on 23 January 1932. A month later listeners could relish her Lakmé, one of her most characteristic roles; Delibes's opera, not heard at the Met for a decade-and-a-half, was revived especially for her chic person and chiming vocalism. Her burgeoning fame is evident in the allotment of four broadcasts in the next season: she opened the radio series as Lakmé, presented the first of her numerous broadcast Lucias, ventured a rare Amina in *La sonnambula*, and capped her radio season with another Pons perennial, Gilda in *Rigoletto*. Her fabled companions in these early years included Gladys Swarthout, Giovanni Martinelli, Tito Schipa, Giacomo Lauri-Volpi, Giuseppe de Luca, Ezio Pinza, and Tancredi Pasero. Thereafter, for a dozen years no broadcast season could be considered complete without a Pons vehicle. After the mid-1940s there were a few lacunae (no broadcasts in 1944–45, 1945–46, 1949–50, and, during Rudolf Bing's tenure, 1952–53 and 1953–54).

The vehicles themselves were few enough. Pons's Met career held only ten roles, of which *Les contes d'Hoffmann*'s Olympia, Linda di Chamounix, and the Queen of Shemakha (*Le coq d'or*) never made it to the airwaves. The paucity of surviving mementos of the broadcasts for the first few seasons not only deprives us of Pons's virginal artistry but denies us the opportunity to hear her in roles that she did not sing in later radio outings. Apparently lost to us are Amina (repeated in 1935) and the 1933 Philine. Of her thirty-one Met broadcasts, twenty-seven centered on the repetition of four roles: Rosina (three broadcasts), Gilda (four broadcasts), Lakmé (six broadcasts), and the oft-recurring Lucia (an amazing fourteen portrayals). A single presentation of her delectable *La fille du régiment* in 1940 provided the only novelty in the final two decades of her broadcast career. Evidently the soprano, like Leonard Warren, subscribed to the belief that all great careers are made by mastering only two to five roles. But then, for the bulk of Pons's career the coloratura repertory that the American public fancied was quite circumscribed.

Pons occupied a prominent, indeed during her first two decades, almost monopolistic, position in that rarefied territory. Apart from an occasional Rosina and Gilda by the enchanting Bidú Sayão, the broadcasts held no real challengers (at least until the coming of Rudolf Bing in 1950). Little-remembered entities like Josephine Tuminia (1941 Rosina) and Hilde Reggiani (1942 Gilda) might appear cometlike and disappear leaving no trail of glory. Now and then Josephine Antoine, Mimi Benzell, and Hjördis Schymberg, reputable but merely serviceable sopranos, figured in the broadcast lists of Pons's favored operas. The precocious Patrice Munsel would appropriate even Lucia for a broadcast or two while Pons was off serenading the troops, but she could not dislodge the queen from the throne. Nor was the right of succession hers. Only New York audiences heard the exemplary Erna Berger's late-career Gilda. Bing repeatedly offered Hilde Güden as Gilda and Roberta Peters as Rosina in the early 1950s, but by that time Pons's occasional appearances in the new manager's production-oriented regime were essentially relics of a lavender-scented past.

The shadowy corners of the bel canto realm were being explored by Maria Callas, whose single broadcast Lucia followed Pons's farewell bride of Lammermoor in 1956. In the 1970s, Beverly Sills would take a stab at claiming the Metropolitan coloratura crown, but by then Joan Sutherland, who first appeared on the broadcasts as Lucia in 1961, had established her hegemony. Her novel combination of virtuosity and vocal size momentarily all but eradicated the image of birdlike soprano that Pons had so captivatingly embodied. But at the half-century mark Pons literally *was* coloratura singing for millions of Americans. Officiating at her final broadcast (*Lucia* on 14 January 1956), announcer Milton Cross confidently proclaimed her "the most famous coloratura soprano now appearing before the international public." The occasion marked her twenty-fifth anniversary with the company. She held on for a few more seasons, as tenacious at maintaining her Met aura as she had been at clinging to her celebrated high Fs, turning up again at a 1960 gala benefit for the welfare fund to sing "Caro nome" two-and-a-half years after her official departure as Lucia on the last night of the 1957–58 season.

The preserved documentation of Pons's radio performances presents a somewhat equivocal aural portrait. While savoring the undeniable charm of her vocalism, one vacillates between, on the one hand, admiration for her bewitching persona (and her skillful marketing of that image) and, on the other, annoyance at technical blemishes and the superficial posture that she perhaps necessarily imposed upon her characterizations. That dichotomy is reflected in the following broadcast critiques, which first appeared in my two-volume history of the early Metropolitan Opera broadcasts, *Saturday Afternoons at the Old Met* and *Sign-off for the Old Met*. There can be no doubt, however, that she held a substantial portion of the American operatic and nonmusical public in thrall for decades.

Lucia di Lammermoor, 27 February 1937: Lily Pons (Lucia), Frederick Jagel (Edgardo), John Brownlee (Enrico Ashton), Ezio Pinza (Raimondo); conducted by Gennaro Papi.

Lily Pons was most acclaimed for her Lucia, the role of her sensational 1931 debut and, over a period of twenty-four years, her most frequent broadcast portrayal. Her repute in the role is well sustained by her first preserved Lucia; she is in excellent form from beginning to end.

Pons is partnered by the reliable Jagel, with Pinza as Raimondo and the Australian baritone John Brownlee making his debut as Lucy's brother. Brownlee, a worthy enough artist in the right roles, had first appeared ten days earlier as Rigoletto, the Metropolitan management having seriously misjudged the nature of his vocal equipment. He is little better suited to the run-of-the-mill bluster of Enrico Ashton (this is in fact his only house performance of the role in his twenty-one Met seasons). He offers a solid, stout portrayal, but all beer and no vino. Brownlee rarely attempts legato, the timbre is inherently wooden, and the top notes turn hollow in Ashton's big opening scene. The audience is decidedly unresponsive. He is a shade more effective in the scene with Lucia where Ashton is allowed to be more sympathetic. Jagel is in good form (for him), occasionally strangled as he approaches the upper range and also short on suavity, but ever the fine musician. Not until the final scene does his portrayal obtain any distinction—there he delivers an excellent "Fra poco a me ricovero" with a neat cadenza, and though Papi allows the orchestra to plod through "Tu che a Dio," Jagel manages the relentless ascent of the final phrases with honor. Papi's tempos are rather unpredictable throughout. In the opening, the chorus is almost routed by the wild brio of Papi's beat, but the slow-moving sextet nearly grinds to a halt in an attempt at grandeur. Pinza is the only one of the afternoon's performers who seems capable of any dynamic modification, though he chooses an uncommonly stentorian heraldic manner for his announcement of Lucia's crime, thundering out "In ciel!" in response to Edgardo's inquiry as to her whereabouts. But his vocal richness is balm in this desert of tonal vacuity.

With Pons one must accept the monochromatic color of her singing and recognize that she knows exactly what she can do with her voice and attempts nothing else. It is folly to look for subtle gradations of tone, vocal coloring in keeping with the text, or any large-scale emotional response either in volume or dramatic emphasis. She is the eternal *jeune fille*, with "pretty" as the only appropriate adjective—but at least "pretty" is not "ugly." One must admire how she utilizes what she has in a secure, professional manner and relish the pleasure which she thereby provides—a pleasure comparable to viewing the most expensive and delicate Meissen figurine, not great art but a wonder of its kind, perfect in its way, as Pons is in this *Lucia*. She never falters, her tones are tremolo-free, few aspirants intrude in fioritura (oddly we hear them in slow cantabile—"Alfin son tu-hoo-a"), she is ever on pitch, her *attacca* is quick and accurate. Her technical arsenal does not include a real trill—the minute ornaments in "Regnava nel silenzio" are indistinct and the longer trills barely acceptable shakes. She etches (as opposed to spins) Donizetti's graceful melodies with utmost care. Even the low-lying cantabile of "Soffriva nel pianto," in which Lucia longs for death, is firmly drawn though far removed from the tragic lament we know it to be. No Gothic mystery shades her tale of the ghostly maiden, but the line of "Regnava nel silenzio" is nicely sculpted and the stratospheric recall of "Verranno a te" in the cadenza of the Mad Scene has surprising fullness of tone. Moreover, she often gains a brilliance in the upper octave and a half that is quite extraordinary, and an occasional upward flight of staccatos (in the Mad Scene) strikes with rapierlike precision. "Our Provençal nightingale," as Cross calls her, concludes the first section of the Mad Scene with a stunning F in alt, brilliant in color, round in tone, and held until the "thunderous applause" drowns her out. But Cross assures us that "her melodious raving" will continue, and it surely does. In fact, every D, E-flat, and F scattered throughout the opera is rung with precision by Pons. A Pons artifice is her habit of pausing a fraction of a beat or more (while the orchestra waits) before launching some of the more spectacular roulades or high notes, thus compelling the audience to join her in a conspiracy of suspense. The audience clearly doted on her and would continue to do so until Maria Callas taught us that we really could care about mad Lucy and her tragic fate.

Lakmé, 6 January 1940: Lily Pons (Lakmé), Irra Petina (Mallika), Armand Tokatyan (Gérald), George Cehanovsky (Frédéric), Ezio Pinza (Nilakantha); conducted by Wilfrid Pelletier.

Lily Pons had followed her heart to Hollywood in the 1930s, but she did not tarry long; her innate chic and notes in alt seemed to need only her own astute promotion to maintain the image of "opera star." No opera was better calculated to exhibit the petite soprano's charms than Delibes's *Lakmé*, a flower of nineteenth-century French exoticism as fragile as the datura blossom whose poison the unhappy heroine consumes at the opera's close. Of course, science has taught us (and Delibes knew it as well) that the datura is not deadly at all—and neither is the opera, though modern critics have almost pummeled it to death.

Before Pons made it her specialty, the Met had known few Lakmés. Patti had sung it in a special season in 1890, but the first Met Lakmé (1892) was Marie Van Zandt (she had created it at the Opéra-Comique), followed by Marcella Sembrich (1906) and Maria Barrientos (1917). Revived for Pons in her second Met season, her portrayal would keep the opera in the repertory for the next dozen years (lapsing only in 1937–38). Two early broadcasts featured distinguished casts (Swarthout, Thill or Martinelli, de Luca, Rothier). But the radio public waited until 6 January 1940 for a repeat, and now the casting, like Pons in person, was decidedly lightweight: only Pinza matched the Nilakantha of Édouard de Reszke or Marcel Journet in those early Met performances. The bass moves with ease from devil to Brahman priest, but unfortunately this is one of Pinza's off days. The voice is oddly unreliable (particularly at the top), though the contrast between the half-voice and full-voice phrases of his second-act aria is telling. Tokatyan makes a brave effort at Gérald's music and is often effective in lyrical passages. He is well matched in vocal weight with Pons, but while the soprano gives a graceful turn to the fleet chains of melody which permeate Delibes's score, Tokatyan too often sends them on motorically. Focus on Lakmé and her Bell Song has rendered the role of Gérald nondescript (for the public), but as the opera proceeds and Gérald's character becomes more feckless, Delibes has quixotically increased the vocal demands. Tokatyan falters in these more dramatic moments (the duet, "Dans la forêt," and the ardent, high-flying phrases which close the second and third acts). In the quieter moments (the opening scenes of act three, for instance) his vocal finesse proves gratifying.

And now for the diva herself. No doubt about it, she is bewitching in this part. In these surroundings her vocal security and elegant phrasing shine. Except for the Bell Song, the part is devoid of coloratura pyrotechnics, and the aria itself relies on nimble staccatos and a pair of high Es rather than intricate roulades. Pons has them ready to hand. The spirited staccatos of "Où tinte la clochette" startle with their dash, and the long concluding E (and its approach) are dead center on. Even more gratifying is the sure control and tonal loveliness of her cantabile; by underlining the contrast between the several moods of the aria she gives it substance. It is her graceful cantilena, in fact, which proves so satisfying throughout the afternoon. "C'est le dieu de la jeunesse" is elegantly phrased, and despite her slight resources, she achieves dynamic contrasts: in "Pourquoi dans les grands bois?" the modulation between lightly floated song and a few brilliantly pointed phrases is carefully planned; in act three she utilizes a pallid, childlike tone as she watches over the wounded Gérald. In short, she actually works at turning Lakmé into a person. The image of Lakmé must have appealed to Pons as a conceit which even her public could accept as a satisfying substitute for Pons, the diva. In any case, her vocal security on this broadcast heralds a welcome period of more agreeable listening for the radio audience.

La fille du régiment, 28 December 1940: Lily Pons (Marie), Irra Petina (Marquise), Raoul Jobin (Tonio), Salvatore Baccaloni (Sulpice); conducted by Gennaro Papi.

On Saturday afternoon, 28 December 1940, the Metropolitan presented a revival of the Donizetti gem *La fille du régiment* as a new vehicle for Lily Pons. Only two Metropolitan Maries had preceded her: Sembrich, at the beginning of the century, and Frieda Hempel (as *figlia*, since the opera was then given in Italian), at the end of World War I. In 1940 all Europe was again engulfed in conflict and France was occupied by the Nazis. When, at the opera's conclusion, Miss Pons advances to the front of the stage dressed in regimental uniform and waving the French flag, Donizetti's pert comedy undergoes a patriotic metamorphosis as the audience rises to its feet. Mr. Cross recounts to the radio audience the "thrilling closing scene. . . . Lily Pons as Marie waving aloft the French Napoleonic tricolors of her twenty-first regiment, and the orchestra and chorus singing those strains of the Marseillaise." An aura of sentiment has accrued to this performance, heightened in memory by the image of the petite Pons as the plucky *vivandière* uttering mild epithets ("Morbleu"), "currycombing one of the dappled wooden horses in its stall," and playing at soldier rather like a grown-up Shirley Temple (remember *The Little Colonel*). Even her most vehement detractors accept Pons's regimental daughter as the pinnacle of her career.

The broadcast captures the actual premiere of the new production, and perhaps the press of rehearsals (which she normally avoided at the Met) took its toll on Pons's slim resources, for she is not in her finest form. For much of the afternoon the brilliant point of the voice is absent, the cantilena (especially in the lower reaches of "Il faut partir") is slightly tremulous, and there is a hint of instability lurking in the unfamiliar patterns of staccatos (add even a slight catch in a high C at the end of the second act—and the Pons high notes were always reliable). But there are a few deft coloratura flourishes along the way, the sentiment is affecting in her farewell to camp life, both tone and feeling are firmly projected in the pathetic "Par le rang et par l'opulence," and her comic touch is sure (she opens the lesson scene in hooty tones and ends it with wild roulades like an overtightly wound-up Olympia). Even unseen, the Pons charm comes through. She is no hoyden tomboy, but the spoiled darling of the troops, and when they return to save her from wealth and decorum, she delivers an assured "Salut à la France!" (with a lengthy cadenza cum flute). Now the familiar brilliant tone reasserts itself, her staccatos firm up (the aspirants more ghastly than ever), and the long high D restores confidence.

The version of the opera which the Met elected (was Papi or Pons the determinant?) is a hybrid. Though sung in the original French, the layout is that of the Italian version which Donizetti prepared for Milan, with sung recitatives replacing the spoken dialogue. Curiously, the composer disemboweled the tenor role in his revision, so Raoul Jobin, new to the Met roster, has no string of high Cs during the first finale nor a go at Tonio's aria in the next act (the Met revival divided the original two-act opera into three acts). All this is regrettable, for Jobin is a very creditable Tonio with his idiomatic French (Canadian-born, he trained at the Paris Conservatoire and was a member of both the Opéra-Comique and the Opéra). His entry to the Met was via the "Metropolitan Auditions of the Air," though curiously not as a winner but snatched for a debut as Des Grieux before the contest was over. He is vocally ardent in the love duet (with Pons appropriately coy). Both he and Pons have the rhythmic éclat for "De cet aveu si tendre," and he delivers some of the afternoon's best vocalism in his plea for Marie's hand ("Ah! mes amis").

The comic roles are in good hands, though generally as much buffa as *bouffe*: Irra Petina (also shorn of her opening aria) doesn't caricature the Marquise; the Duchess of Crakentorp is mercifully played straight and silent by Maria Savage (no star turn by an aged diva, but rather the walk-on of a veteran chorister); and Louis d'Angelo's droll Hortensius displays the good manners of fine comic portraiture. Baccaloni's manners are another matter. His Sulpice is broadly played and trumpeted out in gruff (and highly resonant) tones that could quell an entire French army. But what a lovable old walrus he is, all bluster and big heart, dwarfing Pons not only in avoirdupois but, unfortunately, in volume as well; even Cross calls him "an old friend of ours, by now" (he had been with the company all of three weeks). Papi has the new production well enough in hand, except for some zigzagging between male chorus and orchestra in the drill music which closes the first scene. More important, the *bouffe* high point of the score is muffed—the trio, "Tous les trois réunis," is sadly deficient in panache: Pons is inaudible, Baccaloni gives insufficient point to his threats, and only Jobin is on the mark. One cannot deny the enthusiasm of the audience at the opera's curtain. The Met would keep the work in repertory for three seasons, though the radio audience would wait three decades for another hearing of this delicious French hors d'oeuvre.

Rigoletto, 18 December 1943: Lily Pons (Gilda), Anna Kaskas (Maddalena), Charles Kullman (Duke of Mantua), Leonard Warren (Rigoletto), Nicola Moscona (Sparafucile); conducted by Cesare Sodero.

Throughout this 1943 *Rigoletto* broadcast, Cesare Sodero oversees a curiously bifurcated performance—with Pons and Kullman picture-postcard lovers, Moscona and Kaskas down-to-earth villains. The gentle elegance with which Sodero beguilingly swathed *Traviata*, for example, serves *Rigoletto* less well. We get no sense of the licentious Duke of Mantua's raucous court in the *banda* music, nor is the horror engendered by Monterone's curse caught in the whispered choral response of the courtiers. The flaccid meandering of muted cello and double bass eviscerates Verdi's black comedy when Sparafucile solicits Rigoletto's trade. Sodero adheres to the score's metronome markings, however, and the tepid nature of the performance must be laid equally to Pons and Kullman.

Contributing to the garden party atmosphere of the performance, Kullman is at his most effete, adhering to Verdi's dynamic markings, to be sure, and entirely musical, like the artist he is. But he offers hardly a moment of *slancio* to convince us that this youth is the virile despoiler of women. Perhaps that is the secret of the Duke's success with Gilda (after all, she believes him a poor student), but at least "Questa o quella" could give some inkling of the Duke's character. Kullman does supply a measure of the *eleganza* Verdi calls for, but he seems unduly bored by the whole affair. He summons a modest ardor in the love duet and his suavity is welcome in the cantabile, though he flics a bit out of vocal focus near the end. "Parmi veder le lagrime" is exceedingly well sung within the dolce manner Kullman cultivates throughout the afternoon. He concludes "La donna è mobile" with an oddly manipulated cadenza and a resounding high B (but the tessitura of the quartet pressures him). In the reprise of the aria the tenor negotiates a convincing *morendo* to excellent dramatic effect.

With her childlike tone and manner, Pons is a fitting partner for Kullman. The voice is perilously shaky in the lower octave at her entrance, but soon it settles, the touch of shrillness fading. Her farewell to her father has a lovely simplicity. Occasionally she seems more disposed to play Gilda rather than Pons on this afternoon—her girlish fear at Gualtier's entrance is quite convincing. "Caro nome" becomes an exercise in fermate on high notes, with weak low notes, neat short trills, and an excellent cadenza which houses a secure *messa di voce* before a tenacious high E. Pons's cameo-like delicacy has its charm, but the audience response is surprisingly slight (as it is for everyone throughout the afternoon). In the coda she prefers to ascend in arpeggio fashion to another (even tauter) high E rather than rely on Verdi's effective long trill. "Tutte le feste" has some fine tone, a bit glassy now and then, but overall well controlled, and "Lassù in cielo" is effective in its quiet resignation.

Lucia di Lammermoor, 1 January 1949 (broadcast 2 January): Lily Pons (Lucia), Ferruccio Tagliavini (Edgardo), Francesco Valentino (Enrico Ashton), Jerome Hines (Raimondo); conducted by Pietro Cimara.

"Place aux games" was the order of the day—commercial radio ceded precedence of opera to the New Year's Day football marathons. *Lucia* is the only delayed airing in the history of the broadcasts (in 1955 the problem was averted by passing over the Saturday matinee *Aida* and airing the evening *Traviata*). The *Lucia* broadcast has gained a measure of notoriety as the single occasion where the studio-recording practice of tape splicing invaded the opera broadcasts. Pons had stumbled badly on the high F which ends the first section of the Mad Scene. The second F at the close of the scene went better, and reportedly at the suggestion of the resourceful Cross, the second was substituted for the first as well. Two high Fs for the price of one, not a bad deal for an aging coloratura. From the radio audience point of view, of course, it was one high F where two were ordered, but at least (remembering Flagstad's *Tristan* high Cs à la Schwarzkopf on records, or even the Votipka-Moore broadcast *Tosca* cantata) they were both Pons.

"The Nightingale of Provence" (Cross was singularly inventive in manufacturing sobriquets for Pons) has other problems throughout the afternoon—the pattern of the 1948 *Lucia* repeats itself. In the first two acts her voice is of eggshell-thin fragility, brittle and white; short trills are a squeak, long ones a blur, and the coloratura (especially in "Quando rapito") effortful. Pitch tips to the downside more frequently than on other occasions. If Cross hadn't told us, we would never imagine that Pons likes "the emotional character of Lucia." Valentino, frayed in tone at the beginning, stentorian but hollow thereafter, is at least authoritative. The Lucy-Ashton scene is far from a thing of beauty, though Pons by now has begun to gain in steadiness and quality of tone. When mad Lucy enters we hear a different voice, calmer, warmer, fluent in scales and sure of legato. One feels reassured—evidently Miss Pons can always undergo a conversion for the Mad Scene. But she tires slightly at the very top as she nears the fatal F. In the second section a few upward flights are smudged, and she omits a note or two. The final F (this is the good one) is both thin and flat, but it is *there*. (The first F, as broadcast, is oddly shorter in its reincarnation.)

> *Il barbiere di Siviglia*, 16 December 1950: Lily Pons (Rosina), Giuseppe di Stefano (Almaviva), Giuseppe Valdengo (Figaro), Jerome Hines (Don Basilio), Salvatore Baccaloni (Dr. Bartolo); conducted by Alberto Erede.

Comedy of an old order was on display when *Il barbiere di Siviglia* returned to the airwaves in December 1950 after an absence of seven seasons. The hiatus gives no cause for regret since Edward Johnson's *Barbiere* was an unhappy thing, careless in design, bumptious in spirit, and outrageous in musical style. Bing, in his first season as general manager, had demonstrated his skill at mounting new productions. Would his new broom be stout enough to sweep the cobwebs from repertory opera?

Lily Pons and Salvatore Baccaloni carry onto the airwaves not only enormous reputations but the baggage of years in this initial Bing season. Both are in their early fifties. The basso manages a fair effort (in part aided by a truncated "A un dottore"), for his voice retains a good deal of its imposing size and vibrancy. Tone has survived, though true pitches have not, and his manner projects a delightful sense of the absurd. Pons continued to reign supreme in favor with a large public, for whom her beauty and charm, elegant attire, and skillful career promotion of the opera-diva image compounded their unwavering belief in her song. Undoubtedly, she had something distinctive which commanded loyalty; indeed, I have never neglected an opportunity to hear her recordings—whatever their deficiencies, invariably an ineffable, quite captivating, spell emanates from them. It is a quality (call it a musical charm) which is in short supply today. Now in her twentieth season with the company (though her few appearances each year for the past decade could hardly be called a season), Pons as Rosina had not been heard by the radio audience since 1938. That she had favored the more stratospheric Lucia and Lakmé in her recent broadcasts is not surprising. Rosina's mezzo tessitura, even when transposed upward and greatly embellished with flights above the staff, provokes only glassy, thin tones from Pons's aging throat. As if to contradict nature, the higher altitudes always made her breathe easier, and she ends the Andante of "Una voce poco fa" with a nicely spun top C. She has been over the fioritura hurdles so often that out the roulades will come, but the response is slower and more labored than remembered. Though raised to the key of F by Pons, the aria ends with a tenacious high E which she flicks up to the correct note at the moment of release. In the lesson scene an almost-F concludes Adam's variations on "Ah vous dirai-je maman"; her first variation could well be a parody of a coloratura soprano, for her tones are harsh and aspirated beyond her norm, while the manner is uncharacteristically devoid of the celebrated Pons magic. Only in the cadenza with flute does some measure of the remembered tonal gleam and security in fioriture return. Mercifully, she is nearly inaudible in the ensembles.

Lucia di Lammermoor, 14 January 1956: Lily Pons (Lucia), Jan Peerce (Edgardo), Frank Valentino (Enrico Ashton), Nicola Moscona (Raimondo); conducted by Fausto Cleva.

With Patrice Munsel in the mid-1940s and Roberta Peters in the early 1950s the Metropolitan may appear to have succumbed to the belief that skill in fioriture was the province of youth. After securing Rosina and Gilda, Peters justified her right to the title of coloratura soprano with her first Met Lucia on 1 February 1956. Throughout these decades, however, that often-derided appellation belonged indisputably to Pons, though her defense of the title in the operatic arena had become so rare that it seemed her right to the crown would be lost by default. The paucity and quality of her recent broadcast performances suggest that the astute Pons may have divined that her supremacy was better honored in the breach than in active combat. Two or three Met performances a season had been the norm for almost a decade, with *Lucia* broadcasts in 1951 and 1954 guarantees of her continuing star status. Now a celebratory occasion called her once more into the fray. Management proposed to honor her with a gala on the twenty-fifth anniversary of her Met debut. Pons was eager to oblige. On 3 January 1956, the soprano met the challenge head on by offering the second act of *Rigoletto*, the Mad Scene from *Lucia*, and preferring to end the evening in solitary splendor, arias from four operas associated with her early Met career: *Linda di Chamounix*, *Mignon*, *Le coq d'or*, and *Lakmé*. A few days later (14 January) the diva honored the airwaves with her final broadcast portrayal—Lucia, of course.

Do the ghosts of Lucias past (her own) haunt our celebrant? On commemorative occasions, tradition allows critical judgment to be, if not suspended, at least tempered by good will and, wherever possible, filtered by the recall of former achievements. Still, if one has found fault in the past, to avoid trespassing into hypocrisy requires tact beyond the norm. I take refuge in Pons's earliest recordings—we are concerned with the aural record, though ignoring the visual aspect of this prima donna would be like omitting the fruit from fruitcake. Some idea of the appeal of the artist may be gleaned from contemporary reports, and no better appraiser can be found than Herman Klein, by 1931 an observer of the vocal scene for more than half a century. He had not only heard, but known intimately, Patti, Nilsson, di Murska, Sembrich, Tetrazzini, and, above all, Melba, to name only sisters of the coloratura breed. Writing in the year of Pons's Met debut, Klein judged her recording of the Mad Scene to be an "an excellent *bravura* performance," finding her voice "pure and clear in quality," and her execution "neat rather than phenomenal."[2] A little later that same year, he deemed her Bell Song worthy of comparison in style and timbre with that of Marie Van Zandt ("whose charming creation of Lakmé I witnessed at the Opéra-Comique in 1883"—could one ask for more authentic commendation?). Pons's recording was "quite a perfect thing in its own way," with her staccato "a miracle of delicate flexibility," her tone "sweet and sympathetic."[3] By 1932, Klein found Pons's voice more mature and her technical skill even "surer and more finished."[4] If Pons's Met broadcasts of the 1930s do not always sustain her repute, they do hold valuable souvenirs of her artistry: I have written admiringly of her 1937 Lucia, her 1939 Gilda, the 1940 regiment's daughter, and above all, several outings as Lakmé. Other broadcasts have been less satisfactory, and some have been quite objectionable.

Having paid obeisance to the anniversary diva, I turn my ear to the 1956 broadcast only to discover that I have poured commendatory ink on Pons's beginnings when I might have saved it for her ending. The fifty-seven-year-old prima donna is in remarkably fine voice. Within the limits imposed by her delicate instrument, she is a committed interpreter of Lucia's woes. After gobbling a few introductory recitatives (a common throat massage indulged in by far younger singers), she launches the fountain narrative with assurance, lovely tone, and, best of all, little sign of the tremulousness in the mid and lower range which on past occasions has defaced her cantilena. Unwilling to retreat from her decades-old practice of transposing Lucia's principal arias (up a half step in act one, a full step for the Mad Scene), her topmost notes suffer from this vanity. The E-flat and Fs turn hard and glassy and, in the Mad Scene, fail to reach the pitch—she is ever dedicated in the attempt, however, and the notes never dissolve into a squeak. Occasionally, in the solo arias, she omits a few notes in the lower range to better prepare for the ascent or perhaps merely to marshal breath; admittedly, some of the virtuoso flights which formerly astonished are now taken at a slightly slower pace—they dartle pleasingly well for all that. "Verranno a te" confirms that her virginal tonal color is remarkably intact. She traces its arcs with loving care, executing a grace note with exactitude and thereby subtly enhancing the emotional content of her song. With Pons, the act-two scene with Ashton has always been a way station between pivotal arias, so we need not linger there; but even in these low-lying phrases Pons maintains a steadier flow of tone than she has managed in some earlier broadcasts. For the most part, her Mad Scene replicates her better broadcast efforts. She may drop a few notes in a repeated sequence, snatch a quick breath in a run, or, in the final section (her goal in sight), swoop up to a top note in a welcome fit of exuberance, but her fioriture have their familiar clarity. Moreover, her song is affecting, though "Alfin son tua" is as usual untouched by dolor.

Of her 1948 broadcast bride, I dejectedly wrote that "surely there can't be many Lucias left in this fifty-year-old throat." That occasion was merely the tenth of Pons's fourteen Met broadcasts of the role. Not only had she saved a good one for her anniversary year, but she continued to sing a pair or so for the next two seasons, the last one on the closing night of the 1957–58 season. Her final operatic appearance occurred at Fort Worth (she was a part-time resident of Texas) as Lucia in 1965. The indomitable prima donna resurfaced once again to sing several songs and arias in a Kostelanetz Promenade Concert with the New York Philharmonic. The year was 1972, the soprano was seventy-four years old and evidently still a fair replica of her earlier self. The original vocal lode may have been undersized, but she had mined it with discretion. A turn-of-the-century critic once named a certain coloratura soprano as "the first of her kind, though her kind is not the first." (Wagner fervor was then at its height.) Not so much may be said of Pons, but we wholeheartedly agree with Cross who, during the ovation after the Mad Scene, named her "this fascinating, most chic, and unique artist."

In the early 1950s, when I was in my twenties and associated with the Central City Opera Company, Pons (who was singing a concert at Red Rocks outdoor arena) paid a call on Central City. I, along with others, had the pleasure of showing her the opera house and the historic relics of the old mining town that was home to our festivals. The famed Pons aura was much in evidence. I thought back to the first time that I heard a Metropolitan Opera broadcast; the date was 28 December 1940, the opera was *La fille du régiment*, and the first voice I heard was that of Lily Pons. My ideas about florid song have changed a great deal since then, but I owe her.

CHAPTER FIFTEEN

Lily Pons in Hollywood

James B. McPherson

On 24 October 1933, gossip columnist Louella Parsons wrote in the *New York Herald* that Lily Pons was being pursued for a film contract by both Warner Bros. and Metro-Goldwyn-Mayer. "She reaches Hollywood [on] 31 October," Parsons wrote, "at which time she will decide whether it's to be Warners or M-G-M." As it turned out, RKO Pictures prevailed over both M-G-M and Warner Bros.; Pons would make three films there between 1935 and 1937.

In this chapter, author James B. McPherson, retired music and film critic for *The Toronto Sun*, reviews Pons's Hollywood career. Although her film career did not prove very durable (nor, for that matter, did the genre of the 1930s Hollywood musical), her movie roles, like the Saturday afternoon Metropolitan Opera radio broadcasts, exposed Lily's talents and charm to a broad segment of the American public.

"*A*ND THE OSCAR GOES TO—Miss Grace Moore!"

No, it never happened.

But it might have.

In 1934 Columbia Pictures boss Harry Cohn watched with great astonishment as the film *One Night of Love* become an international hit; it had taken staff music adviser Max Winslow, once-and-future publishing partner of Irving Berlin, a full year to hound the skeptical studio head into approving the project. But this was nothing compared with the astonishment of contemporary opera historians when they discover that the film—an amiable enough bit of nonsense in which the thirty-five-year-old Metropolitan Opera soprano won worldwide celebrity warbling, among other things, "Ciribiribin" and excerpts from *Madama Butterfly*—was actually nominated for five Academy Awards, including Best Picture and Best Actress. Cohn could afford to smile when the Clark Gable–Claudette Colbert comedy *It Happened One Night* claimed both those honors and several others, since that film was a Columbia release, too. And he must have positively laughed aloud at the "opera mania" that infected Hollywood for the next three or four years as a direct result of the unexpected popularity of that little musical picture he had been so reluctant to make.

Even as the Oscars were handed out at the Hotel Biltmore on 27 February 1935, Grace Moore, basking in the more substantial rewards of a greatly increased fee and a percentage of the profits, was at work on her second Columbia film, *Love Me Forever* (in which she would achieve the unique distinction, unprecedented at the Met but unremarkable in Hollywood, of playing both Mimì *and* Musetta in the same "performance" of *La bohème*). Elsewhere around town, Lawrence Tibbett—who, like Moore, had made a few moderately successful features for M-G-M in 1930–31—was back before the cameras as the star of *Metropolitan*, an aria-dappled pleasantry that, although a box-office disappointment, earned a niche in history as the first film ever released by the newly formed 20th Century-Fox. By early summer, veteran producer Jesse Lasky, whose lifelong fascination with opera singers had seduced him into making silent pictures with Geraldine Farrar, Lina Cavalieri, and Enrico Caruso, was supervising *Here's to Romance*, a showcase for boyish Met tenor Nino Martini. Also in the cast, in the formidable role of Herself, was seventy-four-year-old Ernestine Schumann-Heink, "the most spiritual, courageous, wonderful character I've ever met in show business," claimed the worshipful Lasky in his 1957 autobiography.[1]

Nor were bona-fide practitioners of the art the only ones taking advantage of Hollywood's sudden love affair with "grand opera." At Warner Bros., young radio favorite James Melton (it would be another three years before he made his stage debut) found the climate conducive to interpolating a complete perform-ance of "Celeste Aïda," recitative and all, into a Pat O'Brien–Jane Froman frolic called *Stars Over Broadway*. At M-G-M, the Marx Brothers were wreaking havoc on *Il trovatore* as the frenetic climax to *A Night at the Opera* (which time would prove the funniest and most popular of all their films). Meanwhile, at Para-mount, even the redoubtable Mae West got into the act, shoehorning her own hilarious and highly unlikely rendition of Dalila's "Mon coeur s'ouvre à ta voix" into the otherwise forgettable *Goin' to Town*.

But it was the prestige and glamour of authentic opera stars that remained most in demand as studios scrambled to emulate the success of *One Night of Love*. On Saturday, 20 April 1935, Maria Jeritza—still, even at forty-seven and with her Met glory days behind her, undeniably glamorous—made a screen test for M-G-M. Afterward, according to *The New York Times*, "she would not say whether the test had been successful, but she was beaming and said she would have good news for her friends on Monday."[2] Perhaps the good news was that Lily Pons had been signed by RKO Radio Pictures because, although nothing more was heard of Jeritza's bid to grace the silver screen, it was precisely at this moment that the popular French soprano was preparing to join the ever-swelling ranks of divas in Hollywood.

If no longer in the first flush of youth, thirty-seven-year-old Lily was nonethe-less a natural candidate for potential movie stardom. Already a veteran of five Metropolitan seasons, she had won a wide following of adoring fans via radio, concerts, and RCA Victor Red Seal records. The contemporary Met roster may have boasted greater voices—Rosa Ponselle (who would make her own M-G-M screen test the following year) and Kirsten Flagstad (who would contribute "Brunnhilde's Battle Cry" to Paramount's *Big Broadcast of 1938*) for two—but, simply put, few opera stars of her own or any other generation could compete with the petite and graceful Pons photogenically.

Production of her first film, started as *Love Song* but finished as *I Dream Too Much*, was entrusted to the respected Pandro S. Berman, whose previous RKO successes included *Morning Glory* with Katharine Hepburn and *Of Human Bondage* with Bette Davis. James Gow and Edmund North, who had collaborated on *One Night of Love* (it was the twenty-somethings' first Hollywood assignment), were hired to fashion a screenplay from the Elsie Finn–David Wittels story about a French girl whose marriage to a young American in Paris is threatened when her success as a singer eclipses his efforts as a composer. Henry Fonda, then a thirty-year-old Broadway recruit with only two previous films to his credit, was cast as the husband, with other major roles going to experienced character actor Osgood

Perkins (whose son Anthony, then only three years old, would one day make his own mark in the movies) as an impresario, and English-born comic Eric Blore as an eccentric vaudevillian whose fortunes depended on the whims of a performing seal named Duchess. Other amusing moments were contributed by the mournful Mischa Auer, grandson of famed violinist Leopold Auer, as the impresario's staff pianist; the ebullient Billy Gilbert (born in a theater dressing-room in Louisville, Kentucky, where his opera-singer parents were filling an engagement) in an unbilled bit as a chef; the starchy Esther Dale, who had enjoyed modest success as a concert soprano in the 1920s, as a tourist from Tulsa; and a twenty-four-year-old RKO contract player named Lucille Ball as her vacuous gum-chewing daughter.

Although nearing fifty, director John Cromwell, a competent if uninspired veteran of twenty years in the theater and seven on movie sound stages, had yet to make most of the films for which he is best remembered, among them *Abe Lincoln in Illinois* and *Anna and the King of Siam*. Composer-conductor Max Steiner, an accomplished Viennese who had studied with Mahler and whose more than 200 film scores, ranging from *King Kong* to *Gone with the Wind*, would earn him eighteen Oscar nominations over a thirty-six-year Hollywood career, was nominally in charge of musical matters. Jerome Kern, engaged to write four original songs, agreed to do so only if they were orchestrated by Robert Russell Bennett rather than Steiner, while Pons insisted that her current mentor (and future husband) André Kostelanetz be brought in to conduct the two arias chosen for the film, "Caro nome" from *Rigoletto* and the Bell Song from *Lakmé*.[3] (Only a portion of the *Rigoletto* aria was used in the film, while the Bell Song was presented in its considerable entirety in a fully staged "performance" purportedly at the Paris Opéra, where, I believe, Delibes's intimate opera-comique has never been given.)

Kern's partner was Dorothy Fields, daughter of the tall, lanky half of the legendary Weber and Fields comedy team. She had already written lyrics for Tibbett's 1931 film *Cuban Love Song* and would go on to do the same for Grace Moore's *The King Steps Out* (1936) and Ezio Pinza's *Mr. Imperium* (1951). Together Kern and Fields created a varied quartet of numbers to showcase their star. If the film's title song, "I Dream Too Much," was no great improvement on numerous other trite samples of the genre, the team at least produced an engaging pop tune ("I Got Love"), a pleasant Debussyian "aria" ("I'm the Echo") from the nonexistent opera *Echo and Narcissus*, and one genuinely inspired novelty ("The Jockey on the Carousel"). Bolstered by a male chorus and sung by the heroine to comfort a small boy who has been reduced to tears by the bullying of older children, "The Jockey on the Carousel" provided perhaps the best (and best-remembered) moment in the film, the charm of the sequence owing not a little to a delightful performance by five-year-old Scott Beckett. (Already a veteran of more than twenty films, this engaging youngster would also find himself singled out and sung to by Grace Moore in 1937's *When You're in Love*.)

Filming, begun the first day of August 1935, finished in late September. On 6 October, *The New York Times* published an article reporting on the Hollywood experiences of Pons, Martini, and former Met baritone Everett Marshall, who had spent part of the summer making his second (and last) movie, a low-budget Warner Bros. musical called *I Live for Love*.

"Hollywood to work is a nice place," claimed Lily.

To work with so many artists is interesting. The camera men were so kind. It feel like a happy family, you know? In addition to the operatic arias, I 'ave a 'ot song and a 'ot dance. But I tell you, zis part was the thrill in my life. Never 'ave I done it before. Oh, I tell you, it was 'ard work, very 'ard work, but very interesting.

As to the possibility of Hollywood filming a complete opera:

This I think would be a great mistake. To take ze story and modernize it, yes; to modernize the score, yes. But to photograph ze opera entirely, wiz ze story, no. You know, most of ze old opera stories are very stupid, very dull. What zey can do is take some of ze arias and add some new music. Because ze public would become tired of too much opera, no?[4]

On 28 November, *I Dream Too Much* opened at Radio City Music Hall to disappointing business but respectable reviews (although one pained critic promptly dubbed it *I Scream Too Much*). The fatal flaw, according to *The RKO Story*, was the screenplay, "a clumsy melange of high brow artistry . . . and low-jinks comedy . . . further weakened by soggy dialogue."[5]

On 2 December, Lily recorded the four Kern-Fields songs for RCA Victor. "I Dream Too Much" and "I'm the Echo" were issued, "I Got Love" and "The Jockey on the Carousel" were not. Presumably, the lady was as fond of the last-named number as her fans, because fully ten years later she tried it again, for Columbia, this time with success.

On 1 April 1936, *The New York Times* announced that Lily Pons's second Hollywood venture would be a remake of *Street Girl*, a 1929 trifle (the first official RKO production) that starred Betty Compson as a Balkan-born violinist involved with a quartet of jazz musicians. Veteran stage-and-screen writer Jane Murfin, borrowed from Sam Goldwyn to rejig her old story, joined with Dorothy Fields's brother Joseph Fields in transforming the Balkan violinist into a French opera singer, the jazz quartet into a swing band, and renaming the piece *That Girl from Paris*. Pandro Berman again produced, assembling a personable supporting cast headed by Jack Oakie (who had also appeared in the first version), Gene Raymond (six months after the film's release, the twenty-eight-year-old actor mar-

ried M-G-M singing star Jeanette MacDonald), Herman Bing, Frank Jenks, Mischa Auer, and Lucille Ball, the last two far more prominently employed than they had been in the previous year's *I Dream Too Much.*

The film featured a complete traversal of "Una voce poco fa" from *Il barbiere di Siviglia* and a wordless "Tarantella" by nineteenth-century German voice teacher Heinrich Panofka, both conducted by Kostelanetz (who is seen briefly on the podium leading the purported "Metropolitan Opera" performance of the Rossini work while being pelted with spitballs by Jack Oakie). In addition, the film's score, supervised by radio and recording veteran Nathaniel Shilkret, offered Pons in a swing arrangement of "The Blue Danube" (sung in French) and two new songs, "The Call to Arms" and "Seal it with a Kiss," with lyrics by Edward Heyman and music by Arthur Schwartz. Schwartz, in conjunction with his more customary collaborator Howard Dietz, had also supplied numbers for Lawrence Tibbett's concurrently filmed *Under Your Spell.* Three additional Heyman-Schwartz concoctions—"Love and Learn," "Moon Face," "My Nephew from Nice"—were allotted to the bumptious Oakie, who, surrounded by boy choristers, was further called upon to contribute a bizarre falsetto parody of Carrie Jacobs-Bond's "I Love You Truly" to the movie's climactic wedding scene. "Thees Oakie is a very—*comment je dis?*—light and bright boy, don't you know. Always he have spirits,"[6] Lily told an interviewer after the filming, which once again took place during August and September. This time, for whatever reasons, she chose not to commercially record any of the original songs.

On 27 December 1936, four days before the picture's New Year's Eve premiere at Radio City Music Hall, *The New York Times*'s B. R. Crisler reported, in "Film Gossip of the Week," on Pons's status as a bona-fide Hollywood celebrity:

> Her fan mail, of course, has arrived at truly amazing proportions since she became a movie star. The holders of boxes at the Metropolitan are enthusiastic, but they do not write asking advice about life and love and art, or compose whole histories of themselves in six closely written pages. "Fantastique," says Miss Pons. There is, of course, a small percentage of totally insane persons, and then there are certain others, good, steady, dependable writers, to be on whose mailing lists is like subscribing to a periodical. She does not know why people write to her like zees at all.

Oddly, although the silly plot was no improvement on that of Lily's first film, *That Girl from Paris* established itself as "the biggest hit of her movie career," according to Richard Jewel.[7] In 1942, reworked yet again, the venerable property reappeared as *Four Jacks and a Jill* with the leading character, now a nightclub vocalist, played by Anne Shirley.

⊙∫∫∽

In late August 1937, Pons returned to the RKO sound stages to begin work on a film called *It Never Happened Before*. By all accounts, it should never have happened at all. Although the opera-loving Jesse Lasky succeeded Pandro Berman as producer, and André Kostelanetz was elevated to full-fledged music director, they and their star didn't stand a chance against the inane screenplay about a nightclub singer who, in a scheme concocted by her press agent to dupe a wealthy big-game hunter cum opera patron, is persuaded to pose as a twittering, befeathered "bird girl" answering to the name of Oogahunga. Co-authored by Western specialist John Twist, whose previous credits included *Annie Oakley* and *The Outcasts of Poker Flats*, this unpromising material was further handicapped by being entrusted to the celebrated Raoul Walsh, a rough-and-ready "man's man" director more usually found overseeing virile outdoor action dramas. Before filming began, John Howard (best remembered as Ronald Colman's troubled brother in *Lost Horizon*) replaced the originally announced Gene Raymond as Lily's love interest, but "thees Oakie" returned as the enterprising press agent, with old comic hand Edward Everett Horton as the opera-loving hunter. Other roles went to Eric Blore, the English vaudevillian from *I Dream Too Much*; Eduardo Ciannelli, who had sung opera in his native Italy before establishing himself as a familiar character player on the American stage and screen; and Barcelona-born comic actor Luis Alberni, whose countless Hollywood appearances as a manic hair-tearing foreigner included, in this hectic period alone, entertaining bits in Tibbett's *Metropolitan*, Marion Talley's *Follow Your Heart*, and no fewer than three Grace Moore films, beginning with the immortal *One Night of Love*.

In addition to Saint-Saëns's "Le rossignol et la rose," the "Polonaise" from *Mignon*, and a portion of the *Lucia* Mad Scene, the film offered three original songs—"I Hit a New High," "This Never Happened Before," and "Let's Give Love Another Chance"—by lyricist Harold Adamson and composer Jimmy McHugh (this was the third of nineteen films on which the pair would collaborate between 1933 and 1957). Again, Lily eschewed commercial recordings of the new material.

An anonymous wire story, datelined Hollywood, 1 September 1937, gives an appalling glimpse of the indignities to which the star was subjected during production of this ill-conceived project:

> Poor Lily! The movies took off her beautiful clothes and replaced them with a brassiere of white feathers and a short skirt of the same. They painted the rest of her brown.
>
> They dunked her for hours in an imitation river. They put her into an animal cage and spent the rest of the day hoisting her up and down on a block-and-tackle.
>
> They forced her during all these proceedings to sing high C, like a bird made her bite the hand of Edward Everett Horton, the comedian, while Oakie, another such, suggested that a taxidermist be called in to stuff her.

These goings-on left Miss Pons without a single shred of the dignity of an international operatic favorite. They left her weak in the knees, tired, and with trembling lips, from fright, because the pulley slipped once and nearly dropped her to the hardwood floor of the African set.

"Never did I know that Hollywood could be like this," she sighed. "Never did I believe I'd have to do the things I'm doing. I still don't believe it. I'm doing it, but it can't be true. Perhaps it just isn't real. Maybe it's all a dream. . . ."

The jungle scene has real palms and tropical flowers and a river with water from the Hollywood mains. Eleven times Miss Pons descended into this stream and tried to sing to a bird perched on her finger. Eleven times the bird got scared (no insult to Miss Pons's voice) and flew away. The twelfth time the bird stuck it out and the bedraggled star of the opera climbed to dry land.

The costumes and make-up men gave her a new suit of feathers and a second coat of brown paint and the scene shifted to the Horton-Oakie yacht, anchored on the floor nearby. The huntsmen stuffed their captive in a cage, such as explorers use to transport monkeys, and tried to hoist her to their yacht.

They did this time after time before Director Raoul Walsh was satisfied. Once when the cage banged into a palm tree and Miss Pons almost wept from fright, the cameraman cracked: "Well, you said you wanted to be an actress. . . ."

When finally the day's shooting was over, she rubbed the paint from her legs, back and stomach. She put on clothes again and said she intended to take a vacation in Connecticut as soon as the picture was finished.

"Then I will go back in December to New York and the opera," she declared in a voice which makes it seem doubtful whether Hollywood ever would get to do such things again to her.[8]

And it never did. On Christmas Eve, 1937, the retitled *Hitting a New High* opened to disastrous reviews at New York's Rivoli Theater. According to *The RKO Story*, "the film lost a bundle and brought down the curtain on the RKO career of Miss Pons."

Ten years later, Lily would be seen in one further motion picture, but only briefly, and here as herself. *Carnegie Hall*, actually shot in the historic auditorium during the summer of 1946, was a long and lumbering "salute" incorporating guest appearances by many of the music world's most famous names. Independently produced by William LeBaron and Russian-born Boris Morros—who, a decade hence, would be revealed as a counterspy employed by the FBI while masquerading as an agent for the Soviet Union—the well-intentioned project was fatally undermined by its sentimental "framing story." From the pen of silent-screen veteran Seena Owen (who had played the Babylonian princess in D. W. Griffith's *Intolerance*), *Carnegie Hall* tells the story of a cleaning woman who grooms her son to be a classical pianist only to find that, on reaching adulthood, he prefers "pop" music. (Although he accepted an invitation to appear in the film, Arthur Rubinstein remarked "I bet it ends up with Harry James playing the trumpet"—it did.) The film did have the distinction of being the first film to employ stereophonic sound.

Elegantly coiffed and gowned, Lily appeared comparatively early in the 136-minute marathon, singing Rachmaninoff's "Vocalise" (Op. 34, No. 14) and a slightly abbreviated *Lakmé* Bell Song. Except for a single close-up on the last note of the Delibes aria, the forty-eight-year-old soprano is respectfully photographed only in full-length and three-quarter shots.

At its height in 1936—a year that found even Charlie Chan at the Opera   Hollywood's love affair with arias cooled rapidly thereafter. By the end of 1937, Lawrence Tibbett, Nino Martini, and even the inadvertent founder of the feast, Grace Moore, had packed up and left town, never to return. Gladys Swarthout undoubtedly wished she could have followed suit: the elegant mezzo's Paramount contract, signed with high hopes in 1935, ended in 1939 with a non-singing role in a low-budget crime melodrama called *Ambush*. Although opera stars continued to be welcomed on an increasingly cautious and occasional basis—Helen Jepson, for one, briefly graced *The Goldwyn Follies* in 1938—the movie capital would never again embrace "opera mania" on anything like the scale of those few exhilarating years immediately following the surprise success of *One Night of Love*.

As for Lily Pons, many years later she looked back on her Hollywood experience with something less than warm nostalgia:

> You know, for a singer it was very hard because you get up at five o'clock in the morning and pass the gate at seven, and by nine o'clock you are made up and all that, and all day until six or seven o'clock you are singing—so for a serious artist, it was very, very tiring. I made three movies but I didn't like it.[9]

PART FIVE

André

CHAPTER SIXTEEN

Lily

André Kostelanetz

In the entertainment industry, perhaps Mary Pickford and Douglas Fairbanks deserve the credit for legitimizing the "power marriage," a union between two celebrities of equivalent fame. By the late 1930s, power marriages were increasingly common in the entertainment industry—and when Lily Pons and André Kostelanetz proclaimed their vows in June 1938, their marriage brought to the classical-music world a level of media attention that the marriage of M-G-M producer Irving Thalberg to actress Norma Shearer had prompted in Hollywood earlier in the decade.

André Kostelanetz was born in Russia in December 1901. After he received his doctoral degree from the Conservatory of Music in Petrograd in 1922, he emigrated to the United States. In the U.S. he worked as a recital accompanist to Metropolitan and Chicago Opera singers until he became a full-time musician for radio in 1928. His popular radio program, *The Chesterfield Hour*, premiered on the CBS network in 1934. Broadcast from Manhattan's Hudson Theater, the long-running show was the first regularly scheduled radio program to feature a large orchestra and first-rank soloists in both classical and popular music. Rosa Ponselle, the Metropolitan's top-drawing dramatic soprano, was the first diva Kostelanetz persuaded to sing on *The Chesterfield Hour*. Soon, the young conductor convinced Lily Pons to add her name to the program's growing list of celebrity soloists. By the end of the decade, Kostelanetz had become one of the highest-paid classical musicians in the nation.

Kostelanetz's memoirs were published in 1981, six years after Lily's death. Unfortunately, he did not live to see his life story in print; he died on 13 January 1980, at the age of seventy-eight. In this excerpt from *Echoes: Memoirs of André Kostelanetz*,[1] he reflects on his courtship and eventual marriage to Lily.

*I*N 1931 a petite young Frenchwoman named Lily Pons made a spectacular debut at the Metropolitan Opera. There were sixteen curtain calls!

Fate was asserting herself. Just the year before, a serious throat ailment had forced into retirement the reigning coloratura soprano Amelita Galli-Curci. Now, people said, here was her operatic heir. In the few hours it took to sing the role of Lucia di Lammermoor in Donizetti's opera, Lily Pons became a star. Part of the excitement of the evening was the fact that she sang the Mad Scene in the key of F, a tone higher than the original score. Her range was high, even for a coloratura.

I did not hear her sing that night, that season, or even for the next three seasons. It is probably fortunate for me that I did not, because I would most likely have fallen in love with her from afar—as I'm sure hundreds of other young men did—and my modest position in the world then would not have helped me to advance the situation in my favor.

But toward the end of 1934, with the success of [my *Chesterfield Hour*] program, good things began to happen to me and pretty fast. "Mr. Chesterfield" was actually a charming white-haired gentleman named Carmichael who had a taste for classical music—and a belief that it could, if presented by great stars, sell cigarettes. Great stars like Lily Pons.

So when her agent, Frederick Schang, called me I was not surprised. Schang was a founding father of Columbia Concerts Corporation, which later became the huge Columbia Artists Management, and the only agent Lily had for her entire singing career. There would be an immediate demand for Lily by the radio audience, Schang told me, if she could be heard just once on the air. I said fine. He arranged a meeting for the three of us so that we could decide what she would sing.

Schang and I went to her apartment one late evening. She greeted us charmingly, in an amusing mixture of French and English. (Despite the fact that Lily spent virtually all her adult life in the United States—she became a citizen in 1940—French was "nevaire" absent from her speech. I think she sensed how delightful a grace note to her personality it was.) Within a very few minutes I was quietly dazzled and having a little trouble remembering the purpose of the meeting.

The first piece Lily wanted to sing was Gilda's bel canto aria from Verdi's *Rigoletto*, "Caro nome." I sat down at the piano and she began. She sang right through to the end, which is E above high C. What I'd heard was so contrary to what I'd expected! Her voice was shockingly out of tune and there was a wobble in it, two symptoms of fatigue frequently due to a combination of too much work and too exacting a repertoire. A dramatic soprano can sometimes get away with making extra demands of her vocal cords, because they are thicker and can take it, but coloratura is the highest ranging of the soprano voices, and the delicate vocal cords must not be abused, forced. There are only a few operas—*Lakmé*, *Il barbiere di Siviglia*, *Rigoletto*, *La fille du régiment*, for example—that perfectly suit such a voice. I didn't know what Lily's repertoire had been, but her voice sounded as if she had asked far too much of it.

I asked her to sing something else while I tried to figure out how to handle the situation. As a conductor I had an obligation to keep her from showing herself poorly, but how was I going to approach her with this problem? She finished the old English song, "Lo! Here the Gentle Lark," which had gone no better.

We exchanged a few pleasant remarks. I don't remember going to the extreme of complimenting her; I let it go saying how good it was to meet her, hear her sing. But as Schang and I went down in the elevator, I asked him how we could let her sing like this, and on a coast-to-coast network.

I wondered if Lily herself had noticed the deterioration. Singers are not always able to hear their own voices; they rely on the response of the coach or teacher, or the audience. Perhaps there had been times when Lily sensed that something was not quite right—she may even have seen the occasional signals in the press—but simply put it down to her extreme "nervosity," something she suffered from before every performance all her life. And, of course, by the time the trouble became noticeable she was in the very top rank of opera stars, a nice place to be—for everybody. There must have been some among the many people who benefitted from her success who knew something was wrong but were unwilling to give up their profitable participation in her career. And there were probably nights when she sounded better, which made it easier for those people to rationalize their silence. No, it was not difficult to imagine how the situation had developed. The problem was what to do about it. How would Lily take it?

Schang knew there was something wrong, of course, and when I suggested that time be found for her to rest and to resume study with a good teacher, he did not resist. The next day I telephoned Lily and asked if I could see her. We met and talked. She was very approachable, which encouraged me to be direct: did she have a voice teacher? A somewhat nervy thing to ask someone already at the top. But she was absolutely open. She did, although she hadn't seen him for quite some time. It was Alberti de Gorostiaga, who had been her teacher for some years in France. I confessed what my true reaction had been to her singing the night before. To my relief she accepted what I said and agreed that something had to be done.

We sent for Alberti—and what an absolutely delightful man he was! A *Basquais*, slim, mustached, very excitable, and—a priceless quality for the job before him—very frank. If Lily sang a wrong note, he would clap his hand on the piano to accent his "No! No! No!" But if it was good, he would literally jump into the air.

I convinced Schang that Lily should perform as little as possible for a while, and she and Alberti began to work. It was a slow and tedious process. Alberti played fa, Lily sang "Fa," and so on. She did get tired and discouraged but she realized it had to be got through.

Alberti was perfect for her. He understood exactly what her voice could do and what it could not. He believed the mouth cavity, as well as the vocal cords, was part of the whole instrument. And he trained Lily to sing the very high notes not with her mouth wide open—as if she were gargling—but instead with a smaller aperture, almost like a smile. It was Alberti's idea and a very attractive one, I thought. (The complete, perhaps fascinating, but irrelevant details of a suddenly revealed oral cavity can often seriously distract from the beauty of a song, even ruin it altogether, something the photographic intimacy of television has demonstrated!)

Alberti and I conspired to keep Lily's spirits up, to keep her sure of herself. And her confidence was strengthened. She realized she didn't have to sing so often just to prove herself. Or worry about being drowned by the orchestra—"I will be heard again," she would say.

The work went on for almost a year. By the end of that time two things were clear: her voice was on its way back to its full glory, and we were in love with each other.

Our courtship was a whirlwind in one real sense because it kept me in the air a good deal; on the other hand, it lasted four years, much longer than any whirlwind. Lily had been signed to appear in a film called *I Dream Too Much*, for which Jerome Kern had written the score. As usual, all the music was to be prerecorded. The problem with recording the voice is that it must be absolutely note perfect; a mistake is easily noticed and there is no excuse for allowing imperfections onto a record or tape anyway, because the equipment is there to make it right. Lily's voice at that time was still not in the condition to deliver a perfect performance—Alberti had gone with her to California so they could continue working. I recorded the arias and the motion-picture conductor Max Steiner took care of recording the Kern songs.

We began with the Bell Song from *Lakmé*. The problems were apparent right away; one note would be flat, another sharp, and so on. Fortunately, by that time tape was available, which meant that recording could be done in sections. I asked an accompanist I knew, Caroline Gray, to help. The plan was to have Lily sing a song section by section, doing six takes for each. Caroline was in the control room with the score. Her job was to select the perfect notes in each take and mark them with a little cross. At the end we put it all together, note by note. We congratulated Lily on the perfection of the final result, but we never told her how she achieved it.[2]

She made another film, *That Girl from Paris*, I think it was, and so I was flying cross-country virtually every week for almost two years. I never minded the flying; in fact, I enjoyed it tremendously. On one flight a fellow passenger, bound for Tucson and very nervous about flying, I guessed, judging from his talkativeness, asked me if I had heard of this crazy conductor who flew to California every week and actually loved doing it! I told him he was sitting right in front of that conductor. I'm sure his embarrassment took his mind off the fear for a while at least. . . .

In the mid-1930s a transcontinental flight took about eighteen hours. I would leave from Newark about 11:00 PM, fly through the night and most of the next day. When I first started flying, the planes were quite intimate, carrying about fourteen people. Then came the DC-3, which held twenty-one passengers, and finally the DC-4 with four engines, fifty seats, and, best of all, sleeping berths. Whatever I flew, the plane seemed to stop everywhere. Kansas City was always the midpoint and, on the way out, the place to get a morning shave. The plane would land, and when the door was opened there would be the barber ready to freshen you up for a new day. Then up in the air again. The next person to greet me would usually be Lily, who met me at the airport in Los Angeles in her huge Hispano-Suiza roadster.

The newspapers made much of the flying romance. Lily's career and mine, and concert appearances, kept us traveling a good deal. And the fact that we did so openly, and lived together openly, seemed to attract a lot of attention. The big question seemed to be: when would we be married? Our friends wondered, too. The only people who weren't concerned were Lily and I. In fact, I think we were a little hesitant to disturb the situation. Marriage shouldn't change anything, at least not for the worse. Yet I had observed that it often seemed to do just that, as if it were some sort of signal for trouble to start. In any case, we were content to let things slide, until the summer of 1938. By then I think our friends were as surprised as we were to find us married. We told no one except Lily's Metropolitan colleague Geraldine Farrar, who was a stand-in mother for Lily at the small ceremony. As far as the world knew we were simply having a party for some friends at Lily's house in Silvermine, Connecticut.

Our honeymoon turned out to be a semiworking tour in South America. And, of course, we flew. In those days, before World War II made the distinction obsolete, there were two categories of planes: those that flew over land and those that flew transocean. The latter were so-called flying boats, which took off and landed on water and for that reason had to fly only in daylight. On the first day of a six-day trip Lily and I took one of those "boats," a Pan Am Clipper to Puerto Rico, with a stop in Havana. We left at 6:00 AM. The plane seated thirty-four, very comfortably, too. Flying speed was about 160 m.p.h. and the flight was at low altitude, so everything was beautifully visible below.

Our first stop in South America was Paramaribo, the capital of what is now called Surinam but was then Dutch Guiana. From there we went to Rio de Janeiro and then down to Buenos Aires. It was winter there—June and July—and the middle of the music season. Lily sang a number of operas, and I gave concerts. We fell in love with those incredibly beautiful cities.

On the return trip, when we stopped at Paramaribo again, we decided to give a concert for the *libérés* from Devil's Island, the French Guiana penal colony which was then drawing worldwide attention because a fugitive from the colony had written a book exposing the cruel conditions the prisoners, who were mostly political offenders, had to endure there. Feeling was very high because of Belbenois's book. Even Eleanor Roosevelt had taken up the cause of these *libérés*, who were not really free at all; while they were no longer serving time in the prison colony, they still could not leave French Guiana.

We knew there was a fairly large number of *libérés* just across the Moroni River, which separates the two Guianas. Lily and I asked permission to enter French Guiana, but the governor refused, so we thought that in order to come as close to the internees as possible, we would give the concert on a river barge. It was just Lily and I and a piano, and, of course, some men to steady the barge and keep it under control. In the twilight we could make out a small group of people who had gathered to listen. I'm sure, to anyone who might not have known the circumstances of our river concert, we created a rather comic picture. But we wanted to do something simply to show our sympathy and support. A small gesture then, smaller still in light of the long struggle to do away with Devil's Island altogether. Thirteen years passed before the penal colony system was completely phased out.

The theme of the World's Fair of 1939 was "The World of Tomorrow," and the perisphere building contained the Futurama exhibition, which offered views of America as it might look by 1960—sleek car and train models, intricate road- and rail-travel systems, fabulous buildings. It was surrounded by a circular moving aisle that had chairs for the viewing audience. There was a backdrop of motion-picture film which showed men and women walking, presumably into the future, and a narration that had been recorded on tape by a respected newscaster of the day, H. V. Kaltenborn. . . .

On the day in 1939 that the Russians, fresh from signing a pact with Nazi Germany, claimed control of Finland, a touching gesture took place at the Fair. As evening darkened the sky, the tremendous fountain in the center of the International Pavilion displayed in lights the colors of the Finnish flag, and over the loudspeakers people were suddenly hearing Jean Sibelius's *Finlandia*. There were probably some who had not heard the news and could not identify the colors or the music or know its significance, but soon everyone at the restaurants and cafés was standing. For some moments after the last note of music there was silence. A soundless echo touched with prophecy.

The Fair ran through 1940, a year longer than expected. Countries all over the globe had sent their best ideas, their finest expressions of cultural and scientific achievement, to be displayed and admired. They sent, too, their dreams of the future, and thousands of people came to see it all, to be inspired, to dream, to hope for a better world of tomorrow.

Now the dreams were ended. The nightmare of war was upon us.

CHAPTER SEVENTEEN

The Wartime Tours

André Kostelanetz

Lily Pons and André Kostelanetz were performing at a musicians-fund concert in New York's Waldorf-Astoria Hotel on 8 December 1941, when President Franklin D. Roosevelt asked Congress for a declaration of war against Japan. Four months later, Kostelanetz paid a visit to Secretary of War Henry L. Stimson and asked to be assigned to the United Service Organizations (USO) so that he and Lily could entertain troops in Europe and the Pacific.

In his memoirs, Kostelanetz utilized his wartime correspondence to take his readers through his and Lily's USO tours. While he and Lily were logging over 100,000 miles in military-transport planes, jeeps, and armored personnel carriers, André jotted down his impressions in a diary and in letters to Boris Kostelanetz, his younger brother. These hastily written impressions make clear the hazardous conditions under which Lily often sang, and they also establish why she earned the lasting regard of thousands of Allied troops. Excerpted here are portions of André's recollections of their performances in India, China, Burma, and Europe in 1944 and 1945.[1]

10 *December 1944.* Last U.S. broadcast. Off the air 5:00 PM. Home afterward and farewells. Lily and I drive to Queens and the airport through dark dismal Sunday streets. We pass two movie houses. One marquee says *Road to Morocco* and the other *Dangerous Journey!* We take off. Good-bye New York. As we cross the Hudson we open the "sealed orders" envelopes—India, China, Burma, Belgium, France, Germany. The first autograph of this trip is asked for by a woman sitting across the aisle, and to our surprise it is a blank check!

13 December. We leave the shores of the United States at 1:45 PM. Bucket seats greet us once again. The plane is a powerful C-54, and the meteorologist says we will have strong tailwinds. He is right. By the time we approach Bermuda we are traveling at 300 miles an hour with a better than seventy-mile-an-hour tail-wind, establishing a near-record time of four hours and fifteen minutes. . . .

In Bermuda, as in Ascension Island, the men get very little entertainment because most of the performers are rushing on to their designated war theaters. Islands are lonely outposts. Special Services officer asks whether we could drop into a movie—they would stop the picture if we would say a word to the soldiers. But at that moment we are called to board the plane. "Flight 741 to the Azores," booms the loudspeaker.

We taxi ponderously to takeoff position. The plane seems loaded to capacity, and the gas tanks are full for the big hop. With a mighty pull we leave the ground. It is night, and everyone makes himself as comfortable as possible on the floor. For the most part it is either too cold or else the heaters are too active and it gets quite hot. Lily is in her sleeping bag at the front of the plane.

17 December. By 6:00 AM we are flying due east over the Indian Ocean. The sky is full of gold. Sunrise. Hilly coastline below and Karachi.

Trip from Casablanca to Karachi, a total flying time of about forty-eight hours, extremely strenuous—C-46 was packed with passengers, 34, and cargo, which was crowded between the bucket seats and in the center aisle. Impossible to lie down or stretch out. Lily under a ventilator in the roof. At night the heaters went out of commission, and the high-altitude cold air blew on her.

Just before landing we notice our war-painted planes and, nearby, the Parsees's "towers of silence," several of them, about twenty feet high and surrounding a courtyard. The Parsees leave their dead on the tower roofs, where they are devoured by vultures.

Driven to the Hotel Killarney (not a very authentic-sounding name for a hotel in India) and sleep the rest of the day.

At 9:00 in the evening I decide to go out for my first real glimpse of India. I feel it is best to get acquainted with the Orient at night. The mystery and glamour are better retained without the revealing midday sun. I ask to be taken to the railway station so I can see as many different people as possible from all over India. I am not disappointed. It is overflowing with people and color and sound. Trains are jammed with passengers. Everybody seems to be speaking a different tongue. It all makes me think of the second act of *Lakmé*, without benefit of the stage manager. Outside, men, women, and children lie asleep on the sidewalks. Beggars surround me, asking for baksheesh.

23 December. The demand for admission to the opening concert is growing hourly. We planned this tour so that our first concert would be on Christmas Eve and we would continue to play for the rest of the holiday week for the servicemen stationed in and around Calcutta. The orchestra is improving with each rehearsal, and I am notified that we can have some additional strings from the Calcutta Symphony Orchestra. We decide to play indoors since ten thousand soldiers are expected. The dress rehearsal is called at the Eden Gardens. It's a hot and windy morning. Lily rehearses with us, and we try out the speaker system. She has a cold, but we hope by tomorrow it will clear up.

24 December. The big field in the Eden Gardens where we are to play is taken all day for the British cricket matches. Our concert is scheduled for five o'clock. Thousands of soldiers arrive at the Gardens early in the afternoon.

A great disappointment—Lily's cold did not get better, and she is unable to sing. It's announced over the air that the concert will take place without her. I ask Corporal Larry Malfatti[2] of Philadelphia to join us and sing some of the Christmas carols. A record-breaking crowd of over ten thousand Allied troops. On the far fringes of the field we see Hindus in colorful attire and turbans. Concert is broadcast over All-India Radio and American Expeditionary stations. "Holy Night" under Indian sky. The sun sets quickly, and Captain Sherman, Special Services, asks me whether we can finish the concert before the rapidly settling darkness makes the music invisible to the musicians—"Can you play some of the music faster," he pleads, "because the power generator is out of order and we have no lights." I couldn't help thinking of the time that Walter Damrosch had to play the last movement of Tchaikovsky's *Pathétique* allegro furioso in order to catch a train.

It was a beautiful sunset, and as the dark blue-green of the Indian sky deepened, the stars shone ever more brightly. On the triumphant note of "Adeste Fideles" the concert came to a close in almost total darkness, which was filled with the cheers of thousands of soldiers.

Later that evening we drive through blackened Calcutta on the "wrong" side of the street, visiting Red Cross establishments, U.S. canteens, making a few speeches and exchanging holiday greetings with the soldiers, some of whom somehow procured a few evergreens for Christmas decorations.

25 December. Lily is no better. Doctor has diagnosed bronchitis and insisted she stay in bed.

Christmas concert this afternoon in Barrackpur, about an hour's ride from Calcutta. Preconcert lunch with General William Tunner at Hastings Mills, just across the river from Barrackpur. Corporal Leonard Pinnario, excellent pianist, joined us, and I exacted a promise that he will play with orchestra.

Simple, delicious Christmas lunch with very interesting view: the wide Hooghly in front of the house—river traffic included red-sailed junks with occasional U.S. motorboat darting in between them. On the opposite riverbank, Hindu temples. The general is much interested in providing good musical entertainment for his men. On one wall a drawing of him—Christmas gift from his Air Transport Command staff—with inscription: "Mahatma of the Hump."

After lunch we all crossed the river by barge to the concert area. Event coincides with opening of a servicemen's club. Great anticipation. When we arrive, about 4000 listeners are already seated on benches in the broiling Indian sun. Snappy wind helps a bit, until a group of planes begin revving their motors on the windward side. Before long, orchestra and audience can scarcely see or hear for the dust and noise. This does not create much discomfiture—everyone realizes the planes are going on missions that will be sure to shorten the war.

The Christmas carols were greeted with much enthusiasm. The local Special Services officer supplied jingle bells (where ever did he get them?). Considerable *ooh*ing and *aah*ing over announcement of "Rhapsody in Blue" and the "Ave Maria," which is, so far, the most often requested song on both tours.

Much autographing after the concert, usually of paper money. GIs prefer to have it on money instead of anything else. In some countries, where there is considerable inflation and the money is not worth anything, they usually remark, "Now it's worth something!" after we have signed the bank note.

Driving home through Indian villages I notice banners in the shape of sails, with white and blue predominant. This is the Pakistan Moslem banner, emblem of a Moslem state which they hope to achieve. Another banner was also in evidence—the red flag with hammer and sickle of the Communist Party.

Lily and I have Christmas dinner in our hotel room in the evening. The stone floors make the room damp and chilly.

Can't help thinking about all the terrible hunger in this city. Ironically, in many cases the hunger is a result of people's unwillingness to accept any food that they are not accustomed to—or that their religion forbids.

1 January 1945. Letter from a GI in China includes question: "Why do you let us down and omit China from your schedule?" For some days now we have been trying to investigate all possibilities for getting into China. It is a great disappointment to us to be told that China is closed. We volunteered for the CBI theater, and to be so near to China and not be able to get there seems inconceivable. The tactical situation is precarious, and civilians are not permitted to enter—just the opposite, they are being evacuated from China. But now we have additional ammunition—this soldier has put the issue at our door. Of course, the schedules are made up by the Special Services of the theater, and nine times out of ten the artist goes to places that he has never heard of before. We ask for a meeting with General Neyland. He tells us that our admission to China depends on the China commander. He agrees to send a wire himself. We also send a wire. There is considerable suspense in this waiting.

New Year's Day concert at a hospital in Calcutta, in an open square. Some patients sit in wheelchairs outside; others listen from windows. Major Gillis, who is treating Lily's cold, is the hero of the day since he has just about cured her, making it possible for her to sing today. To close the concert I conduct "Auld Lang Syne" and the chief doctor motions for all those who can stand up to do so. I turn and conduct the audience. Lily and I are close to tears. It is not the first time. There is something about concerts in hospitals that sets them apart.

19 January. We are getting farther into the jungle, traveling slowly. From the train window elephants, monkeys, and crocodiles are on view. The monsoon left quantities of puddles and small lakes. Snakes are everywhere. Dinner with General Yount, thirty-seven years of age, who runs this great supply road. We missed him by five days at Teheran, on our first overseas trip, where he did a great job on the Iranian railroad.

Luxuriant foliage, egrets, rice paddies. Kanchenjunga, in Himalayas, is visible. It is third-highest peak in world. Train is carried across the Brahmaputra on old-fashioned barges, which take quite a few hours. Impossible to build a bridge due to monsoon rains.

We are getting into Assam. The British tea-plantation word for siesta here is "lay-back," one hour each afternoon.

Joint U.S.-British audiences that night. The British applaud "Stars and Stripes Forever" vociferously. That day there was a news flash of the capture of Warsaw, and I made an appropriate announcement before we played the Warsaw Concerto, which was greeted very warmly.

20 January. We are delighted—a wire just came in from the deputy commander in China theater, asking us to come for twenty-five days!

Playing for the smallest audience of our overseas career, 300 or so. A theater of the Gay Nineties type—all wood, with enormous overhanging balcony. Deafening enthusiasm. A few miles from this place there is a camp with many more soldiers, and we are wondering why they are being bypassed. It is getting rougher in every sense. "Rough" is one of the most often used words overseas.

24 January. Colonel Baker, our pilot to China, says this will be his 111th crossing of the Hump. We are first USO troupe to go to China since ban on civilians.

Weather unusually clear. Short briefing on use of parachutes and oxygen masks. This is first flight so far where parachutes are necessary. Someone remembers joke about then: at end of parachute briefing the inevitable question —"What happens if the chute doesn't open when I pull the cord?" Answer— "Well, just bring it back and we'll issue you a new one!"

Take off and begin gradual climb. Valley after valley with drifting cottony clouds above them. Seemingly endless snowy ridges to be crossed. Shining narrow ribbons far below—the Salween and Irrawaddy rivers. Ever higher—time for oxygen masks' grotesque disguise. In cockpit I see we are 13,600 feet and still climbing. Pilot points to a house on mountaintop, at 12,500 feet. How was it ever built way up here? Tibet, the roof of the world, to our far left.

Now, terraced grounds in regular designs below. Baker signals this is China. Descent bumpy.

We have landed in Kunming, capital of Yunnan province. First impressions: many women all dressed in blue coats and carrying little baskets filled with small stones—they maintain the airport runways. Reddish earth. Chinese soldiers, Special Services officers, all smiles. *Ding-ho!* Thumbs up!

Driving through Kunming to General Cheves's home. This is a different world. Stores and markets full of food, especially vegetables, but we are told prices are very high. Inflation terrific: 500 Chinese dollars to 1 U.S. [dollar].

Talk to General Cheves about my desire to bring string players to China. He tells me the situation is difficult—transportation scarce and billeting quarters in the camps we are going to so meager. It will be impossible. With great regret we let the players know the bad news.

26 January. First concert in China, at a hospital near Kunming. Lieutenant Colonel Leonidoff, chief doctor of the hospital, tells me of his experiences as medical adviser to the Chinese. There is much disease here. Incidentally, the cost of constructing a hospital is enormous. Land is $10,000 an acre; one windowpane, $8; a simple chair, $15.

The band played very well, and when we signed autographs after the concert we were showered with fine comments.

Driving in moonlight back to Kunming was beautiful. Tall trees throwing black shadows on the countryside. But the bright light of a full moon is not welcome in this part of the world. It is perfect for bombing.

29 January. Begin our tour today. I now have twenty-one players, the smallest group of musicians so far, and no strings. The scores for brass band I packed are now being put to use. The limitation is coloring our selections, of course—we do a lot of marches—but we get around it. Particularly nice is a version of "Begin the Beguine." And we always have our "regulars"—Lily's accompanists Theodore Paxson, piano, and Frank Versaci, flute.

On the flights there are twenty-eight people: three crew, Lily and me, two Special Services officers, and the twenty-one musicians. The C-47 seems overloaded, the tail is jammed with instruments and baggage. Pilot has never landed at airfield we are headed for, which is in the Hump, 8000 feet up and complicated to reach.

Landing strip surrounded by mountains. We hit tail-first, then nose goes up and down again, all in a matter of seconds. In a plane not equipped with safety belts you have to hang on to whatever you can—but, as the saying goes, "Any landing from which you walk away is a good landing." Special Services' greetings as we emerge from plane: "We thought you would all be killed." The plane was obviously overloaded.

Concert starts at 4:15. The sun goes down early. During the last part of the show it is extremely cold, wind blowing. Indoor "rec" (recreation) halls too small to accommodate audiences wishing to hear us. Everyone frozen. Lily looks blue. The C.O. offers us an extra plane to help us out, and his chief pilot, Major Watson. As we drive to the airport I notice a forest fire on one of the ridges—I'm told that Japanese sympathizers started it to pinpoint the airport. There doesn't seem to be any possibility of controlling it due to the enormous spaces involved. Take-off in the dark, Major Watson at the controls. (He is a pleasant fellow with a Southern accent. He bets me a hundred dollars I will not recognize him when he comes to see me in New York.) I go into the cockpit and from time to time see more of those fires burning. The major's pet dog is with us in the plane, a brown mongrel. He yawns on takeoff to clear his ears. Fine landing; everybody applauds the major. In the other plane went the piano and baggage.

Lily stays with two Red Cross girls in a nicely appointed place. Orchestra and I go to unfinished quarter—plenty "rough." We are now a third of the way up the Hump. Extremely cold night—five blankets.

4 February. Great day! Over a hundred vehicles coming through. General Lewis A. Pick, builder of the Ledo Road since October 1943, in the first Jeep. Big, jovial, looks and speaks like Walter Huston. Face extremely sun- and wind-burned.

At the gates where the road ends are enormous pictures of President Roosevelt, General Stilwell, and Generalissimo Chiang Kai-shek. The spittoons in the Custom House are glistening, and bunches of grass have been spread around to keep the chill away. Dignitaries of both nations on dais. The Governor of Yunnan appears with a cigar in his hand and three enormous stars, decorations, on his chest. Ceremony to begin with our playing of "The Star-Spangled Banner." General Davidson, commander of the Tenth Air Force, has told me that the Chinese felt that since we are the guests we should play first. So the moment Lily cuts the ribbon I start to conduct the first notes—and at the same moment the Chinese band begins their anthem! Everyone doubles over. According to tradition, once a national anthem is begun it must be finished. No stopping. Well, the second we finish the Chinese stop, too. Very strange—because you can start any music together, but to finish together is almost impossible. (Later I asked General Davidson if simultaneous playing of two anthems made terrible confusion. "Not really," he said. A very important Chinese general had turned up at the last moment, inquired about the procedure, and was told we were to play first. That was not right, he said, because if Americans play first they will feel awful that they make us lose face—so play at the same time. And, out of courtesy, the Chinese stopped when we did, although they hadn't finished their anthem!)

First truck rolls through. The Chinese play "Polly Wolly Doodle All the Day." The Generalissimo announces that the Ledo Road will henceforth be known as the Stilwell Highway. Then many speeches—and translations—last of which I make, finishing with two Chinese words I know very well because they are the names of our Tibetan dogs at home: *Shan Lo! Wah Ping!* Peace and victory. After that Lily and I invited to a hut by two colonels and a major—they are OSS—and eat (devour!) whole box of Blum's chocolates, which the major magically produces. Lily confesses she thought for a split second that I was calling our dogs in Connecticut when I yelled their names. The longing for home is always just under the surface, struggling with the desire to be *here* and make some contribution, some sacrifice, for the cause. How must these boys feel who have been so long away and face death every single day.

16 February. Breakfast with General Cheves at 7:00. We will leave China with regret.

The Tenth Air Force sends in a C-47 which takes my China Band over the Hump. We go in another plane. All our friends are at the airport. Weather is clear. A good flight—on oxygen.

Land in Myitkyina (it's pronounced Mishino) on the Irrawaddy River. This is the town where the old Ledo Road joined with the Burma Road. Completely different weather, really hot. China Band has not arrived, so in the afternoon I start rehearsing the band here, teaching them the same numbers that the China Band played so I can join the two if the China players arrive at the eleventh hour. Everyone now very much concerned about their plane. There are no reports.

We give the concert with the Burma Band for enormous crowd outdoors. After concert news comes that China Band landed in Bhamo, 120 miles south.

17 February. Fly south over jungle at an altitude of only few hundred feet. Lily points out elephants in a clearing. Follow the Irrawaddy, winding through the thick growth, land on improvised airfield—recently vacated by Japanese.

Concert set for afternoon, and we are asked to give first broadcast over station WOTO (Wings Over the Orient) that night. (WOTO theme song is "Road to Mandalay.")

China and Burma bands play together for concert. Very effective performance for huge gathering of soldiers. Afterward, visit to recent battlegrounds. Jungle growth churned up by explosives. Some temples greatly damaged because the Japanese had established a radio station close by. Small temples everywhere, most in disrepair—it is apparently an act of devotion to erect one but not to see that it is kept up.

Major General Davidson is our host at dinner, and we meet Admiral Louis Mountbatten, head of Southeast Asia Command and commander of Allied operations against Japanese in Burma. Talk centers around Indian and Chinese music. Consensus is Orientals understand Western music better than we do theirs.

Lieutenant Bert Parks, former CBS announcer, is emcee for broadcast, which is given in a small portable station. Everyone squeezes in. I close with a short farewell speech, for we are on our way tomorrow for the European theater. General Sultan asks for "Ave Maria." I give baton to Sergeant Jack Kollon, my assistant throughout China tour.

Walls of house we are billeted in are made of jute and strung on bamboo. For privacy all lights must be put out—the jute is almost transparent. Cries of peacocks sound through the night, which is very cold.

18 February. Leave Burma early morning for long day's flight. Everest visible—enormous masses of snow about 60 miles away. At sunset we see the incredible Taj Mahal below. Land in New Delhi.

First tub bath in two months.

24 February. To El Adem, near Tobruk, then across the Mediterranean to Athens. Weather very bad. We fly fifteen miles from enemy-held Crete. The Turks declared war on Germany today. We wonder whether the Germans in Crete will react, but all seems quiet.

Naples by evening.

25 February. Leave Naples early. Over Corsica and the coast of France—Riviera, Lily's birthplace, is clouded over. It is the first time in seven years she has seen her native land and she is much moved. At Dijon a crew of shot-down American flyers who walked out of Germany join us for flight to Paris.

In Paris streets deserted. Whatever shops are still in business are closed as it is Sunday. City impressive and dignified, but like someone dazed and not yet recovered.

Full moon in evening as we walk through the quiet streets. We had been told there were no air alerts here, but all at once all lights go out and sirens wail. The first alarm in months, but the all clear sounds soon.

26 February. We are going to play at the front in Germany! Briefing at USO headquarters at Chatou. Nonfraternization highly emphasized—reports of young boys and girls shooting and knifing Americans. We are issued gas masks and steel helmets. There is quite a problem about the organization of the orchestra, and I am busy getting it together.

A tale of Paris. When the Nazis were ready to leave Paris they camouflaged their vehicles with greenery. The next day everyone from small boys on bicycles up to men in trucks did the same thing.

One of General de Gaulle's aides tells us the General likes to listen to Lily's Mozart records. Meet Mrs. Anthony Eden in a smart British uniform—gray and red, with service ribbons. She asks for our autographs for her son.

Lily and I lunch with Marlene Dietrich, who says the table will now be known as the "Lily-Marlene" table!

2 March. Six months overseas; we are due for our first stripe—"hash mark."

By car through France to the forward areas in Belgium. Lunch at Rheims, near the sandbagged cathedral. Intermittent sun, rain, snow. It is strange to go through Château-Thierry, Belleau Wood—cemeteries of the great sacrifices of the last war. It is an all-day drive, and we see the first German prisoners working on the roads, and our soldiers guarding them with rifles. Driver watches constantly for enemy strafing.

13 March. Three-hour drive to Krefeld, Germany, captured 5 March. It is a few miles from the Rhine, opposite Duisburg. Drive through Aachen, Julich, and many other cities and villages now famous as battlegrounds. Everything destroyed—houses leveled, dead cattle and horses. There are many minefields—some of them marked by Germans, some by us. Enormous quantity of burned and overturned tanks. A few German civilians.

Arrive at house in Krefeld where we are billeted. Nearby, a road sign: Düsseldorf—20 kilometers. Essen—18 kilometers. In front of house is burned German truck, and on the spring grass lie German bazookas and mortars. Deep roar of steady, heavy artillery, with occasional particularly loud blast. We are about three miles from the Rhine and front lines.

Owners of the house at the door, greet us with exaggerated obsequiousness. On drive to the Mess for dinner we see that Krefeld did not escape—most of its buildings are laid waste but still bear, in enormous white letters, statements of allegiance to Hitler: We Will Not Capitulate. Victory or Siberia. What Did You Do Today for Germany? Innumerable Heil Hitlers and, of course, countless swastikas. Many white flags, obviously hastily made, hanging out of windows or affixed to what remains of the houses. We are less than 4000 yards from the Rhine. At the Mess hall there is suddenly a tremendous concussion and explosion. The soldiers hasten to explain that it is our 155 howitzer battery, located close to the Mess hall, going into action.

Krefeld was taken only about a week ago, so it is suggested we get home before dark—there are still snipers around. German civilians are off the streets at five o'clock, and it gets dark about seven, but conversation with the men who do the fighting makes us late for curfew, and we drive at night. No lights on the streets or car, so it takes us some time to locate our house. Steady cannonade. An eerie feeling to drive in this dead town. We creep along, careful not to get off the road and into possible minefields.

Candles inside of the house. Windows rattle at every blast.

14 March. In bomb shelter adjacent to house are several people in German uniforms, obviously discards by Nazi soldiers. MPs are posted at the house to keep out all unwanted visitors.

The German couple in our house excessively and artificially solicitous. They just can't do enough for us. This morning Lily opened the door to a room near our bedroom and discovered about ten Nazi uniforms lying about, as if hastily discarded. Sometime during the night, despite the U.S. soldier guarding the house, some Nazis must have slipped in, changed to civilian clothes, and slipped out again. A little disconcerting. We realized then that you could never tell just by looking at someone whose side he was on. . . .

Visit a dugout next to a battery of 155 howitzers where the officers are surrounded by radios and phones. A target is selected, and Lily writes with chalk on a big shell, "Catch this one, Hitler!" It is loaded. Terrific roar. When noise subsides, a sergeant says blandly, "Hitler, count your soldiers."

Security does not permit any announcement of concert, but I see little posters in a few places with an arrow pointing to Caserna, which is where we are going to play. It is a huge building, probably once a warehouse, with many holes in the ceiling and walls.

Concert is in afternoon because of evening curfew. Enormous gathering of combat GIs overflows through the many doors. We are greeted with tremendous enthusiasm. Throughout the concert, cannonade persistent. Airplanes overhead continually. The audience sits with rifles and battle helmets within easy reach. Rapt attention—I do not think they are nearly as conscious of the bombardment as we are.

16 March. Colonel Barret tells us there will be an artillery barrage on Duisburg and wants to know if we would like to see some of the battle action. We drive for half a mile along the Rhine and climb to an observation tower 400 yards from the river. From the platform we see the German lines on the opposite bank. Factory section of Duisburg very well outlined, despite rain and some fog. One of the guns will be a German 88 manned by a crew of our soldiers who were wounded by this type of gun. Colonel Barret orders antitanks to attack first. A few seconds later we see bright flashes and the antitanks reveal their location in a clump of trees. A smokestack is hit. Then a set of cannon open up on pillboxes on the far shore. Flashes from all sides, explosions. Once 12 batteries—120 guns—fired 2 shells each simultaneously—240 explosions in less than a minute. They burst over the entire riverfront.

18 March. Visit the displaced persons' camp. Every nationality seems to be represented.

Wonderful to have 100-piece orchestra. After concert a soldier says, "War is misery, but you brought us joy." Lily and I feel humbled. . . .

Ominous silence tonight, broken now and then by small-arms fire quite close to the house. A sergeant rushes in and calls Lieutenant Rooney and myself to the phone, which is across the street. Message: the concert in Cologne is set—2:30 PM, 20 March! Overjoyed, we step back outside into the pitch-darkness. After a few paces I ask Rooney if he knows the password for the evening. He says no and stops in his tracks. We start to retrace our steps. Suddenly a guard appears from nowhere and follows us. For some reason he doesn't ask any questions, and we are relieved to reach the telephone post, where we are given the night's password. Luckily. As we went back home we were stopped abruptly and challenged. Last night a general was out walking and was challenged. He didn't know the password, so he began explaining who he was. One MP interrupted with, "Who is Frank Sinatra?" "A damn poor singer," said the general. The MPs laughed and let him pass.

20 March. Morning drive to Cologne. Delayed en route by enormous military traffic going forward. Finally reach outskirts of the battered city. Cathedral spires visible on horizon. No time for lunch. Go immediately to concert location, New University. Much battered—the rear stage wall is gone; a cloth hangs in its place. But there are 2500 GIs gathered, each one holding a gun. The German line is only three-quarters of a mile away, across the Rhine. As I greet the audience and announce the "American Patrol," there is a great blast that jolts the stage. I'm sure the beginning of that piece—bass drum and snares—has never sounded so feeble! Smell of cordite fumes on the stage and, as I go off after the first number, someone shouts, "It's an outgoing!"—a 155 howitzer battery behind the thin stage wall attending to the serious business of war. Throughout the performance there are firings at the most unexpected moments, which release dust from the ceiling each time. Atmosphere triumphant. American music for American soldiers on the banks of the Rhine. . . . The men cheered us on, and we added encore after encore.

Our request to visit the cathedral causes a conference of MPs. Finally we are driven off in a Jeep through the shambles of the city. Opera house in ruins. A narrow winding street, made even narrower by rubble, brings us to the great cathedral. Everything around it is down. Cathedral looks particularly light in color because of the battle dust that has settled on it. There is some damage, but the fact that it stands at all is testimony to the skill of the Allied fighting men and fliers.

Lily and I cross narrow street and move nearer the cathedral, in front of which a giant burned-out German tank is standing. "Make it fast," the MPs tell us. A few shells fell during the day, and the big square is out of bounds.

Long drive back to Belgium and a most welcome dinner. Sirens start just as we sit down, but it is a short alert and everyone relaxes.

21 March. Receive message that the great United States Army Band and Major Glenn Miller's orchestra will be combined for our two concerts in Paris. I look forward to conducting them. In the now relatively peaceful town of Namur, on the Meuse, we give our closing concert in Belgium, in old opera house. Soldiers are everywhere—in the orchestra pit and on stage. A cold evening, and there is a draft on the stage. When I ask the stage manager whether he can remedy the situation, he points to the roof and says only "V-one." There is much destruction in this part of the world from a weapon that made its first appearance at the tail end of Hitler's career.

22 March. General Simpson's Ninth Army not to be first in Berlin, after all, so concert tonight is our last USO appearance overseas—the 112th. Phone rings about six o'clock, a friend telling us to turn on the radio—a broadcast of the recording made of our concert on the Rhine.

Opera house is jammed to the rafters. The musicians absolutely fill the stage. No heat, so Lily wears her coat throughout evening. The moment I begin to conduct the electric power fails. Emergency lighting equipment for about half an hour, then lights come back on.

Cheers and whistles of GIs in appreciation of music unrivaled in our professional life. Encore after encore. "The national anthems!" announces Lieutenant Rooney. We start with the "Marseillaise," then "God Save the King." Turning to the audience, I conduct "The Star-Spangled Banner." Everyone sings.

CHAPTER EIGHTEEN

Lily Pons: An Essay in Astro-Economics

Charles O'Connell

ℰ⫯⟋ Neither André nor Lily could have imagined that, soon after the war, a colleague from the recording industry would charge in a controversial book that their wartime tours and the dangers they faced had been inflated considerably, and that their main purpose in entertaining the troops had really been to enhance their images and fatten their bank accounts. In fact, author Charles O'Connell went so far as to question the artistic merits of both Pons and Kostelanctz in the pages of his book, *The Other Side of the Record*.

As a recording executive, O'Connell had served at both RCA Victor and Columbia Records. His association with RCA, however, had ended as a result of his quixotic dealings with best-selling recording artists. Pianist Arthur Rubinstein, whose complaints to RCA founder David Sarnoff contributed to O'Connell's firing, dismissed him as "a nice Irishman to talk to but not to work with."[1]

O'Connell's book was released on Friday, 10 October 1947, and was hotly debated in newspaper columns for the next several weeks. Gossip columnists Walter Winchell and Louis Sobol kept the controversy alive in their widely read columns—Sobol noting on 21 October that Kostelanetz was "roaring mad" at O'Connell, and Winchell writing that same day that O'Connell's "inflammable stuff" was "too Gee'Whiz for the printed page."

The chapter from O'Connell's book in which he criticizes Pons and Kostelanetz is entitled "Lily Pons: An essay in astro-economics with special reference to the Kostelanetz constellation—Lily, André, *Coq d'or*, Coca-Cola, and Chrysler." It is reprinted here in full.[2]

*A*STRO-ECONOMICS is a very abstruse science, of which I am neither a professor nor a very close student. I am, however, familiar with its basic thesis, which is, stripped of detail, simply this: if one star can make a lot of money, two stars in conjunction can make a lot more. Some pairs of stars, especially those who know the uses of that adversity which descends upon us all on [income-tax filing day] annually, make money that can be represented only by appropriately astronomical figures.

There have been some remarkable partnerships in the arts and sciences. One may think of Tchaikovsky and Mme von Meck, Marie and Pierre Curie, Clara Wieck and Robert Schumann, Richard and Cosima Wagner, Elizabeth Barrett and Robert Browning, Lynn Fontanne and Alfred Lunt, Charles and Mary Beard; but for complete, rounded perfection and effectiveness there is, there has been, no astral conjunction quite in a class with the constellation of the planets, Lily Pons and André Kostelanetz. I shouldn't refer to these stars as planets, I suppose, because (and this is without checking up on my celestial physics) planets shine only by reflected light; and though it is true that André and Lily glitter with uncommon brilliance under the fierce light of publicity in which they live and breathe and have their being, it would be grossly unfair to deny either or both of them the extraordinary talents that are theirs.

These talents are by no means entirely musical. Pons, in addition to being a coloratura soprano of notable accomplishments, has studied a charming role and acts it to perfection every day of her life. She has a flair for the extraordinary and fantastic in couture, and with unerring acumen ferrets out those productions and those producers that are the most sensational; and she wears her remarkable clothes with a manner. The association of the coloratura soprano voice and the sounds—I will not call them songs—of birds is a "natural" for the publicity man; and Lily readily admits a passion for our feathered friends, especially the rare and costly varieties. In her New York apartment I have often observed a cage full of the creatures, which, happily, were never vocal when I was present. The bird motif is worked pretty hard. Indeed, I recall a cocktail party that Lily and André gave for the unveiling of one of her many portraits, which—surprise!—represented her with an archaeopteryx, or something, perched prettily on her finger. I almost expected to see a caption under it—"Can *you* sing?"

You could not be with Lily very long without observing evidence of her well-publicized superstition concerning the number thirteen. Most people who have any superstition about this mystic number regard it as unlucky. Obviously, for Mme Pons, in whose life nothing average or ordinary has ever happened except birth, it would have quite the opposite significance. Thirteen has many a happy association for her. It appears, together with the initials LP, on the license plate of her car; and just to be a spoil-sport, let me add that in the "Nutmeg" state you too could have your initials for a license number if you are well-behaved. In the state of Connecticut (charming country, readily accessible from New York—and no state income tax), the Utopia of so many tax-conscious professional people, where Lily has a charming house, anybody may have his initials or any reasonable arrangement of figures or letters on his license plate as long as he obeys the motor laws. Thus the LP13 on Lily's Brewster-bodied Ford. But thirteen is even more important for Lily. According to the press agents, Mr. Kostelanetz proposed thirteen times before she bestowed her hand.

Lily claims the south of France as her birthplace, but it remained for U.S., long before she became a citizen, to name a post office, Lilypons, Maryland, after her. (Another distinction is, I believe, that she is the first Metropolitan prima donna to display her umbilicus in that fortress of propriety. The costume was for *Lakmé*.) It is related that she first studied piano with a career in prospect, and that her remarkable voice was discovered quite by accident. I hope she and her admirers will forgive me if I cannot wax enthusiastic about Lily's voice, for the reason that the coloratura type has absolutely no appeal for me as a musician. I have admired only one, and that one not for its coloratura qualities but for its remarkable rather sultry sweetness and lyrical loveliness. That was the voice of Galli-Curci. The singing of a coloratura is a cross between a cackle and a whistle, and performers on the vocal high wire and trapeze are utterly devoid of musical interest to me. As coloratura voices go, I think that Miss Pons has one of the best extant. She has extraordinary range, some warmth in the lower register, and she often negotiates the inhuman difficulties of the great coloratura arias with quite accurate intonation.

I remember when Lily first came to this country as the pupil and protégée of Maria Gay and Giovanni Zenatello—not as the pupil of Alberti de Gorostiaga, as was intimated in the authorized article in the *Saturday Evening Post*. She looked then essentially very much as she does now, except for the color of her hair, which has always been variable. At that time it was quite black. She is very short in stature; this she compensates by wearing the highest of high heels. I think this is not so much that she wishes to be tall, since diminutiveness is one of the attributes her press agent so enthusiastically dotes on. I think it is rather to distract the eye from rather generous dimensions in the horizontal planes. (I once knew a music critic who lost his job when one of his readers got out the dictionary to discover what the critic meant by a certain expression in his review, to wit: "the steatopygous Schumann-Heink." I think that I would be on safe ground, however, if I content myself with the word "kallipygian" which must be complimentary since a smart Fifth Avenue women's shop not long ago spent a great deal of money in selling the idea to its clientele.) Miss Pons has the swarthy skin of the Mediterranean peoples, but unusually generous and skillful *maquillage* obscures her natural epidermal tint and texture. Her legs are so frail as to be almost birdlike, and her feet, the tiniest I have ever seen on a mature person. She wears such extraordinarily short-vamped and high-heeled shoes that she must perforce walk almost on the balls of the toes. The effect is certainly to make her feet seem tinier than they actually are; it also suggests to unbeglamored and dis- illusioned eyes a case of *talipes equinus*.

If these remarks seem unchivalrous or malicious, let me say at once that they are not so to be construed. No one on the operatic stage and few in any theater anywhere can look so delectably young, or radiate more bewitching charm, or seem so precious, so fragile, so completely and perfectly fashioned by some kind of magic, out of zephyrs and flowers of spring. If it is true that Lily's magnetism for an audience is a work of artfulness, it is likewise true that it could never be convincing if it did not originate fundamentally in a warm, simple, sunny nature. I have known the lady for quite a few years, offstage and on, at work and at play, and sometimes under circumstances both trying and unflattering, and in all my acquaintance with her, she has invariably been *"gentile, aimable, et douce."*

Working with Lily

I am happy to have had some influence in bringing about Pons's engage- ment for Victor records, and this, incidentally, was tantamount to gambling a lot of Victor's money, for she had at the time made no appearances in the United States and had no public here. Though I was not then directly concerned with the production of Victor recordings, I was consulted in this particular matter and on hearing an extraordinary recording of Miss Pons's voice which Mme Gay presented, I, with a group of other Victor people, recommended a contract for Miss Pons. I did negotiate subsequent contracts with her, always without diffi- culty, until the last time the contract was up for renewal, when I was outbid by Columbia. This was a matter of regret to me and to my employers, who valued Miss Pons very highly as an artist, though on a purely dollars-and-cents basis her services were never, for us, a good investment. I do not believe they are prof- itable to Columbia either, although sales of Pons's records have been substantial. That they were profitable to Miss Pons, both in cash guarantees or advances against royalties and in a great deal of costly advertising, goes without saying.

It has always been very pleasant to work with Lily. She is a good musician, she is always well prepared, and never, so far as I can recollect, has had to can- cel or interrupt a recording session because of any vocal indisposition. She is amiable, docile, cooperative, and gracious. Usually I engaged Wilfrid Pelletier to conduct for her, and that assured an agreeable situation—which was by no means true later on when we were required to engage Kostelanetz.

Here was a rather awkward situation. I had three reasons for not wanting

André to conduct for Victor recordings, and I could not with discretion discuss them with Lily. The first reason was that I wanted an abler conductor. I do not mean to disparage André at all, for he is a first-class workman; but we were doing opera, not the Coca-Cola hour, and I wished to have not only a first-class operatic conductor but one associated with the Met, as Lily was, and one reasonably conversant with the opera. Secondly, Kostelanetz was, at the time, rising as the bright particular star of our competitors, and I didn't warm to the idea of advancing the prestige of a Columbia artist at the expense of Victor. Finally, André required an orchestra so large as to be unreasonably expensive, actually impracticable in relation to the size and acoustic character of our studio, and in bad taste musically. We finally decided, nevertheless, to accede to Lily's wishes and engage Kostelanetz. The results were not too happy. The records were fair, but the incident brought to a crisis a situation which had been existent for some time between Lily and André. He may have used it to give extra pressure to the influence he was bringing to bear on Lily to transfer her devotion from Victor to Columbia. This she was quite unwilling to do, but André, wisely as it turned out, eventually persuaded her. Furthermore, André, who is as touchy as "the fretful porcupine," was deeply offended when I protested what seemed to me the senseless waste of time and talent in recording, for which he was directly and solely responsible by reason of his grossly inflated orchestra and the agonizing slowness of his recording methods. He retired into typical Russian sullenness for a day or two and then, as a final expression of pique, warned us solemnly that we must not use his name as conductor on the records. I was only too willing to be restrained by this prohibition.

"To Hell with Mr. O'Connell!"

Lily, as I have said, is quite amiable, and furthermore, I suspect her of having a sense of humor. I am sure she enjoyed, as I did myself on reflection, the most embarrassing moment of my life. It happened like this:

The Democratic National Convention which nominated Franklin D. Roosevelt for his second term met at Philadelphia. The climax planned for the convention was to come on the last night, when Roosevelt was to appear at Franklin Field, the stadium of the University of Pennsylvania, to make his speech of acceptance. Immediately preceding the President's appearance there was to be an hour's concert by the Philadelphia Orchestra with a soloist. Mr. [Leopold] Stokowski discreetly declined an invitation to conduct this concert, but very considerately suggested me as a substitute, and Reggie Allen, then manager of the orchestra, engaged me as conductor and Lily Pons as soloist. It had rained most of the day, but as concert time approached the Pons luck asserted itself, the skies cleared, and we rushed to Franklin Field, where 110,000 wild-eyed Democrats awaited the arrival of our Chief Executive. I was mightily excited—

by the character of the occasion, the imminent appearance of the President, the sight of the multitudinous audience, the knowledge that every radio station in the United States would be tuned in, the pleasure of conducting the Philadelphia Orchestra, and by no means least, the honor of conducting for Miss Pons. Besides, she called me "Maestro"!

The inimitable sang-froid of Jim Sauter, who was in charge of entertainment and probably of everything else at the Democratic Convention, calmed me down somewhat and I went to work with a will. I might as well have stayed home. I assure you that 110,000 people can make more noise than 110 musicians, and there were moments during that concert when I literally could not hear the orchestra; in fact, when I had finished conducting the "Rhumba" movement from Karl McDonald's Second Symphony the trombones still had a couple of bars to go. As nobody heard them, it didn't matter much except to the trombones and myself.

When the soloist appeared, however, the audience quieted as if by magic, and in ten seconds Lily had them in the hollow of her little hand. I don't remember all we did, but among other things there was Bishop's "Lo! Here the Gentle Lark." The solo flute, John Fischer of the Philadelphia Orchestra, the solo soprano, the orchestra, and myself managed to finish neatly together. This was Lily's concluding number, and when the applause quieted, Mr. Sauter, master of microphones, delivered himself of an announcement. "And now," he cried into the enormous void of silence, "and now the Philadelphia Orchestra will play Beethoven's Consecration of the House, under the direction of Mr. O'Connell." Whereupon an anonymous Stentor, in a voice far-carrying as a coyote's on the plains, perfectly audible to 110,000 Democrats and via radio to 110,000,000 other citizens, gave out with "To hell with Mr. O'Connell; give us some more Lily Pons!" Lily was sweet enough not to want to laugh and gave me a most sympathetic look, but when she saw that both Sauter and I were in convulsions she had a good laugh out of it too. Later there were tragicomic happenings of one sort or another, including the difficulties of getting the orchestra started at the right moment on "Hail to the Chief"—but we were talking about Lily and André.

Super-Salesman

André is the shrewdest man in the music business. No one can match him at capitalizing an asset or suppressing a liability. He is possessed of a ferocious acquisitiveness, yet has the courage to spend money in great amounts in order to *make* money in greater. If the money is supplied by a radio sponsor or a recording company, so much the better. Indeed, it is the investment of such money in André's unique talents that has made him a very wealthy man. I am sure he earns more from radio and record royalties than any conductor in his or any other field. He has surely, shrewdly, and cautiously developed and impressed on the public mind the Pons-Kostelanetz association, each of the two artists edging over little by little from his and her respective side of the tracks, until ultimately, like all parallel lines, they will seem to converge; merge in that wonderful common ground of music, the musical *pons asinorum* traversed by the low-highbrows, the high-lowbrows, and the myriad middlebrows.

To this numberless mass André is the master musician of all time, and therefore, he has doubtless been to Chrysler what he was to Coca-Cola—the master salesman. Like all good salesmen, he knows how to work both sides of the street and across the tracks too. He knows, as few musicians or even businessmen know, the uses and the value of exploitation, promotion, and, above all, publicity. He knows what is to be exploited and what shouldn't be; that Lily's French accent is cute and that his own, which is of the Gregory Ratoff variety, might be regarded as funny; that Lily's diminutive charm and glamorous stage appearance are assets, whereas his own personal charms are perhaps less obvious. He knows that Main Street likes to read of Lily's mink and sable and chinchilla, and that such luxuries are really not luxuries at all, but useful and convincing "props" and sound investments from any viewpoint. Furthermore, he knows music. He knows how to arrange it, beglamorize it, conduct it, and sell it, because he knows up to forty decimal places the common denominator of musical taste in the radio audience. The Pons-Kostelanetz combination has been mutually advantageous and fantastically profitable. Lily brings to it the glamour of the Metropolitan, a touch of what the lowbrow thinks is highbrow, a picturesque personality, vocal fireworks, and musical talent of no mean order. André contributes really sound musicianship, extraordinarily shrewd commercial sense, crafty showmanship, sometimes good and often cheap music, but all of it, always, hand-decorated and chromium-plated.

André, deplorably, is showing signs of going "longhair"—figuratively, of course. This comes about, I think, partly because of suppressed desires, partly from much the same impulse that underlies a rich brewer's donation of stained-glass windows to the church, and partly out of financial considerations. Many a millionaire gets religion after he's got enough money to afford it. André can afford it. André has doubtless made all the money that he wants, or at least all that he can use; and it would perhaps bring our symbols *Coq d'or* and Coca-Cola a little closer into line if he were to graduate into the symphonic field. This no doubt would be attended with some difficulty for any man so long and intimately associated in the public mind with crass commercialism and with what, in the sense that it appeals to the mass, one may call vulgate music. But I think André will be able to wangle it by judicious application of the assets at his disposal; and indeed he has already made moves in this direction. There have been discreet offers, to various of the major orchestras during their summer season and to at least two of the major orchestras in their winter season, of the services of Lily as soloist, and at very special fees, but necessarily, of course, with André conducting.

161

Pension funds and pension-fund concerts are likely to benefit from the ministrations of André and his partner—that is, the pension funds and the pension-fund concerts of the more prosperous and more important orchestras, whose names will bring new prestige to Kostelanetz publicity. I shall be surprised if he does not accept, at least for what part of the season he can spare from the more remunerative commercial field, the co-conductorship of an American symphony orchestra.

When I juxtaposed *Coq d'or* and Coca-Cola I was, of course, speaking figuratively. I meant to indicate that the conjunction of two stars in their respective fields results in a combination for money-making unparalleled even in these mad years; that the combination of what Lily has, plus what André has, plus André's knowledge of how to exploit what they both have, is invincible.

André's musical background is obscure. I have been told that he was an opera conductor in Russia prior to his taking up residence in the United States, but this I do not believe. If we are to take at face value the assertions of all the émigré musicians and refugeniuses, it must be that Italy, Central Europe, and Russia were populated exclusively by conductors. I know more than one imported musician who made a precarious living as a *chor-répétiteur* or accompanist in some provincial European opera house but who on arriving here at once has achieved a nice fat job on the basis of having been a well-known European opera conductor.

This was not the case with André. Whatever his European background, the experience and the practical musical education that developed him into the excellent musician that he is were gained in this country. He had valuable and ultimately highly profitable experience as a routine arranger and transcriber for the Judson Radio Company, forerunner of the Columbia Broadcasting System, where Eugene Ormandy was at the same time principal conductor. I am given to understand, by an unimpeachable authority, that André learned what he knows about conducting from Mr. Ormandy. This would hardly be surprising, since Mr. Ormandy is technically one of the soundest and most expert men ever to lift a baton in this country, and both able and generous in helping other musicians in their work.

How to Make Music Better Than It Is

If you had been accustomed to listening to André's Coca-Cola hour via radio and had later been present in the broadcasting studio, you would probably have been startled to find that the live orchestra doesn't sound at all like what goes out on the air. So many microphones, echo chambers, and every other electronic and mechanical gadget that can be employed come between the actual performance and the broadcast that the finished product you hear via radio really has little resemblance to the raw material developed in the studio. André has skillfully and with imagination, if not always with good taste, exploited every resource that radio science can offer. The extraordinary clarity which is sometimes noticed in the Kostelanetz strings is accomplished, first, by the curious style of Kostelanetz orchestration, which so often requires all the strings to play in unison in the upper register; and secondly, by an electromechanical operation which gives the sound a floating and spacious quality. The whole orchestra is treated not as a unit but as a number of small groups, each with its own microphone, each controlled more by the flow of electric current than by the baton. I do not like, nor can any musician of cultivated tastes like, the character of the orchestrations which André has had made for him, but I do admire their cleverness and adroit employment of orchestral color and the skill with which the type of orchestration and the mechanical gadgets are made to operate together to produce a unique effect. As I have pointed out, André is keenly aware of every possible detail that can be used to make his work distinctive and popular. The question of his taste is not at issue. I dare say he is not playing to satisfy *his* taste but rather to tickle that of a certain broad level of the listening public. Whether that is good or bad is probably of no interest to the conductor so long as he satisfies it.

The techniques of recording have been employed to the great advantage of Lily also—though no more so than with other singers who have appeared in the movies. Sound-film recording is a priceless boon to any performing musician because it makes it possible that the public will never hear any but the artist's best—and there is no reason why the public should ever hear any but an absolutely perfect performance. The reason for this is that ten or a dozen or a hundred sound film recordings can be made, and indeed are made sometimes, of each selection. These can be synthesized into one finished recording by the simple expedient of cutting up the film and pasting one hundred or one thousand fragments together to make a perfect whole. "A good note here, a good note there; here a note, there a note everywhere a good note!" A perfect performance in public almost never happens, but even if it does happen, it is lost forever. In film recording perfect performances can be and are manufactured out of dozens or scores of imperfect performances, each one of which has something in it that is good. That is why movie crowds are so impressed and concert audiences so often disappointed when singing stars of the films appear in person. The various vital helps that the film record can give are absent. A voice that seems full and resonant on the screen may actually be small, pinched, and cold. There may be in reality a few or many lapses from pitch, but on the screen there are none. Film recording is the great deceiver, but I don't know that we should quarrel with it if its only crime is making things better than they are.

The versatility of film recording was rather amusingly demonstrated when Deanna Durbin was making the picture *100 Men and a Girl*. The orchestral recordings were all to be made in the Academy of Music in Philadelphia, where a very elaborate multi-channel film-recording system had been set up. Mr. Stokowski was to conduct the accompaniments for Miss Durbin. The day came for Deanna to record her songs with the orchestra, and it happened that the young lady was indisposed and decidedly not in good voice. In addition, she was scared to death. The recorders were nothing daunted. They recorded the accompaniments anyway and later on recorded the solo voice in Hollywood, combining the two in a final "dubbing," or re-recording, for the finished film. If you saw the picture, you heard Deanna singing in Hollywood and her accompaniment being played in Philadelphia.

I have been told that over a hundred "takes" were made on one number which Lily Pons sang in her last film. I don't know that this is true, but it could be, as this is common practice. I did not see or hear the film and consequently don't know the results from personal experience, but I am sure they were perfect.

Something for the Boys

I was personally disappointed in the wartime activities of many musicians. At least as far as those in the upper brackets are concerned, their USO activities were often conditioned upon their estimate of their tax situation or of the amount of exploitation that could be applied to their camp appearances. A good many singers and instrumentalists have achieved those income brackets where it is determined that additional earnings will be unprofitable. Entertainment at camps, with all expense paid and all transportation provided to remote corners of the world, with the opportunity for subsequent, impudent advertisement of patriotic effort and uproarious success among the boys, suggested to many wealthy entertainers a handy way of continuing to work, to keep in the limelight, to have the extraordinary experience of visiting war theaters in wartime, and to avoid additional taxes. (New Delhi, India, Oct. 24 [UP]—The British Army newspaper *Contact* today praised its American counterpart, the *C.B.I. Roundup*, for criticizing Hollywood entertainers who find the Far Eastern theater too "rugged," and asserted that the same criticism applies to many British stage, screen and radio performers. Like the *C.B.I. Roundup*, *Contact* agreed that entertainers have done a great deal in this war. But it is also agreed that they had no right to make undeserved publicity out of their trips to the front at a time when men were risking their lives fighting the enemy in Europe and the Far East.—*Philadelphia Inquirer*, 25 Oct. 1944.)

I do not, of course, mean to suggest that all the musicians who have given their talents to entertain the armed forces have been actuated by such sordid motives. A few fine artists who happened to be of draft age went to their military duties without protest, deferment, or lamentations; and I must cite in this connection the most honorable of them all—Albert Spalding, the American violinist, veteran of the air force in the first World War and in his fifties, who without

164

fanfare, without the specious pretext of entertaining the soldiers, undertook a man's job with the armed forces and disappeared completely from the concert stage. Spalding, rather than accept a factitious commission, rather than pose in uniform or perform as a player, joined the armed forces under an assumed name. His identity was not disclosed until 6 May 1945, after a broadcast of the program called "We the People," during which his work in Italy was described—his daily broadcasts to the Italian people, his instructions for sabotaging German installations, secreting food, equipment and arms from the enemy, and other such matters. (Nevertheless, there were a surprising number of able-bodied young orchestra players who managed, after being drafted or enlisted, to establish themselves in sinecures in and about New York, in the Army, Navy, Coast Guard, and Maritime Service; and to make about as much money as ever from radio and recording dates. Sometimes they were in uniform, sometimes not.)

The Pons That Depresses

It was inevitable that André and Lily would eventually, sometime before the end of the war, do something romantic and spectacular—for the boys. I am sure that with their usual thoroughness they overlooked no angle. Iran, from whence we had heard no harrowing tales of bloodshed or hardship, was chosen as the locale most in need of the services of the conductor and the coloratura. I know of no other instance where the appearances of a radio performer for the entertainment of our soldiers were exploited through a commercial radio hour, as happened in the case of André. "On tour with the Armed Forces," Coca-Cola repeatedly told us. Some people were critical of the exploitation—first of their camp shows and then of the retaking of Paris—which was engineered when they returned to New York on 23 August 1944. With customary foresight, an interview had been arranged at Lily's suite in the Waldorf. Photographers were on the job; and the *New York Herald Tribune* and other newspapers printed a two-column cut of the returning ambassadors of music, both in the slickest of uniforms, Lily modestly confining the number of decorations in her lapel to four. The press reported Lily "in ecstasy" and already planning concerts for Paris. "Everything in my home is Paris and everything in my heart is French," she cried, "and now we do not have the feeling of captivity any longer." A rather startling statement, I thought, for one whom America has kept for years in fabulous luxury and whom France scarcely knew at all before the war; one to whom America has provided everything she has, including recently obtained citizenship with its freedom, and a refuge. Lily added that she couldn't go to France for at least three months for "she must sing the opera in New York and San Francisco" (advt.) "because I am [an] American too."

But nothing that publicity agents have ever accomplished could have pleased them as much as what happened on the editorial page of the *New York Herald Tri-*

bune the following day. This was, I suppose, fortuitous, and without the collaboration of press agentry. In one column the *Herald Tribune* excoriated the publicity seekers of our own Ninth Air Force, and in the adjoining column, under a headline that included Miss Pons's name, gave the lady and her husband the benefit of a pontifical editorial—the most astonishing piece of free publicity I have ever seen.

Even this was not the climax. Ten days later the *Saturday Evening Post* in the issue dated 2 September 1944, with an article entitled "Main Street Moves to Amirabad" printed a picture two thirds of a page wide and six inches deep, purporting to show "Appreciative soldiers of the Persogulf Command raising the roof after some high-grade warbling by little Lily Pons. André Kostelanetz conducted the 46-Yank orchestra." This photograph, you will note, appeared less than ten days after Pons-Kostelanetz returned from their Persian campaign.

The *Post* goes to press from four to six weeks in advance of publication date. Making due allowance for time consumed by travel and by mails, André must have had this picture made almost the instant he set foot on Persian soil. Of course, the interviews, news stories, and editorials, timed with the return of Pons and retaking of Paris, the ready suite at the Waldorf capable of accommodating a sufficient number of the press and supplying them with entertainment (though Lily's apartment a few blocks further north might have served the purpose) and finally the *coup de grâce* of a feature picture in the *Saturday Evening Post*—all this may have been a series of coincidences and not a prelude to André's and Lily's reappearance on the Coca-Cola hour the next Sunday afternoon, 3 September; but to me it seemed like insensitive commercial exploitation of our young fighting men for the benefit of those very American darlings of the American public who can say to that American public: "Everything in my home is Paris and everything in my heart is French."

PART SIX

Milestones

CHAPTER NINETEEN

Silver Gilt for Lily

Mary Jane Matz

On the evening of Tuesday, 3 January 1956, the Metropolitan Opera House was the scene of a gala performance celebrating Lily Pons's twenty-fifth season with the company. The program that night included the second act of *Rigoletto* and the Mad Scene from *Lucia*. Lily concluded with four arias: "O luce di quest' anima" from *Linda di Chamounix*, "Je suis Titania" from *Mignon*, "Chant du Rossignol" from Stravinsky's *Le rossignol*, and the Bell Song from *Lakmé*. In the New York *Journal-American* the next day, a prescient Miles Kastendieck wrote: "She is, perhaps, the last of a long line of coloraturas who made their singing the be-all and end-all of their art." Author Mary Jane Matz covered the event in the pages of *Opera News*.[1]

$\mathcal{L}$ILY PONS, who celebrated her twenty-fifth anniversary at the Metropolitan earlier this month, is more than just a singer; Lily is a phenomenon. Lily is the tiniest, the liveliest, the best dressed, the most chic. Lily, the conscientious. Lily, the indestructible. Lily, the unique.

More has been written about Pons in the last quarter of a century than about any singer of the generation. She has left the mark of her tiny foot and the echo of her voice in every corner of the world, has been interviewed by thousands of reporters. Yet when *Opera News* spent an afternoon with her last week, Lily Pons had something new to say.

Looking back across twenty-five years, Lily says simply: "I cannot believe it. Going around the world, learning, studying, singing, always busy. Where have they gone, these years? It seems like ten, perhaps, or fifteen at the most." A singer obsessed with conscience, Lily goes to bed at nine, gets up at seven, has breakfast at eight and delights her friends with Pons maxims: "Health comes first," "If you don't have fun before midnight, you will not have it after midnight," "If you smoke and drink, you cannot sing." Lily is a teetotaler, a devotee of big steaks and fresh fruits and vegetables. She is allergic to smoke, avoids parties at any cost and admits that she neglects her friends shamefully.

"Of course I like to go out and dance, like everybody. But a singer is a highly skilled laborer. Singers must be like athletes. If you are not strong, you get colds. A ballerina or pianist can perform with a cold. A singer—never. It is always my rule, no matter how important the performance, never to sing with a cold. Better to cancel and be replaced, better to disappoint the public than to sing badly and have people whisper, 'What has happened?'" Yet Pons's ironclad conscience forbids her to cancel, "because too many people's lives are involved." Only in the rarest emergency has she done it, "thanks to God and my health, which is wonderful."

When Lily came to the United States twenty-five years ago and first stepped onto the Metropolitan stage, she weighed exactly ninety-eight pounds. "It was a revolution!" she laughs delightedly. "I was the first soprano of that size to sing at the Metropolitan. People said, 'If she can sing well with her figure, then why suffer these padded prima donnas?' Women subscribers who had been fat for years began to reduce. Rich gowns began to look more chic on slenderizing women." Lily, who now weighs 109 pounds, says roguishly she is "a big woman now." She isn't!

Serene in spite of her inexhaustible energies, Lily has spirit without temperament. No prima donna in the pejorative sense of the word, she is truly a diva, in full command of the world around her. She moves like a queen through snow-slides in the Alps, train crashes in Siam, fan mob scenes in all parts of the world. Nothing disturbs her unruffled calm; yet she has firm convictions, by which she stands—precepts by which she lives. Only that old bugaboo, stage fright, bothers her. "No matter if I have only a little radio concert to sing. I am sick all day. Until I get on the stage and feel my public, I am sick, like on the sea. The public gives me courage and a push forward. Then my nerves are forgotten."

In twenty-five years Lily has sung roles and concerts in the thousands. Sitting back to survey her artistic life, she recalls *Lucia* with love, casts a warm glance at *Lakmé*.

"I cannot resist the color, the beauty and the very Frenchness of *Lakmé*. I feel somehow that it belongs to me, for each singer has one or two roles which he makes his very own. I feel so deeply the little nature of that Hindu girl, although I know in my own heart that the opera is not great music. Yet *Lakmé* is pleasing, the ballet is colorful. And the story of *Lakmé*, her love and her father's rage, is full of human appeal."

When Lily sang *Lakmé*, she had the materials and jewelry for the costumes chosen in India. "I was very interested in that epoch, in the correct dress for it. All my life I have been very particular about that."

Lily Pons's love for *Lakmé* has its roots in the petite coloratura's passion for Oriental art and culture. Her homes are filled with her famed collections of Oriental pieces. In her Palm Springs house, she "lives in saris, sarong dresses and Chinese gowns." It comes as no surprise, then, that she is fascinated by Oriental operatic heroines such as Constanza of the *Seraglio*, the Queen of the Night and the Queen of Shemakha.

She finds time, too, to love Western heroines: Gilda, for her touching ingenuity; the Doll in *Les contes d'Hoffmann*, for her infantile charm; Cherubino, for his freshness. Of the roles she has sung, she dislikes only Philine in *Mignon*. "I never sang it after Mr. Gatti left the Metropolitan," she asserts with a determined tilt of her tiny chin.

Of the roles she considers for the future, Mélisande interests her the most. "It is the most beautiful thing in opera: pure expression and magnificent poetry. But one must retire from the world for six months to learn so difficult a part." Lily Pons would also like to create a role which would be written especially for her; but she has little hope. "Modern composers write first for orchestra and second for voice, but never for coloratura. That bird does not exist any more!"

The one role which she would love to sing and will not is Carmen, "that wonderful, expressive part." Carmen needs to be understood, Lily Pons says; someone must sing the role who knows all about gypsies—"the most proud people in the world, with their terrible vanity, their power." Lily Pons has ideas about Carmen, who should not be "a cabaret *demoiselle*, a nightclub dancer. She is violent, like a piano wire. If only Carmen Amaya had a voice!" Lily wails.

Today, she confides, she has reached a point where she turns to herself and says, "Oh, *mon Dieu*! What have I missed during these years!" But Lily has a conscience which never lets her rest.

"I believe every artist has a message for the public. I think I have conveyed mine. I love my public and they love me. I have been rewarded richly. Since 1931 many coloraturas have come and gone at the Metropolitan, but Lily—she is still here!"

CHAPTER TWENTY

The Legendary Lily

Irving Kolodin

Forty-one years separated the beginning and end of Lily Pons's operatic career in America. In May 1972, she achieved a milestone in the history of singing when she emerged from retirement at age seventy-four to sing a one-time concert at New York's Philharmonic Hall. Irving Kolodin, whose apprenticeship as an opera critic was spent under the tutelage of W. J. Henderson, published this essay review of the historic concert in *The Saturday Review*.[1]

*T*HE ETERNAL MYSTERY of what makes one performer average, another un-usual, and a third exceptional casts an unexpected fascination over one of this year's Philharmonic Promenades at Lincoln Center, conducted for the tenth year by their inventor and only exponent, André Kostelanetz. It was clearly some form of what the French term *blague* that prompted Kostelanetz to deco-rate the event with the reappearance, after years of nonsinging, of a soprano described as Lily Pons.

A likely story, sneered the cynical; the true Lily Pons celebrated the end of twenty-five years of Metropolitan Opera singing more than fifteen years ago, sang only a few concerts thereafter, and has since enjoyed a well-earned retire-ment in the playgrounds of the well-to-do. At one time it was Palm Springs, California; at another in the area of Dallas, Texas. Why should she even consider exposing her still lovely neck to the chopping block of a New York appearance at an age—admittedly sixty-eight and perhaps unadmittedly more—when most sopranos are content to teach what they can no longer preach? Clearly this was an impostor to lure the gullible.

But the program made apparent at least one "why" of this happening. Nine-teen seventy-two has been the year of Joan Sutherland's great triumph [at the Met] as Marie in Donizetti's *La fille du régiment*. When the work was last per-formed at the old Met, in 1942, it was with Lily Pons as Marie. As has been noted in conjunction with other roles they share—Amina in Bellini's *La sonnambula* as well as Lucia in Donizetti's sad tale of the Ashtons and Ravenswoods—there are as many ways of stitching together the notes of these parts as there are of embroi-dering a precious fabric. To Pons, there was only the one, the authentic kind of needlework, and that was petit point.

For my suspicious mind, it was at least to demonstrate that whatever form of homespun Sutherland practiced it was petit point that Donizetti demanded, which caused Miss Pons to begin her four-part effort with "Chacun le sait" and end it with "Salut à la France!," both from *La fille*.

Radiating chic, as ever, beautifully clad in pink and white organza lace, coiffed in what appeared to be a lacquered black wig, and cosmeticized to an almost doll-like finish, Miss Pons made an entrance that could only have been the product of nearly fifty years' practice in perfecting the unreality that is every true prima donna. The exquisite way in which she was turned out assured her a triumph by sight alone.

If those who know her long and well could scarcely believe what they saw, they were truly taken aback by what they heard. Take it from one who grew up in the critical business listening to, wondering at, and sometimes complaining about Lily Pons, she had, literally decades ago, often done herself less justice than she did this 31 May. It was a kind of afterglow, a final flaring up of the barely smoldering vocal flame, a stirring about of the all but exhausted embers that recalled the equally memorable exhibition and perhaps the last previous one of its kind—that the great baritone Giuseppe de Luca gave in Town Hall in 1947, aged seventy.

Some who had never heard the Pons voice in its prime might have concluded that what they heard in Philharmonic Hall, charming as it sounded and discreetly amplified as it was, could hardly be more than a pale echo of the quality with which a great reputation had been made. The fact is that hers was always a sound for which, as well as to which, one had to listen. Exquisite in its purity, it was really no more in quantity than one might have expected from the tiny frame out of which it emerged.

Was this Promenade performance some form of artifice, manufactured for the occasion? Not really. Let's guess that it was very carefully prepared, painstakingly rehearsed, and produced out of a considerable background of vocal rest and rejuvenation. When Miss Pons was new to the Met a mere forty years ago, an eminent critic of the time attributed her unexpected success—she came carefully unheralded—to "the astonishment and delight of an assembly which found on the Metropolitan stage a new singer who could actually sing."

In paying tribute to a soprano with "a technique far above the slovenly average of today," the same critic (W. J. Henderson) added: "Miss Pons has precious gifts. Someday she may be a great singer." Had Henderson lived to hear her sing Bachelet's "Chère nuit" or Ponce's "Estrellita" at this Promenade with more artistry at nearly seventy than when she was "getting by" on her "precious gifts" and a "technique far above the average" at forty, that same connoisseur might have said, without either malice or surprise, "Why not? Lilli Lehmann was singing Violetta at sixty, Mattia Battistini was giving recitals in London at sixty-six, and old Schumann-Heink could still declaim Erda's part in *Siegfried* at the Met when she was past seventy."

What is too seldom remembered about singing is that, basically, it is a form of muscular discipline like any athletic endeavor. Durability is as much a part of the exceptional singer as it is of the exceptional ballplayer, and, at bottom, the name of both games is technique. Miss Pons had it at twenty-six, and she still has it at sixty-eight, as her lively version of Delibes's "Les filles de Cadiz," among other encores, demonstrated. It was, in all, a fine night for the human body, with Miss Pons—whose performance, it is understood, was being filmed for possible television use—preceded by dancers Patricia McBride and Edward Villella in a vital sequence of excerpts from Khachaturian's *Gayne*. Kostelanetz did his share of the evening's work with a rapport bred of twenty years' domestic as well as musical partnership with the former Mrs. K.

PART SEVEN

The Last Prima Donna

CHAPTER TWENTY-ONE

The World of Lily Pons

Edgar Vincent

Longtime publicist Edgar Vincent, whose client roster has included numerous opera and concert stars, began his career at the Muriel Francis agency's New York headquarters on Fifth Avenue, where he was assigned to the promotion of Lily Pons. In an interview conducted for this book, Vincent's candid yet affectionate depiction of Pons's masterful use of the media provides a firsthand glimpse of the soprano's shrewd and often amusing self-promotion.[1]

*T*HROUGH THE Muriel Francis agency, where I began my career in the music business, I was assigned as a young staff member to help publicize Lily Pons. Although Lily was then nearing the end of her Metropolitan Opera career, she was still *the* prima donna. Yet she had perfected the art of being a prima donna to such a degree that it was utterly charming to be around her.

Lily lived in a world entirely her own—a world of glamour, fashion, money, and celebrity. She was the center of that world, and she had learned the value of publicity very early in her career. She knew how to make it work for her, and she certainly knew how to get it. But she also had a sense of humor about herself, and that was part of her charm.

My good friend Humphrey Doulens, who was Lily's tour manager at Columbia Artists Management and who had known her in the 1930s, used to tell me great stories about the publicity stunts he arranged for her. One time, Lily was scheduled to sing a concert in Greensboro, North Carolina. Since Humphrey's job was to get maximum publicity for her concert tours, he came up with an idea that would tie in her concert appearance with the World Series, which was in progress the day she was scheduled to sing in Greensboro. Lily didn't know the first thing about baseball, but Humphrey asked her to go along with the ruse he had planned.

As he explained it when he met her at her train, he had told the Greensboro newspaper that Lily was a baseball fan and was following the World Series with great interest. This was in the early days of television, and the game was being telecast all over the country. The newspaper latched onto this and not only sent a photographer but also assigned the sports editor to interview Lily.

The sports editor didn't know any more about opera than Lily knew about baseball, so Humphrey basically told him what questions Lily would want to be asked. Then Humphrey told Lily what the questions would be, and she agreed to play along with the script and act as if she was practically glued to the television set during the World Series.

The sports editor greeted her and said, "Miss Pons, I understand that you are a great baseball fan, is that right?" So far, so good; he was following Humphrey's script.

"*Oui*, I certainly am! Yes, I am a very beeg baseball fan," Lily said in that charming accent of hers.

"Are you going to watch the game this afternoon?" the sports editor then asked.

"*Oui*! Most certainly, I will be watching the beeg game!" Lily answered, right on cue.

Apparently, the sports editor forgot his next question because there was an embarrassing pause, and Lily thought she ought to fill it by saying something.

"By zee way," she said nonchalantly, "who eez playing?"

Well, that betrayed the whole ruse, of course, and everybody got a big laugh out of it. Humphrey Doulens didn't know what to do, but Lily was quick-minded and in her good fashion she turned the whole situation around. First, she told the sports editor that all baseball players have to learn to breathe the same way that great singers do. "They have to breathe down to *here*," she explained, pointing to her diaphragm and running her hand down to her tiny waist. Then she demonstrated her deep-breathing techniques for the photographer. The next morning, that interview became a front-page headline story!

Lily was such a celebrity that royalty often courted her, which always made for good press. André Kostelanetz and the Shah of Persia had become great friends, and the Shah took a great liking to Lily. He was scheduled to visit New York, and Lily called me to tell me about it. "The Shah will be coming to the Metropolitan to hear my Lucia," she told me, "and I want all the photographers there so that every newspaper will get the story."

In those days there were about seven or eight newspapers in New York City. I called around to the photo desks to arrange for the coverage, but I couldn't get any enthusiasm for it. They all said, "Yeah, if we can spare a photographer, we'll send one to her dressing room and get a couple of shots." That didn't sound good, so I hired my own photographer instead.

The Shah didn't stay for the whole opera. He decided to come backstage to see Lily right after she finished the Mad Scene. I got lucky because I had my photographer there, and also the Associated Press photographer was backstage, too. But there was a problem because Lily's mother, whom she always called "Maman," was with her in her dressing room, and it was creating a problem for Lily. If she didn't include her mother in the photographs, it would have been rude—but if she did include her, the photos would be less newsworthy because the Shah greeting Lily was what the photographers were after.

Seeing what was happening, I had to find a way to tactfully move Maman to another dressing room while the photos were being taken. Everything got done, one way or another, and the photographers did their work—but the next day there was absolutely nothing in any of the papers. Another day went by, and still nothing. So I called the city desk and asked why the photos hadn't been printed as yet. The answer I got was, "Look—it's no longer news. The Shah has been photographed everywhere in the city, visiting places, cutting ribbons, and all of that. He's just not news anymore."

I was getting desperate, so I called my contacts in the society columns and asked them to run the photos. They all liked Lily, and when I asked if there was any chance of the photos being used, they all said they would give it a try. But they also called back and told me that everybody was tired of running stories and photos of the Shah of Persia.

On the third day, I got a call from Lily. "*Dites-moi*," she said—and when she began a question with *dites-moi*, it usually meant she was going to put you on the spot. And she had other ways of letting you know where you stood, too. She would call me "Edgar" when I was on her good side, but "Vincent" when she was mad about something. Well, that particular day it was "*Dites-moi*, Vincent, what happened to the pictures of the Shah and me?"

"Well," I said, "those idiots at the press keep telling me that the Shah is no longer news because he's been photographed with this person and that person already, so he's no longer good copy."

"But," she interrupted, "the Shah has not been photographed with *me*!"

When it came to publicity, or for that matter anything that had to do with the management of her career, Lily was all business. She would call you on the carpet if you weren't doing things that she thought you should be doing.

I overheard a phone call that Lily made to Constance Hope, who was then managing her publicity. "Constance, *dites-moi*, what are these things that you call 'sundry expenses' in the bill for your services?" Lily asked. Constance patiently explained each and every item, and why she thought they were justified.

"I do not pay zeez 'sundry expenses,'" Lily answered nonchalantly, and she hung up.

She could be that hard-nosed in her personal life, too. However good or bad the marriage was between André and Lily, once the marriage was over, it was *really* over from Lily's standpoint. When they were living at Gracie Square, André had bought her a famous Renoir painting of a little girl in a meadow. That painting had its own special niche in their home, and André developed a great fondness for it over the years.

When they got divorced, Lily basically cleaned out Gracie Square; she took nearly everything. André was wealthy, so he didn't say much—except when it came to that Renoir painting. He wanted to know if Lily would let him keep it, even though he had originally bought it for her.

"Yes, of course you can have it," she said to him. "But you must buy it back from me first. And at the current market price."

Whenever I think of Lily, though, it is her charm, her warmth, and her humor that keep coming back to me. Once when she was on a concert tour, I saw a demonstration of all those facets of her personality, and I also witnessed how her perfectionism could get her into funny situations.

She was to sing a concert someplace in the hinterlands, and the hall she was to sing in was a converted high-school auditorium. That's par for the course in some smaller towns, and she didn't mind at all what the place looked like. But what she did mind were the thick red-velvet curtains that surrounded the stage.

She was worried that they would absorb too much of her voice, which wasn't very large anyway.

She sent word to her concert promoter that those curtains would have to come down. He sent word back to Lily that the manager of the hall did not want to remove them because the backstage area was very cluttered, and there wasn't enough time to clean it up properly. But she insisted that the curtains had to go.

Finally, the manager of the hall asked to see her in person. She received him very pleasantly, and he said to her, "Miss Pons, I am very, very sorry but there is such a clutter backstage that we cannot—"

She didn't let him finish the sentence. "No!" she said firmly, "I do not sing unless zeez curtains are taken away!"

She had the last word, and down came the red-velvet curtains. What the manager of the place didn't tell her, however, was that the curtains had been put up to cover a very large sign that had been painted on the back wall of the stage. So, at eight o'clock that night, Lily sang a wonderful concert in front of a huge sign that read, RESTROOMS—THIS WAY.

CHAPTER TWENTY-TWO

Lily Pons: 13 April 1898– 13 February 1976

Francis Robinson

In the 1949–50 Metropolitan Opera season, incoming general manager Rudolf Bing appointed to his senior staff a seasoned publicist, Francis Robinson, whose mellifluous Tennessee-tinged voice would grace numerous Metropolitan intermission features on radio for decades to come. Robinson's sentiments as a writer and broadcaster were anchored in the Metropolitan's distant past, in the so-called golden age of Caruso, Galli-Curci, and the era of World War I. In his popular "Biographies in Music" installments during the Metropolitan broadcasts, Robinson profiled many of these legendary singers, including Lily Pons, one of his personal favorites.

Early in 1976, Lily was diagnosed with pancreatic cancer. The cancer ravaged her very quickly, and on 13 February 1976 she died at the age of seventy-seven. Word of her terminal illness reached Robinson while he and Anthony A. Bliss, whose familial association with the Metropolitan Opera began in the 1890s, were visiting Dallas in conjunction with the annual Metropolitan tour. Two months later, Robinson contributed this obituary essay to *Opera News*.[1]

*M*R. BLISS and I were on the circuit ahead of the tour. We were checking into our hotel in Dallas late the afternoon of 11 February 1976. "He's here now," I heard the clerk say, and she handed me the telephone. It was a mutual friend to tell me Lily Pons hadn't long to live. She had taken her to St. Paul's Hospital for tests one month to the day before. The verdict was cancer of the pancreas, and Lily never went back to the beautiful apartment which, with the house in Palm Springs, had been home for the past fifteen years.

She was conscious but was seeing no one except her sister, who had come from Cannes. We somehow couldn't take it in—Lily, so full of life, so full of the joy of life, which are not always one and the same. We completed our rounds and flew back to New York barely more than twenty-four hours later. Next morning she died. It was Friday the thirteenth, a number she was superstitious about in reverse. She swore by it. Her license plate was LP13.

The world without Lily? Definitely duller. But how much more dull if we had never had her.

I first met her on Easter Sunday 1933. She was singing in Nashville the next night. It was my first year on the Nashville *Banner*, and I was sent to interview her. It was cold and rainy for that time of the year, but the magic and glamour that attended Lily Pons, offstage as well as on, dispelled all clouds. Surrounding her, but not too much, were her manager, Paul Stoes (this was even before Humphrey Doulens), her secretary, her flautist and her pianist, Giuseppe Bamboschek, who had been Giulio Gatti-Casazza's musical secretary. History here, past, present and future.

The hour was early, but Pons was—as she remained throughout more than forty years before the public in this country (she made her last appearance in New York on 31 May 1972)—the epitome of chic. She was wearing the simplest of outfits, a close-fitting suit of gray sharkskin with a narrow fur neckpiece and a not too wide-brimmed but floppy hat, which in the photograph in my file looks as smart today as it did then.

Whether by chance or design, all this simplicity was the perfect opposite for the shock—a South American jaguar named Ita, with not a leash in sight, already too big and aggressive for comfort. Miss Pons gleefully displayed a fingerless pair of gloves. "It's the ninth pair she has eaten," she said. Not too long afterward Ita was retired to the zoo. Human flesh would have been next.

Lily Pons made her Metropolitan debut at a Saturday matinee, 3 January 1931. She was an immediate and sensational success. Like Galli-Curci, who retired from opera just a year before, she had come to this country unheralded.

Mr. Gatti purposely kept her under wraps. There was not even a picture of her in the papers the Sunday before her debut.

Beginning as a pianist, she had studied at the Paris Conservatory and had acted at the Théâtre des Variétés when she was engaged by the opera house at Mulhouse in Alsace. Maria Gay and Giovanni Zenatello brought her to this country and to the attention of the Met. She sang 198 performances of ten roles in New York and another eighty-five performances on tour. The last new role she undertook was Marie in *La fille du régiment*. Valentina made her costumes, and Lily broke out a tricolor half the size of the stage to point up her interpolation of the Marseillaise. Less than a year later, we were in the war too.

Nothing like Lily had ever happened in opera before. Edward Johnson said she and Gladys Swarthout had a contest as to which could bare the most midriff in *Lakmé*. Both won, but Lily got there first, and with a rhinestone in the strategic spot. A town in Maryland was named Lilypons. Needless to say, it had a pond with a lot of lily pads, and she and her husband, André Kostelanetz, had their Christmas cards postmarked there. She sang for our soldiers in China, Burma and India under a sun so sweltering she had to hold wet towels to her head between numbers. Her uniform was a strapless evening gown, just as though she had been in Carnegie Hall.

Lily's silver jubilee, twenty-five years to the day after her debut, was one of the great nights in the history of the Metropolitan. She sang the second act of *Rigoletto* and the Mad Scene from *Lucia* with the full company. At intermission she got flowery speeches and several times her weight in silver. The final third of the program she carried alone in billowing white before a curtain of pale blue with hundreds of tiny gold fleurs-de-lis. There were arias with full orchestra by Thomas, Donizetti, Stravinsky and Delibes, with a Strauss waltz as encore.

The spring before all this she was on tour with us and already planning the big night. No other prima donna had achieved such a record at the Metropolitan. I was sitting next to her at a Guild luncheon in Memphis. She was looking as only Lily Pons could, in navy-blue linen with white piping and a straw hat of the same colors. The entire conversation, or I should say monologue, was programmed to the gala eight months away. General de Gaulle would be invited, as would President Eisenhower. They never got there, but no matter: it was a great night just the same.

"And," Lily concluded in the famous staccato, higher by a couple of tones than usual, "this will not be a *farewell!*"

It wasn't; and neither is this piece. She is an authentic entry in the pantheon of singing. Worth more than all the encomiums heaped on her by honest critics or the heartfelt shouts of her fans are three sentences from the autobiography of Giulio Gatti-Casazza: "It is said that the art of bel canto is finished. But this is not true. Artists like de Luca and Rosa Ponselle, Elisabeth Rethberg and Lily Pons demonstrate the truth of what I assert."

CHAPTER TWENTY-THREE

Lily Pons

Lanfranco Rasponi

Lanfranco Rasponi (1914–1983) was a Florentine educated at the University of California and the Columbia School of Journalism. He blended four careers in postwar New York City: writing about opera and opera singers (for *The New York Times*, *Opera News*, and other periodicals), representing them as a publicist (Renata Tebaldi, Franco Corelli, and Licia Albanese were among his clients at various times), writing about New York society (for *Vogue*, *Town and Country*, and other magazines), and also managing the Colony and Quo Vadis, two popular Manhattan restaurants of the day.

In *The Last Prima Donnas*, based on the author's firsthand experiences with legendary sopranos, Rasponi presented a collection of his interviews with great singers, from Amelita Galli-Curci and Lucrezia Bori to Renata Tebaldi and Maria Callas. In his incisive summary of the life and career of Lily Pons, Rasponi drew upon his thirty-year association with the diva.[1]

*T*HE FRENCH WORD *"chic"* has become part of the English language, but in French *"avoir du chic"* means something more. It is difficult to translate, for it implies a combination of several very positive traits: character, correct behavior, and style. And the best description of Lily Pons is just she had *"du chic."* Everyone loved her, from her secretary, Margherita Tirindelli, to her manager, Humphrey Doulens, from her colleagues to the stagehands and the CBS men with whom she made many recordings. She was a professional through and through. She accepted no nonsense from anyone, but she never expected people, even at the height of her fame, to accept any nonsense from her. Thus she won everyone's respect during her long time before the public. Although she stopped singing at the Metropolitan Opera in 1959, after twenty-eight years on the roster, this did not mark her retirement. She went on, singing less and less, until the mid-1960s. Then at the age of sixty-eight she made a most unexpected appearance at Philharmonic Hall in New York City, under the baton of her ex-husband, André Kostelanetz. She sang six arias to delirious acclaim, and the concert became part of a television documentary dedicated to her.[2]

Thoroughly French, she was always aware of how to earn money, keep it, and enjoy it. For control was the secret of her long career and her lack of errors in judgment. "I started really earning some cash," she once told me, "when I was approaching the age of thirty, and I knew that the time ahead for a coloratura was not long. Actually, because I treasured and protected what God had entrusted to me, the silver flute in my throat lasted much longer than I could ever have hoped or anticipated."

She was a very special phenomenon and fitted into no category. When she became an overnight star in January 1931 with a matinee performance of *Lucia di Lammermoor* at the Metropolitan, she had almost no background to speak of; her only experience was in minor provincial theaters in France. Galli-Curci's forced withdrawal from the United States's leading opera house (due to the inexorable advancement of a goiter) had left the coloratura throne vacant, and Gatti-Casazza was desperately searching for someone to replace the crippled Italian nightingale. Toti dal Monte was still smarting from the manner in which she had been treated, because of Galli-Curci's jealousy, by the management at the Met during the 1924–25 season; Lina Pagliughi's figure was considered impossible for the standards of such a sophisticated audience; and Mercedes Capsir was no longer in her prime.

Giovanni Zenatello and his wife, Maria Gay, two former great singers who ran the summer seasons in the Arena at Verona and had become prominent agents, took a big chance and brought Pons to America to audition. Her credentials were so unimpressive that it took a great deal of patience to persuade Gatti-Casazza to listen to her. The famous general manager thought the French soprano represented a considerable gamble, but he decided to take it. The voice was tiny, and after the solid coloraturas of Sembrich, Barrientos, and Galli-Curci, he wondered how the public would respond. But in her favor were her dark looks, small waist, a piquant charm, and very assured high Es and Fs. He saw to it that she came on with no fanfare whatsoever; the press department was ordered not even to send any advance photos of the new singer to the newspapers. His astuteness brought unhoped-for results. The public, totally unprepared, was dazzled by the purity and daring acrobatics of the diminutive voice, which, because of infallible schooling (she had studied in Paris with Alberti de Gorostiaga), always managed to reach the last row of the gallery, however big the theater. The Mad Scene was a triumph, and in the excitement no one could recall how many curtain calls there were.

Despite the drama of the Depression, lines formed at the box office of the theater where the new nightingale would sing. Pons had come at just the right psychological moment, as she herself admitted with total frankness. Those were the days when films had been revolutionized by sound, and being so personable and attractive, she was immediately signed up for several motion pictures. *I Dream Too Much* and *That Girl from Paris*, among others, were not artistic successes, but they helped enormously to project her unknown name all over the world. With her keen intelligence and shrewdness, she became the darling of all the women's pages. Her large, spectacular apartment on Gracie Square and her country house in Connecticut were eminently suited for photograph sessions, and with her unfailing taste she became one of the world's best-dressed women. She started collecting paintings by Renoir, Matisse, Braque, and Chagall, among many others, when the prices were still fairly reasonable. She was so well known that a town in Maryland was named for her and for many years her Christmas cards carried the postmark "Lilypons, Md."

Her every appearance, on- and offstage, was eagerly anticipated because of her innate elegance and the glamour she projected. She learned to keep her figure trim—for most of her career she weighed around 104 pounds, and she was a little less than five feet tall—and make the best of a really not well-proportioned figure (she had a long waist too, and rather short legs) by wearing just the right kind of clothes. She became part of the society circuit, but when she worked she rarely attended parties. Her marriage in 1938 to André Kostelanetz, the conductor, always remained a mystery even to her close friends. Was it a love match? Most people near her did not think so but suspected it was a sensible union between two persons who had many interests in common and whose joint appearances brought in very high fees. This was particularly true of the summer al fresco concerts, such as those held at the Hollywood Bowl, Philadelphia's Robin Hood Dell, and New York City's Lewisohn Stadium, where year after year Pons was heard by tens of thousands. After their divorce she and Kostelanetz remained on excellent terms, and while he remarried, she never did. Like Grace Moore and Gladys Swarthout, Pons never had any children, and in later years she did not regret it. "When I look around and see the despair of so many of my friends who have been so disillusioned and deceived by their sons and daughters," she once said to me, "I realize that I have been lucky."

Because she was so deeply admired by her friends, the gossip of her love affair with a Texan whom she could not marry was always discussed sotto voce. But no one was surprised when she left New York and took an apartment in Dallas. She suffered terribly from nausea before every performance; and as singing in public held little pleasure for her, the more financially independent she became (she was one of the highest-paid singers of the century) the more she curtailed the number of her appearances. With the Metropolitan, where she sang from 1931 to 1959, she appeared 198 times in only ten different operas, and eighty-five times on tour with the company. So in the space of twenty-eight years she sang an average of only ten times per season. In the latter period of her career she was determined to spend the three winter months in her desert home in Palm Springs, California. And though she also sang for twenty-seven years with the San Francisco Opera whose seasons were always in the early fall, she wanted to remain at the Metropolitan because of the prestige the name gave for her concert tours. Several coloraturas came, some went, others stayed; but her star kept shining, for she was a special case, the Lily whom everyone had learned to love and could not do without.

Everyone in her large entourage knew the terrible nervous ordeal she went through before performances. She told me that she had been to see many specialists and no remedy had ever been found to soothe her stomach, which never stopped being affected by her public appearances. But with the enormous discipline she imposed upon herself, she went on bravely, knowing that the torture must be endured silently. As she became increasingly famous, she concentrated on fewer roles, until in the second part of her career they were reduced to five. In the first years at the Metropolitan she undertook Olympia in *Les contes d'Hoffmann*, Philine in *Mignon*, the title role in *Linda di Chamounix*, Amina in *La sonnambula*, and the Queen in *Le coq d'or*, which she and Ezio Pinza, as King Dodon, turned into a huge commercial success. Then she stuck to Rosina, Gilda, Lucia, Lakmé, and Marie in *La fille du régiment*. These last two were her crowning glory, for somehow even her acting seemed more spontaneous, and in the Donizetti part she showed humor and spirit. It was she who, with conductor Gennaro Papi, convinced Edward Johnson to stage this long-neglected opera, and it became a smash hit.

She never attempted the Queen of the Night,[3] for she knew she did not possess the lower range to do it justice, and she abandoned Violetta in *La traviata* after trying it out in San Francisco, for she realized that her instrument was too limited in scope for the drama of the role. While the first act was right for her, the rest demanded a larger, more expressive type of voice. She also spoke to me about Mélisande, but later told me that after going over the score, she had found it lay too much in the middle.

Her career, with few exceptions (she sang at Covent Garden in London in 1935, at the Paris Opéra, at the Colón in Buenos Aires, and at the Bellas Artes in Mexico City), was mainly American. And during the war she braved the stifling summer heat in Burma, China, and India—and always dressed in beautiful evening gowns—to sing for the GIs. Being intelligent and a realist, she knew that the American public was exceedingly loyal and that in the United States she had become an institution. Abroad, it was a different story: competition was intense, and the smallness of the voice was a drawback. It was crystal clear, delicate, somewhat colorless, and she had an effective way of hitting the high Es and Fs that made one realize what a feat she had accomplished. And although she usually had no trouble with her pitch, the expression was practically nonexistent given the lack of palette in the sound. I attended several of her Carnegie Hall recitals and was always impressed by the choice of her selections, keeping her programs on the highbrow side. Despite the meticulousness of the preparation and the musicianship, though, the general impression I received was one of monotony. But she was a musician to her fingertips; she was a pianist before she turned to singing. In fact, Darius Milhaud, whom she asked to coach her in his *Chansons de Ronsard*, declared how surprised he had been at how beautifully she could sight-read. Limited as an actress, she relied on her personality, which always came to her aid.

In an interview she gave me for *The New York Times* in 1941 when she became an American citizen, she spoke at length about how she was finally satisfied with the way her type of voice sounded in the numerous radio broadcasts she made. "Before they perfected the system," she declared, "the vibrations of the upper register were terrible, and any note above a high C sounded metallic. People never get tired of listening to vocal acrobatics, and radio audiences are no exception. So I have had to include over and over again the Mad Scene from *Lucia*, the Shadow Song from *Dinorah*, 'Una voce poco fa' from *Il barbiere di Siviglia*, and the Bell Song from *Lakmé*. For three years I went on once a week, and of course this was commercially excellent, as it brings your voice and name into millions of homes. The sale of the recordings also increased astonishingly. I have always felt, however, that the standard of the selections could be improved upon and always had discussions about them with the sponsors. The public is more hip than it is given credit for. I had avalanches of mail from both Americans and Canadians after the broadcast of *La fille du régiment*, all congratulating me for taking on a new opera and giving them the opportunity to get acquainted with a delicious, forgotten score."

In 1946 I interviewed her again, for *Opera News*, and the occasion was her assuming the title role of Lakmé for the opening night of the season, having reworked her conception of the part after her stay in India. It was interesting that her predecessor Galli-Curci had told me, ten years before, how she had hated the Delibes opera and how trashy she thought the music was. But Pons's point of view was entirely different. "This is the first time I will be singing the Hindu priestess in New York City since my having visited India. I must confess that although I had been singing the part since the beginning of my career, I was never very clear as to the very intricate patterns of Brahmanism. The simple love story of East and West can't meet always appealed to me, but I had never looked into any hidden significance behind Lakmé's and Nilakantha's motives."

During her long wanderings around India while she sang for the American troops in 1944, she explained, she became terribly aware of the curse of the caste system. The hopelessness hovering over all Hindus derives from the fact that they know from birth that theirs is a narrow path from which it is impossible to deviate. Lakmé's tragedy, therefore, is in the best Greek tradition. Fate is against her from the very minute the curtain rises on the first act, and although in her youthful emotion she tries to counteract it, she is doomed from the start.

"There is little evolution in Lakmé's soul and heart," she continued, "during the course of the opera, and that is how my interpretation differs now. From the first moment she appears with Mallika in the flower duet to the dying scene, she is a willowy instrument in the hands of her gods. Formerly I built up her character to a series of climaxes. But that was wrong and not according to the Hindu mentality. While death to us of the West is an important step, to Easterners it is not. When Lakmé drinks the juice of the poisonous exotic flower, she is only facing karma and reincarnation. I am underplaying her now emotionally, keeping in mind her closing sentence: 'Love, you have given me beauteous dreams.'

"The opera should be visualized and interpreted as a series of vignettes in the Persian-Hindu miniature style of the eighteenth century. It should be stylized and never leave the dream world. From the temple of the first act to the square of the second and the jungle of the third, the three different Eastern moods should always be underlined. There should be no attempt at desperate histrionics or heavy dramatic accents on the part of anyone, even the infatuated hero, Gérald. He is never deeply in love. In fact, in the end he is quite willing to leave the priestess who has sacrificed everything for his welfare and go back to his garrison.

"As for the costuming, it is one of the most difficult I have for the heroine belongs to one of the highest castes, and she must at the same time convey a great simplicity of line. Heroines can be visualized in most cases as color or as emotion. While Gilda's shade is pastel, Rosina's is a Goya red or yellow, and Lucia is white and black. But in the case of Lakmé, there is no definite color that can be applied to her. Her motive is one that escapes definition, for she is like a flower, whose span of life is very brief indeed. The mood is one of mist and tenderness, of delicacy and withering ecstasy. Lakmé is, strangely enough, best known for the Bell Song, but to an interpreter that is not really the most important part. I don't mean vocally, of course. Its fireworks are extremely difficult, but they do not reveal anything of her character. The 'Pourquoi dans les grands bois' is infinitely more revealing and poetic, for in this lyrical outburst the young priestess gives vent to her delight in nature. And throughout the third act there are pages of haunting loveliness."

The last time I saw Pons was in New York City in 1972, and I never dreamed that she had so short a time ahead to live. She had come from out west, where she divided her time between the house in the desert in Palm Springs and the apartment in Dallas, and was on her way to spend her usual two months in France, visiting her sister in Normandy and spending some time at her flat in Cannes, where she had been born in 1905 [*sic*]. It had been a long time since we met, but I was not surprised to find her looking beguilingly petite as ever, not an extra pound in sight, her hair dyed blond and superbly coiffed, and dressed in a becoming blue *tailleur*. We always spoke French together, for despite all her years in the United States, English did not come easily to her; nor did Italian, which I always found surprising, since her mother had been Italian. What she said to me that day impressed me enough that I wrote it down in my diary that night.

"You and I know," she said, "that the best is behind us. We are fortunate to have lived when there was still a certain amount of style and manners, and people still had a heart." In saying this she pointed to her own. "Now it's all so cheap, tawdry, shoddy, and people do not seem to have any feelings left.

"As for the world of opera, I cringe. Everyone is singing what is not suited to their voices; they all look like unkempt gypsies. That is why I am happy to live in the desert many months of the year, in contact with the sun and nature. The air is pure, and Westerners are rough but nice people. Come and see me there and we will talk about the old times."

Alas, I never went, and in February 1976, at the age of seventy-one [*sic*], she died in Dallas, quite suddenly, of cancer of the pancreas. I was told that from the time the cancer was discovered until she passed away, barely a month had elapsed. If she had to go, I am happy that she could go quickly and, I hope, with as little pain as possible. For a nightingale who had given such infinite pleasure to so many people deserved not to be caged, but to fly away into the beyond, leaving behind only pleasant memories.

Notes

Introduction

1. "Lily Pons—Press Kit," bound typewritten document prepared by Humphrey Doulens for the Constance Hope agency and Columbia Artists Management, Inc., 1946. (Courtesy of the Ludecke-Pons Collection.) Variations of the same content pervade other press kits that the Hope agency and Columbia Artists prepared for Pons.
2. Irving Kolodin, "The Legendary Lily," *The Saturday Review*, 24 June 1972, p. 76.

One

1. This article is compiled from a typewritten manuscript prepared by William Seward from handwritten notes of Lily Pons, which was then edited by her. The manuscript is held in the Ludecke-Pons Collection.

    Between 1943 and 1956, Pons, through her secretary Margherita Tirindelli, prepared notes that were to be used in articles by or about her. Portions of this chapter are similar to an article entitled "The Birthday Party that Shaped My Life," which appeard with Pons's byline in the January 1956 issue of *McCall's*. In a letter to Flora Adler dated 5 December 1948, Tirindelli explained how articles that appear with Pons's name as author came about: "I ask what she would like to say (write) and I take down notes carefully as she tells me what her thoughts are. I type up the notes and I either give them to Lily to go over and mark up, or Miss [Constance] Hope would do that and then we would have Lily review the script and have us take this or that out or put this or that in." (Courtesy the Ludecke-Pons Collection.)
2. Perhaps it would have been expecting too much for the perpetually young-looking Pons to have given her actual birth year to encyclopedists and interviewers. Contrary to the variety of dates she and her publicists gave over the years (1904, 1905, and 1907 seem to have been the preferred ones), birth records in the *Registres des Actes de l'Etat Civil Déposés aux Archives de la Mairie*, Draguignan, confirm that Lily Pons was born at 1:00 AM on 12 April 1898, and that she was christened Alice Joséphine Pons. (Believing thirteen to be her lucky number, she would always cite

13 April as her birthday, claiming—perhaps correctly—that the midwife recorded the correct time, 1:00 AM, but forgot that it was technically 13 April, not 12 April.) Her mother's name appears as Marie Pétronille Naso, and her father's as Léonard Louis Auguste Antoine Pons. (The authors are grateful to Bill Park for furnishing a copy of the birth certificate.)

3. The date, circumstances, and details of Auguste Pons's participation in the Paris-to-Peking marathon varied widely in press accounts after his daughter became famous. A 1947 monograph, *Lily Pons: A Souvenir Life Story*, edited by Humphrey Doulens and published by Columbia Artists Management, has her father "driving a Panhard from Paris to Peking in 1914, being stalled on the Mongol desert." Among other sources, David Ewen's *Men and Women Who Make Music* (New York, 1939) has the elder Pons racing for Peking in 1907 in an "amazing stunt of driving a Sizaire-Nandin car from Paris to Peking," during which he "lost his way in the Urals [and] starved for a while in Tibet" (p. 126). *The New York Times*, in the obituary for Marie Pons (11 June 1963) listed the date of the marathon as 1914. Shortly after Lily's Metropolitan debut, *Time* magazine wrote (19 January 1931) that Auguste Pons had achieved "a certain notoriety by motoring from Cannes to Paris and back when automobiles were practically unknown."

4. In the article "The Birthday Party that Shaped My Life," published under her byline in the January 1956 *McCall's*, Pons says that her father "died on the blood-drenched fields of Ypres" (p. 21), a more dramatic version than what she and her mother told the press in most of their interviews. On occasion, Lily was also less exacting about the year of her father's death: in an interview conducted by Josephine LeSueur for a feature article in the January 1936 issue of *Photoplay*, Lily cited 1925 as the year of Auguste Pons's death. Other sources, including several of the New York dailies of the early 1930s, stated that Pons's father died in the summer of 1930, only weeks before her Metropolitan audition.

5. The name is spelled variously as "D'Erly," "DeArly," and "Dearly," among other versions, depending on the context. For consistency, "D'Erly" is utilized throughout this book.

6. In addition to Lily's typical exaggeration of her youth (she would in fact have been twenty-three when she and Mesritz married, not sixteen as she claims here), conflicting information surrounds the date of the marriage. A 1968 copy of a marital-record entry in the *Registres des Actes de l'Etat Civil Déposés aux Archives de la Mairie* at Draguignan lists Pons as having married August Mesritz on 15 October 1930, a date that varies completely from every published account of their marriage and subsequent divorce. The Associated Press reported their divorce on 30 December 1933, prior to which the major newspapers had reported the impending divorce on 20–21 December 1933. The *Chicago Tribune*, among others, stated (20 December 1933) that the marriage had lasted seven years, whereas other press accounts cited ten or even eleven years, often giving Pons's age as nineteen when she married Mesritz. The October 1921 date that Pons gives in her notes is consistent with recollections of family members.

Two

1. The reviews quoted in this chapter are contained in a scrapbook owned by discographer Bill Park, to whom Pons gave it, through William Seward, as a remembrance of her friendship with the Park family. The author joins the editors in extending thanks to Mr. Park for providing access to the scrapbook for the preparation of this chapter.

2. Pons's own account of this event appears in Chapter 1, page 23.

3. From undated handwritten notes by Lily Pons. (Courtesy of the Ludecke-Pons Collection.)

4. *L'Alsace*, 27 November 1927.

5. Unidentified clipping, with the note "Montpellier, 1929/30" pencilled in the Pons scrapbook.

Three

1. Giacomo Lauri-Volpi, *Voci parallele* (Milan: Aldo Garzanti, 1955), pp. 12–21. This chapter is adapted from an unpublished English translation by George Nyklicek. (Courtesy of Thomas G. Kaufman.)

2. Actually, Galli-Curci's first Met Gilda took place on 26 November 1921, with Mario Chamlee as the Duke.

Four

1. This chapter was compiled by James A. Drake from his interviews with Nina Morgana Zirato in August 1972, February 1973, and June 1977.

2. Frederick H. Martens (1874–1932) wrote, among other works, *The Art of the Prima Donna and Concert Singer* (New York: Appleton and Company, 1923). His wife is listed among the attendees at a musicale sponsored by Mrs. E. Berry Wall, held at the American Women's Club in Paris on Wednesday, 21 November 1928. The names of attendees appear in newspaper accounts in the *Chicago Tribune* and *New York Herald*, 22 November 1928.

3. Bidú Sayão once asked Pons how she could hold the high notes "so much longer than anyone else did." According to Sayão, "Lily said that she had a trick for those notes. She sang her high notes in a type of falsetto, never in full voice." (Interview of Bidú Sayão by Kristin Beall Ludecke, October 1997.)

4. According to the audition card in the Metropolitan Opera Archives, Pons's audition took place on 29 March 1930. (Courtesy of Robert Tuggle, Director of Archives, Metropolitan Opera Association.)

5. Zirato's agreement with Pons is dated 26 March 1930. In it, Pons authorizes Zirato to receive a five-percent commission for "transacting for me all my business in connection with my artistic services . . . in the United States of America, Mexico, Cuba and Canada," but on the condition that he must "act in perfect agreement and accord with Maria Gay Zenatello, my advisor and general representative, as to terms and conditions of contracts to be signed by me with concert, operatic or other managers or impresarios." The agreement was to expire on 15 May 1935. (Courtesy of the Ludecke-Pons Collection.)

6. The Galli-Curci incident to which Morgana refers took place in the 1916–17 opera season and became for Gatti-Casazza, in the words of historian Robert Tuggle, "the greatest embarrassment of his professional career." In a May 1917 letter to Otto Kahn, Gatti was forced to account for his inability to secure Galli-Curci before the Chicago Opera had signed her and catapulted her to stardom as Gilda in *Rigoletto*:

   > Last year during the winter I received a letter from Cuba from the husband of Mme Galli-Curci, in which he asked me if there would be a possibility for an engagement for Mme Galli-Curci. . . . I replied that . . . there was no position for her. This is all! Since then I never heard anymore from Mme Galli-Curci and no one else approached me, neither directly nor indirectly, regarding this artist.

   The full text of the letter is quoted in Tuggle, *The Golden Age of Opera* (New York: Holt, Rinehart and Winston, 1983), p. 143.

7. A letter to Gatti-Casazza from Maria Gay, dated 20 October 1930 and now housed in the Metropolitan Opera Archives, reads in part: "We leave with Lily Pons on November 12 for New York on the *Ile de France*." Touching upon the commitment Gay had made to Zirato to oversee personally Pons's bel canto schooling, she reassured Gatti that Lily had "worked very hard during the summer with an Italian pianist, Zecchi, at our home in Verona and I can tell you that she's made great progress and you'll be very happy with her." The letter is quoted in Tuggle, *The Golden Age of Opera*, p. 220.

8. Morgana is probably referring to the 13 December 1930 performance of *Norma*, with Ponselle, Telva, Lauri-Volpi, and Tancredi Pasero as Oroveso. In the early 1970s, when Pons began making notes for the book that William Seward was planning to write about her career, she recalled the event: "My first performance was with Rosa Ponselle. She was in *Norma*. She was so beautiful [and] when I saw that [performance] I thought, 'What am I doing here?'" (Courtesy of the Ludecke-Pons Collection.)

9. Pelletier's first name was typically spelled "Wilfred" in Metropolitan Opera programs and in most U.S. newspapers. In his autobiography, however, he utilized the original spelling, Wilfrid. In keeping with Pelletier's apparent preference, the latter spelling is used throughout this book.

10. When speaking of Maria Galvany in interviews, Morgana invariably pronounced the singer's last name "Gal-va-*nee*," accenting the last syllable. When reminded that most opera commentators place the accent on the first syllable, Morgana replied curtly, "Well, perhaps Madame Arkel deliberately mispronounced Madame Galvany's name when she introduced me to her in 1910!"

11. Morgana's Victor test recordings were made in New York City on 29 April 1920 with Josef Pasternack as her accompanist. The only known copies are housed in the Stanford Archive of Recorded Sound. (The editors are grateful to William R. Moran, founder of the Stanford Archive, for providing the date and location of Morgana's Victor recording session.)

12. For a complete list of the singers who appeared as special guests, see *The New York Times*, 17 April 1966. The gala performance took place the previous evening.

13. Bruno Zirato died at the age of 88 on 28 November 1972. Pons's Philharmonic Hall concert appearance took place on 31 May 1972.
14. The program aired on 14 September 1974. (Courtesy of Merv Griffin Productions.) The "young admirer" that Morgana refers to here was William Seward.

Five

1. "Lily Pons Cheered at Metropolitan Debut," *Musical Courier*, 10 January 1931.

Six

1. Oscar Thompson, "*Lakmé* Returns to the Metropolitan with Pons as Star," *Musical America*, 25 February 1932.

Seven

1. Rose Heylbut, "Miracles Do Happen, Says Lily Pons," *The American Magazine*, October 1931, pp. 36–37, 156–158.

Eight

1. W. J. Henderson, *The Art of Singing* (New York: Dial Press, 1938), pp. 409–417. The article originally appeared in Henderson's column in the New York *Sun* on 7 February 1931.
2. New York *Sun*, 4 January 1931.

Nine

1. P. K. Thomajan, "A Lady Who Can Scrimshaw a Melody," *Literary Digest*, 31 January 1931, pp. 15–17.
2. Letter of Lily Pons to W. J. Henderson, 9 February 1931. (Courtesy of the Ludecke-Pons Collection.)

Ten

1. Lily Pons, with R. H. Wollstein, "Fame Overnight!," *The Etude*, June 1931, pp. 393–395.
2. Although Pons refers to operatic performances in Milan and elsewhere in Italy, the documentary record shows that she sang almost exclusively in France prior to her Metropolitan Opera debut. See Chapter 2, "Lily Pons in France," by Andrew Farkas.
3. In most other sources, Pons gave her age as thirteen, rather than fourteen as she states here, when she entered the Conservatoire.

Eleven

1. Lily Pons, with Juliette Laine, "The Girl Who Wants to Sing," *The Etude*, November 1933, pp. 731–732.

Twelve

1. Rose Heylbut, "Profitable Vocal Study: A Conference with Lily Pons," *The Etude*, October 1943, pp. 631–634.

Thirteen

1. The typescript of this Hope agency press release is held in the Ludecke-Pons Collection. In the early 1970s, William Seward had proposed to write an article for *Opera News* using this material. Correspondence between Seward and Frank Merkling, editor of *Opera News* at the time, establishes that Seward prepared the piece, with Pons's direct assistance and approval, between February and April 1970. There is no correspondence from Seward or Merkling, however, to indicate why it was never published in *Opera News*.

Fourteen

1. Excerpted, with new introduction, from Paul Jackson, *Saturday Afternoons at the Old Met: The Metropolitan Opera Broadcasts, 1931–1950* (Portland, Oregon: Amadeus Press, 1992) and *Sign-off for the Old Met: The Metropolitan Opera Broadcasts, 1950–1966* (Portland, Oregon: Amadeus Press, 1997).
2. Quoted in William R. Moran, ed., *Herman Klein and The Gramophone* (Portland, Oregon: Amadeus Press, 1990), p. 504.
3. *Ibid.*, p. 507.
4. *Ibid.*, p. 534.

Fifteen

1. Jesse L. Lasky with Don Weldon, *I Blow My Own Horn* (New York: Doubleday & Company, 1957), p. 248.
2. *The New York Times*, 22 April 1935, p. 14.
3. In his autobiography, *Echoes: Memoirs of André Kostelanetz*, Kostelanetz claims that Lily was experiencing vocal difficulties at the time the film was made. His rather extraordinary account of how these difficulties were overcome on the soundtrack recordings is reprinted in Chapter 16 of this book (see pages 138–139).
4. Quoted in *The New York Times*, 6 October 1935.
5. Richard B. Jewel with Vernon Harbin, *The RKO Story* (London: Octopus Books Limited, 1982), p. 91.
6. Quoted in *The New York Times*, 27 December 1936.
7. Jewel and Harbin, *The RKO Story*, p. 114.
8. *The (Toronto) Evening Telegram*, 1 September 1937.

9. From undated handwritten notes prepared by Lily Pons at the request of William Seward for the proposed biography he intended to co-author with Claire Lily Girardot, Pons's niece. (Courtesy of the Ludecke-Pons Collection.)

Sixteen

1. André Kostelanetz, in collaboration with Gloria Hammond, *Echoes: Memoirs of André Kostelanetz* (New York: Harcourt Brace Jovanovich, 1981), pp. 85–94.
2. Audio tape was certainly not available in 1935, but recording experts say that it might have been possible at the time to perform this now commonplace feat using optical film.

Seventeen

1. Excerpted and condensed from Kostelanetz and Hammond, *Echoes: Memoirs of André Kostelanetz*, pp. 129–175.
2. Lorenzo (Larry) Malfatti, founder and associate artistic director of the Opera Theater of Lucca, Italy, and professor emeritus of music at the Cincinnati Conservatory of Music, was chosen by Kostelanetz and Pons to sing at their Christmas concert in Calcutta in December 1944. "Unbeknownst to me," Malfatti told Kristin Beall Ludecke in a 1997 interview, "my commanding officers, Col. John Trutter and Walter Galyon, had arranged a sort of secret audition for me" by inviting Pons and Kostelanetz to one of Malfatti's solo engagements with the U.S. Army Concert Band. After the Christmas concert in Calcutta, Lily and André encouraged Malfatti to audition at the Juilliard School, where he was awarded a merit scholarship. Kostelanetz and Pons continued to guide his study, recommending him to Mack Harrell and the legendary baritone Giuseppe de Luca for further coaching. With Aaron Copland, David Diamond, and Lee Hoiby, Malfatti became one of the first Americans to win the Fulbright Award; from there, he began a professional career in opera and also sang on radio. Years later, Malfatti would learn that Kostelanetz and Pons had paid for most of his schooling.

Eighteen

1. Arthur Rubinstein, *My Many Years* (New York: Alfred A. Knopf, 1980), p. 447.
2. Charles O'Connell, *The Other Side of the Record* (New York: Alfred A. Knopf, 1947), pp. 17–33.

Nineteen

1. Mary Jane Matz, "Silver Gilt for Lily," *Opera News*, 9 January 1956, pp. 5–7.

Twenty

1. Irving Kolodin, "The Legendary Lily," *The Saturday Review*, 24 June 1972, p. 76.

Twenty-One

1. Compiled from an interview with Edgar Vincent by Kristin Beall Ludecke, August 1997.

Twenty-Two

1. Francis Robinson, "Lily Pons: 13 April 1898–13 February 1976," *Opera News*, 3 April 1976, pp. 38–39.

Twenty-Three

1. Lanfranco Rasponi, *The Last Prima Donnas* (New York: Alfred A. Knopf, 1982), pp. 423–430.

2. The television special to which Rasponi refers was first reported by the *Dallas Times Herald* in a feature story on 16 July 1972. The documentary, written and directed by Charles Blackman, former associate conductor of the Dallas Symphony Orchestra, was to be released by Blackman's own company, Charos Productions, with Pons's and Kostelanetz's cooperation. The resulting film, which contained excerpts of Lily's 1972 Philharmonic Hall concert, was neither aired nor released. Blackman, still living in Dallas at this writing (1997), owns the film footage as well as the rights to its release.

3. Pons did, however, sing the Queen of the Night in her homeland in 1928, before she came to the attention of the Metropolitan management. See Chapter 2, "Lily Pons in France."

Lily Pons:
A Selected Bibliography

Andrew Farkas

$\mathcal{A}$ S IS THE CASE with most singers of world renown, Lily Pons achieved an artistic stature during her career that obliged other biographers and auto-biographers to mention her presence in the life and career of her contemporaries. Thus, inevitably, Pons is often referred to in the musical and biographical literature, but because of the near-obligatory inclusion of Lily Pons's name in biographical dictionaries and other reference works dealing with opera and its practitioners, publications of this type would be too numerous to list and thus are omitted from this selected bibliography. Only those titles that mention her in a context of some significance are listed here.

Aguilar, Paco. *A orillas de la musica.* Buenos Aires: Editorial Losada, 1944.

Benton, Joseph. *Oklahoma Tenor: Musical Memoires of Giuseppe Bentonelli.* Norman, Okla.: University of Oklahoma, 1973.

Björling, Anna-Lisa, and Andrew Farkas. *Jussi.* Portland, Ore.: Amadeus Press, 1996.

Bloomfield, Arthur. *50 Years of the San Francisco Opera.* San Francisco: San Francisco Book Company, 1972.

Briggs, John. *Requiem for a Yellow Brick Brewery.* Boston: Little, Brown and Company, 1969.

Brockway, Wallace, and Herbert Weinstock. *The World of Opera.* N.p.: Pantheon Books, 1962.

Celletti, Rodolfo. *Le grandi voci.* Rome: Istituto per La Collaborazione Culturale, 1964.

Current Biography. New York: Wilson, 1944.

Davidson, Gladys. *Opera Biographies.* London: W. Laurie, 1955.

Davis, Ronald L. *Opera in Chicago.* New York: Appleton-Century, 1966.

Dizikes, John. *Opera in America: A Cultural History.* New Haven, Conn.: Yale University Press, 1993.

Domingo, Plácido. *My First Forty Years.* New York: Alfred A. Knopf, 1983.

Douglas, Nigel. *More Legendary Voices.* London: André Deutsch, 1994.

Drake, James A. *Richard Tucker.* New York: Dutton, 1984.

———. *Rosa Ponselle: A Centenary Biography.* Portland, Ore.: Amadeus Press, 1997.

Eaton, Quaintance. *Opera Caravan.* London: Calder, 1957.

———. *The Miracle of the Met.* New York, Meredith, 1968.

Emmons, Shirlee. *Tristanissimo.* New York: Schirmer, 1990.

Ewen, David. *Living Musicians.* New York: H. W. Wilson, 1940.

———. *Men and Women Who Make Music.* New York: Thomas Y. Crowell, 1939.

———. *Musicians Since 1900: Performers in Concert and Opera.* New York: H. W. Wilson, 1978.

Farrar, Geraldine. *Such Sweet Compulsion: The Autobiography of Geraldine Farrar.* New York: The Greystone Press, 1938.

———. *All Good Greetings.* Pittsburgh: University of Pittsburgh Press, 1991.

Fitzgerald, Gerald. *Annals of the Metropolitan Opera: Chronology 1883–1985.* 2 vols. Boston: The Metropolitan Opera Guild/G. K. Hall, 1989.

Flanner, Janet. *An American in Paris: Profile of an Interlude Between Two Wars.* New York: Simon and Schuster, 1940.

Gatti-Casazza, Giulio. *Memories of the Opera.* New York: Charles Scribner's Sons, 1941.

Gigli, Beniamino. *Memoirs.* Translated by Darina Silone. London: Cassell, 1957.

Harvith, John, and Susan Edwards Harvith, eds. *Edison, Musicians and the Phonograph: A Century in Retrospect.* New York: Greenwood Press, 1986.

Henderson, William James. *The Art of Singing.* New York: The Dial Press, 1938.

Herman, Robert. *The Greater Miami Opera: From Shoestring to Showpiece, 1941–1985.* Miami: GMOA, 1985.

Jackson, Paul. *Saturday Afternoons at the Old Met.* Portland, Ore.: Amadeus Press, 1992.

———. *Sign-off for the Old Met.* Portland, Ore.: Amadeus Press, 1997.

Kesting, Jürgen. *Die grossen Sänger.* 3 vols. Düsseldorf: Claassen, 1986.

Kolodin, Irving. *The Story of the Metropolitan Opera, 1883–1950.* New York: Alfred A. Knopf, 1953.

———. *The Metropolitan Opera, 1883–1966: A Candid History.* New York: Alfred A. Knopf, 1968.

Kostelanetz, André, and Gloria Hammond. *Echoes: Memoirs of André Kostelanetz.* New York: Harcourt Brace Jovanovich, 1981.

Lamparski, Richard. *Whatever became of . . . ?* 2nd series. New York: Crown, 1968.

Lauri-Volpi, Giacomo. *Voci parallele.* Milan: Aldo Garzanti, 1955.

Levy, Alan. *The Bluebird of Happiness: The Memoirs of Jan Peerce.* New York: Harper & Row, 1976.

Matz, Mary Jane. *Opera Stars in the Sun*. New York: Farrar, Straus & Cudahy, 1955.

Mayer, Martin. *The Met: One Hundred Years of Grand Opera*. New York: Simon and Schuster, 1983.

Mercer, Ruby. *The Tenor of His Time: Edward Johnson of the Met*. Vancouver, B.C.: Clarke, Irwin, 1976.

Merkling, Frank. *The Golden Horseshoe*. New York: Viking, 1965.

Merrill, Robert. *Once More From the Beginning*. New York: Macmillan, 1965.

Mordden, Ethan. *Opera Anecdotes*. New York: Oxford University Press, 1985.

Noble, Helen. *Life with the Metropolitan*. New York: G. B. Putnam's Sons, 1954.

O'Connell, Charles. *The Other Side of the Record*. New York: Alfred A. Knopf, 1947. Reprint, Westport, Conn.: Greenwood Press, 1970.

Pahlen, Kurt. *Great Singers From the Seventeenth Century to the Present Day*. Translated by Oliver Coburn. New York: Stein and Day, 1974.

Patrón Marchand, Miguel. *100 grandes cantantes del pasado*. Santiago: Andrès Bello, 1990.

Pelletier, Wilfrid. *Une symphonie inachevée. . .* Ottawa: Leméac, 1972.

Pleasants, Henry. *The Great Singers: From Jenny Lind and Caruso to Callas and Pavarotti*. London: Victor Gollancz, 1971.

Ponselle, Rosa, and James A. Drake. *Ponselle: A Singer's Life*. Garden City, N.Y.: Doubleday, 1982.

Rasponi, Lanfranco. *The Last Prima Donnas*. New York: Alfred A. Knopf, 1982.

Rosenthal, Harold. *Sopranos of Today*. London: Calder, 1956.

———. *Two Centuries of Opera at Covent Garden*. London: Putnam, 1958.

Rushmore, Robert. *The Singing Voice*. New York: Dodd, Mead, 1971.

Shaman, William, William J. Collins, and Calvin M. Goodwin. *EJS: Discography of the Edward J. Smith Recordings: "The Golden Age of Opera," 1956–1971*. Westport, Conn.: Greenwood Press, 1994.

Sills, Beverly. *Bubbles: A Self-Portrait*. Indianapolis: Bobbs-Merrill, 1976.

———. *Bubbles: An Encore*. Indianapolis: Grosset & Dunlap, 1981.

Sills, Beverly, and Lawrence Linderman. *Beverly: An Autobiography*. New York: Bantam, 1987.

Simpson, Harold. *Singers to Remember*. Lingfield: Oakwood Press, [1974].

Steane, J. B. *The Grand Tradition: Seventy Years of Singing on Record*. London: Gerald Duckworth & Company, 1974. Reprint, Portland, Ore.: Amadeus Press, 1993.

Taubman, H. Howard. *Opera Front and Back*. New York, Charles Scribner's Sons, 1938.

———. *The Pleasure of Their Company*. Portland, Ore.: Amadeus Press, 1994.

Tuggle, Robert. *The Golden Age of Opera*. New York: Holt, Rinehart and Winston, 1983.

Valenti Ferro, Enzo. *Las voces: Teatro Colón, 1908–1982*. Buenos Aires: Arte Gaglianone, 1983.

Walsh, T. J. *Monte Carlo Opera 1910–1951*. Kilkenny: Boethius Press, 1986.

Weinstat, Hertzel, and Bert Wechsler. *Dear Rogue: A Biography of the American Baritone Lawrence Tibbett*. Portland, Ore.: Amadeus Press, 1996.

Selected Periodicals

(Note: The + sign after pagination indicates that the article is concluded elsewhere in the magazine issue.)

"Another View." *Opera News* 57 (5 December 1992): 41.

Baird, J. E. "Coming Through the Air." *Life With Music* 2 (May 1949): 16–18+.

Beatty, J. "Hitting the High Notes in Cooking; Lily Pons Invites You to Her Favorite Dinner." *American Magazine* 132 (December 1941): 46–48+.

"Biographical Note." *Musical America* 73 (October 1953): 13.

"Biographical Sketch." *Musical America* 76 (1 January 1956): 4.

Bronson, A. "Met to Fete Lily Pons With Gala; Only Femme Star for 25-Year Run." *Variety* 201 (21 December 1955): 52.

Coleman, E. "Petite But Permanent Pons." *Theatre Arts* 40 (March 1956): 82.

"Country Life in Her Norman Farmhouse at Silvermine, Connecticut." *House and Garden* 73 (January 1938): 41–43.

Desbordes, J. "Lily Pons, Chanteuse." *Les Annales Politiques et Litteraires* 102 (11 May 1934): 506.

d'Houville, G. "Lily Pons dans La Femme en Cage." *Revue des Deux Mondes* 45 (15 May 1938): 458–459.

"Durable Lily." *Time* 60 (14 July 1952): 57.

"Durable Lily Pons." *Newsweek* 47 (16 January 1956): 50+.

Eaton, Q. "Petite Prima Donna Idol of Thousands." *Musical America* 54 (10 April 1934): 6–7.

Evans, W. "Set Your Home to Music: Interview." *Better Homes and Gardens* 20 (January 1942): 38–39+.

Eyer, R. "Metropolitan Honors Lily Pons on Silver Anniversary." *Musical America* 76 (15 January 1956): 3.

"Fashion With an Operatic Flair." *Holiday* 25 (February 1959): 70–73.

Fitzgerald, G. "Lily." *Opera News* 37 (10 February 1973): 16–19.

"The France I Love." *American Magazine* 156 (July 1953): 38–41+.

Frost, R. "Lily Pons: Diva in Art." *Art News* 45 (August 1946): 34–37.

Gardner, M. "Leetle Leely; Profitable U.S. Corporation." *Saturday Evening Post* 215 (24 April 1943): 9–11+ and 215 (1 May 1943): 16–17+.

Heylbut, R. "Miracles Do Happen, Says Lily Pons." *American Magazine* 112 (October 1931): 36–37+.

———. "Profitable Vocal Study." *Etude* 61 (October 1943): 631–634.

———. "New Thoughts on Voice Care." *Etude* 64 (May 1946): 264+.

Hughes, C. "Pons and Kostelanetz, First Family of Music." *Coronet* 27 (April 1950): 130–134.

"I Live in the Country." *Arts and Decoration* 44 (February 1936): 6–9+.

Jellinek, G. "Lily Pons, Coloratura Assoluta." *Stereo Review* 38 (May 1997): 114.

Kolodin, I. "Music to My Ears." *Saturday Review* 39 (21 January 1956): 44.

———. "The Legendary Lily." *Saturday Review* 55 (24 June 1972): 76.

Kostelanetz, A. "Lily's Bedroom." *House and Garden* 85 (January 1944): 37–39+.

Kramer, A. W. "Discovery of Lily Pons." *Outlook* 158 (6 May 1931): 21.

Landry, R. J. "Lily Pons, 68, Queen of Geriatric Divas." *Variety* 267 (7 June 1972): 2+.

"Lily Pons." *Musical Courier* 145 (15 February 1952): 31.

"Lily Pons—Gala Performance." *Musical Courier* 153 (15 January 1956): 10–11.

"Lily Pons nie zyje." *Ruch Muzyczny* 20 (no. 10, 1976): 18.

"Lily Pons, 1904–1976." *Buenos Aires Musical* 31 (no. 485, 1976): 1+.

"Lily Pons's New Film Uses a New Route to an Old End." *Newsweek* 6 (7 December 1935): 41.

"Lily Pons' New York Apartment." *House Beautiful* 79 (May 1937): 58–59+.

"Lily Pons 'Studied' for Video by Dallas Firm." *Variety* 265 (29 December 1971): 2.

"Lily Pons Talks About Beauty." *Pictorial Review* 34 (November 1932): 48.

"Lily Pons, 28 Years at Met Opera, Dies at 71; Made Three Films." *Variety* 282 (18 February 1976): 110.

"Lily's Back." *Time* 48 (25 November 1946): 63.

"Lovely . . . Engaged . . . Uses Pons." *High Fidelity* 4 (July 1954): 39.

Matz, M. J. "Silver Gilt for Lily." *Opera News* 20 (9 January 1956): 4–7.

"Metropolitan Honors Lily Pons on Silver Anniversary." *Musical America* 76 (15 January 1956): 3.

Miller, P. L. "Lily Pons in Retrospect; Coloratura Assoluta." *American Record Guide* 40 (May 1977): 49–50.

"Music Among the Stars." *Arts and Decoration* 47 (December 1937): 16+.

Needleman, J. "On Tour: Lily Pons, Emil Niosi, and Wells Hively—Memories of Emil Niosi." *Flutist Quarterly* 14 (Winter 1989): 27.

"New Look at Lily." *Life* 29 (23 October 1950): 52.

"New Opera Star." *Woman's Journal* 16 (February 1931): 5.

"Obituary." *Newsweek* 87 (23 February 1976): 91.

"Obituary." *Opera News* 40 (3 April 1976): 38–39.

"Obituary." *Opera* 27 (April 1976): 336–337.

"Obituary." *Time* 107 (23 February 1976): 61.

"Now It Is 'Dr. Pons'." *Voice* 6 (May–June 1950): 2.

Park, B. "Lily Pons" and "A Lily Pons Discography." *The Record Collector* 13, no. 11–12 (April 1961): 245–271.

"Personalities: Awarded Hunter College's President's Medal for Distinguished Achievement." *Musical America* 76 (1 January 1956): 13.

Phillips, J. C. "Portrait of a Singer." *Collier's* 88 (26 December 1931): 21+.

Pons, L. "A Plea for Better U.S. Stage and Concert Facilities." *Variety* 181 (3 January 1951): 272.

———. "The Birthday Party That Shaped My Life." *McCall's* 83 (January 1956): 20+.

———. "Day I'd Like to Live Over." *Good Housekeeping* 142 (April 1956): 209.

———. "The Coloratura—A Rara Avis?" *Music Clubs Magazine* 36 (November 1956): 8+.

———. "From Piano to Song." *Music Journal* 18 (January 1960): 18+.

Pons, L., with J. Laine. "The Girl Who Wants to Sing." *Etude* 51 (November 1933): 731–732.

Pons, L., with R. H. Wollstein. "Fame Overnight!" *Etude* 49 (June 1931): 393–394.

Pringle, H. F. "Little Lily." *Collier's* 99 (22 May 1937): 36+.

Rasponi, L., ed. "Post-War Engagement in Monte Carlo." *Travel* 87 (August 1946): 26–27+.

Robinson, F. "Lily Pons: 13 April 1898–13 February 1976." *Opera News* 40 (3 April 1976): 38–39.

Rosenfield, J. "Texas Gusher." *Opera News* 27 (5 January 1963): 34.

Sabine, L. "That Elusive Something; Interview." *Independent Woman* 13 (March 1934): 71.

Schauensee, M. de. "Robin Hood Dell Opens Brotherly Love Summer." *Musical America* 72 (July 1952): 17.

Schaumkell, C. D. "In Memoriam Lily Pons." *Opernwelt* no. 4 (April 1976): 53.

Schonberg, H. C. "Facing the Music. (Lily Pons Taking Her First Ballet Lesson)." *Musical Courier* 143 (1 February 1951): 4.

"Sentimental and Brisk; Recording of Conversation Piece." *New Yorker* 26 (3 February 1951): 26–27.

Slater, M. "Music on the Peninsula." *Opera and Concert* 15 (December 1950): 32.

Smith, C. "Opera in San Francisco." *Musical America* 71 (1 November 1951): 24.

"Soul! Color! Chic!" *Newsweek* 46 (25 July 1955): 26.

Sutton, H. "Tours for Divas." *Saturday Review* 37 (4 September 1954): 35.

"Thirteen for Lily." *Musical America* 74 (1 February 1954): 6.

Thomajan, P. K. "A Lady Who Can Scrimshaw a Melody." *Literary Digest* 108 (31 January 1931): 15+.

———. "Lily Pons, a Temperament-Silhouette." *Musician* 40 (January 1935): 5.

"Triller in Uniform." *Time* 36 (30 December 1940): 30–31.

"Where Are They Now?" *Newsweek* 64 (26 October 1964): 26.

Woolf, S. J. "Lily Pons in a New Role: Interview." *New York Times Magazine* (5 January 1941): 9+.

The Films of Lily Pons

James B. McPherson

I Dream Too Much

RKO Radio Pictures, Inc.
Working title: *Love Song*
Length: 97 minutes
New York premiere: Radio City Music Hall, 28 November 1935
Producer: Pandro S. Berman
Director: John Cromwell
Story: Elsie Finn, David G. Wittels
Screenplay: James Gow, Edmund H. North
Music director: Max Steiner
Original songs: Dorothy Fields, Jerome Kern
The cast:

Annette Monard . . . . Lily Pons
Jonathan Street . . . . Henry Fonda
Roger Briggs . . . . Eric Blore
Paul Darcy . . . . Osgood Perkins
Hubert Dilley . . . . Lucien Littlefield
Gwendolyn Dilley . . . . Lucille Ball
Darcy's pianist . . . . Mischa Auer
Uncle Tito . . . . Paul Porcasi
Boy on merry-go-round . . . . . . Scott Beckett
Mrs. Dilley . . . . Esther Dale
Jail official . . . . Etienne Girardot
Chef François . . . . Billy Gilbert (unbilled)

That Girl from Paris

RKO Radio Pictures, Inc.
Working title: *Street Girl*
Length: 105 minutes
New York premiere: Radio City Music Hall, 31 December 1936
Producer: Pandro S. Berman
Director: Leigh Jason
Story: Jane Murfin ("suggested by" a story in *Young's Magazine*)
Adaptation: Joseph A. Fields
Screenplay: P. J. Wolfson, Dorothy Yost
Music director: Nathaniel Shilkret
Original songs: Edward Heyman, Arthur Schwartz
The cast:

Nicole "Nikki" Martin	Lily Pons
Whammo Lonsdale	Jack Oakie
Windy McLean	Gene Raymond
"Hammy" Hammacher	Herman Bing
Butch	Mischa Auer
Claire Williams	Lucille Ball
Frank	Frank Jenks
Coat-room girl	Patricia Wilder
Reporter	Vinton Haworth
Immigration officer	Willard Robertson
Paul DeVry	Gregory Gaye
Nikki's uncle	Ferdinand Gottschalk
Marie, Nikki's maid	Rafaela Ottiano
Purser	Harry Jans
Ship's captain	Landers Stevens
Photographer	Edward Price
Justice of the Peace	Alec Craig
Opera conductor	André Kostelanetz

Hitting a New High

RKO Radio Pictures, Inc.
Working title: *It Never Happened Before*
Length: 85 minutes
New York premiere: Rivoli, 24 December 1937
Producer: Jesse L. Lasky
Director: Raoul Walsh
Story: Robert Harari, Maxwell Shane

Screenplay: Gertrude Purcell, John Twist
Music director: André Kostelanetz
Original songs: Harold Adamson, Jimmy McHugh
The cast:

Suzette/Oogahunga .... Lily Pons
Corny Davis .... Jack Oakie
Jimmy James .... John Howard
Cedric Cosmo .... Eric Blore
Lucius B. Blynn .... Edward Everett Horton
Andreas Mazzini .... Eduardo Ciannelli
Luis Marlo .... Luis Alberni
Carter Haig .... Jack Arnold (formerly Vinton Haworth)
Jevons .... Leonard Carcy

Carnegie Hall

Federal Films, released by United Artists
Length: 136 minutes
New York premiere: simultaneously at Winter Garden and Park Avenue,
    2 May 1947
Producers: Boris Morros, William LeBaron
Director: Edgar G. Ulmer
Story: Seena Owen
Screenplay: Karl Kamb
Music adviser: Sigmund Krumgold
The cast:

Nora Ryan .... Marsha Hunt
Tony Salerno, Jr. .... William Prince
John Donovan .... Frank McHugh
Ruth Haines .... Martha O'Driscoll
Tony Salerno, Sr. .... Hans Yaray
Olin Downes .... Olin Downes
Anton Tribik .... Joseph Buloff
Henry .... Emile Boreo
Tchaikovsky .... Alfonso D'Artega
Walter Damrosch .... Walter Damrosch

Guest artists, in order of appearance: Bruno Walter, Lily Pons, Gregor Piatigorsky, Risë Stevens, Artur Rodzinski, Arthur Rubinstein, Jan Peerce, Ezio Pinza, Vaughn Monroe, Jascha Heifetz, Fritz Reiner, Leopold Stokowski, Harry James.

In 1989, Turner Home Entertainment released *I Dream Too Much* and *That Girl from Paris* on video as part of "The Lucille Ball Signature Collection." (What unwary Lucy fans thought on discovering that Ball's screen time in the first film amounts to less than five minutes can only be imagined.) In 1995, the New York-based Bel Canto Society released an unauthorized duplication of *Carnegie Hall*. According to the Society: "Original 1947 versions of *Carnegie Hall* differed from one another. Some were released with certain musical selections abridged or omitted; some omitted portions of dialog. We pieced together our print from four sources to include all the material." The video plays for 144 minutes, eight minutes longer than the film's official running time. To the best of this writer's knowledge, *Hitting a New High* has never been made available on video in either an authorized or a pirated edition.

The Recorded Legacy
of Lily Pons

George Jellinek

⊙§§~ Longtime host of the nationally syndicated weekly program "The Vocal Scene," musicologist George Jellinek is author of *History Through the Opera Glass* (1994) and *Callas, Portrait of a Prima Donna* (1960), as well as numerous articles contributed over the years to *The New York Times*, *Stereo Review*, *The Yale Review*, *Opera News*, and other major periodicals. He is also a Grammy Award winner.

In his contribution to this book, Jellinek traces the long career of Lily Pons through her numerous commercial recordings. The discography by Bill Park that follows serves as a companion to Jellinek's analysis, providing the details on Pons's numerous recordings for Odeon, Victor/ H.M.V., and Columbia.

*T*HERE WAS the generation of the legendary nightingales—Sembrich, Melba, Tetrazzini, Galli-Curci, and Hempel—whose accomplishments are impressively documented on records. Then Joan Sutherland emerged on the scene in the late 1950s, setting new standards. In the intervening quarter century or so, the dominant singer in what is generally considered the coloratura soprano repertoire was Lily Pons. She was by no means the best among her contemporaries. As Pons was achieving international prominence, the spectacular Maria Ivogün (1891–1987) was already ending her career. But there were Toti dal Monte (1893–1975) and Lina Pagliughi (1907–1980) in Italy and Erna Berger (1900–1987) in Germany, outstanding singers but lacking the sparkle and theatrical presence that turned Lily Pons into a media-mesmerizing *star*. Contemporary listeners, mindful of that visual image, frequently found her failings as a singer relatively unimportant. Future generations unacquainted with the Pons persona will, of course, judge her singing through a clearer and more objective lens.

It must be kept in mind that when Pons began her career in the French provinces in 1927, she was already thirty years old, a trained and virtually "finished" artist. Her first recordings (for French Odeon in 1928–29) disclose a somewhat fragile tone of innate girlishness and a bravura technique manipulated with playful ease. In the *Rigoletto* duet with the mellow tenor of Enrico di Mazzei, her Italian is still a bit tentative, but her native language choices show much more promise. "Air de Rosine" from *Le barbier de Séville* is full of infectious joy, freely embellished, with flights up to an E-natural. Her first recording of Olympia's "Doll Song" from *Les contes d'Hoffmann* also reveals splendid coloratura facility, though she leaves a few passages in the *Mireille* Waltz rather indistinct. A suggested expansion of her repertoire is indicated by her early Odeon recordings of arias from *Les noces de Figaro* and *La bohème*, which are performed with impressive style and musicality but with less than pinpoint intonation. Pons's first recordings from *Lakmé*, her future signature role, also date from 1929. Her tone is still somewhat brittle and the trills are unspectacular, but the expression is sensitively shaded, the high E-natural is easily negotiated, and the cleanly articulated staccatos, which continued to distinguish her singing, are firmly in place.

The Victor Recordings

In 1930 Lily Pons came to America with a rejuvenated birth year (1904), attended by her enthusiastic mentors, Maria Gay and Giovanni Zenatello, and with a bright prospect for a Metropolitan audition. Actually, the Victor Company (later RCA Victor) signed up the vivacious newcomer on the basis of a test recording; the Metropolitan contract followed a few days later, on 29 March 1930.

Pons remained under contract to Victor for the next ten years. Never an adventurous opera singer, nor one to expose herself in unfamiliar repertoire, Lily Pons limited herself to only ten roles during her long career with the Metropolitan Opera, although she did impersonate her special favorites (Lucia, Lakmé, Gilda, Rosina) on more than two hundred occasions in the house and on tour. The abbreviated Mad Scene from *Lucia di Lammermoor*, recorded in 1930, transposed upward, now boasts a climactic high F; her Italian sounds more assured, the trills are facile, scale passages are, if not pearly, entirely fluent, and the conventional embellishments are neatly executed. The two arias from *Lakmé*, also recorded in 1930, display brilliant E-naturals and a midrange noticeably fuller than was exhibited on the earlier Odeons. Gilda's two arias reveal the proper contrasts: "Tutte le feste" is pleadingly inflected, and "Caro nome," with its customary concert ending culminating in a high E-natural, displays her trademark accurate staccatos. These recordings date from 1931. Some years later (1940), in the duet "Il nome vostro ditemi," she was paired with the mellow baritone of Giuseppe de Luca, who had briefly returned to the Metropolitan at age sixty-four. Their voices blend admirably, as they do on the duet from Rossini's *Il barbiere di Siviglia*, an equally happy product of that same 1940 session.

In 1935 she recorded Rosina's "Una voce poco fa," this time in virtually idiomatic Italian, with clean attacks and carefree embellishments. Her whole approach radiates joyousness, retailing her girlish spirit of 1929 but now enriched by a more solid tone. A firm high F shines over it all: a triumphant note her audiences by then were accustomed to hear and appreciate.

The role of the Queen of Shemakha in Nikolai Rimsky-Korsakov's *Le coq d'or* was added to Pons's Metropolitan repertoire in 1937. Three years later she recorded for Victor the familiar "Hymne au soleil" (Hymn to the Sun) at a somewhat hurried tempo, dictated by the limitations of the 78 rpm disc. Otherwise, hers is a conventional treatment decorated with a fanciful cadenza rising to a high F. Pons's last year for Victor also produced a virtuosic "Ombre légère" from *Dinorah*, a Meyerbeer opera that neither the Metropolitan nor any other company produced in those years. Her *Dinorah* disc displays clean attacks, feathery lightness, lightning staccatos—the works. On a more restrained side, and somewhat surprisingly for 1940, came the Handel aria "Alma mia" from *Floridante* with a chamber-group backing.

Pons's growing concert repertoire makes up much of the rest of her Victor recordings. They fall into two categories: French songs and coloratura showpieces. Sung in her favorite high keys, Debussy's "Green" and "Mandoline" perfectly suited her vocal personality, as did "Il pleure dans mon coeur" (which was released for the first time on the RCA Victor compact disc *Lily Pons: Donizetti -

Verdi - Debussy - Rossini - Delibes, 09026-61411-1). Fauré's "Les roses d'Ispahan," tastefully and stylishly done, rounds out this part of her recorded encores. The remaining recordings are devoted to coloratura crowd pleasers highlighting her stratospheric notes, Victorian fare by Bishop and Benedict featuring her fast staccatos with some flute-accompanied warblings, and a couple of even more forgettable items.

The 1940 Victor release of "Je suis Titania" from Thomas's *Mignon* is a souvenir of the Metropolitan's revival of that opera. The flighty Philine, a role Pons did not retain very long, was nonetheless perfectly suited to her vivacious stage personality.

A CD released by the Metropolitan Opera Guild, entitled *Portraits in Memory* (MET 213), contains two previously unreleased items from the soprano's Victor years: Debussy's "Fantoches" and Rossini's "La promessa."

The Columbia Recordings

In late 1940 Lily Pons ended her ten-year association with the Victor Company and followed her husband, conductor André Kostelanetz, into the Columbia fold. The erstwhile debutante had become a box-office bonanza, a concert favorite nationwide, and a budding movie star. The many demands on her services reduced her operatic appearances, but she did add an important new role to her repertoire: Marie in Donizetti's *La fille du régiment*, revived for her by the Metropolitan in the wartime year of 1940. It was a role that she triumphantly repeated in San Francisco and Chicago, and it served as her introduction as a Columbia recording artist—most appropriately on Bastille Day, 14 July 1941. The recording session featured four of Marie's arias. "Chacun le sait" finds Lily at her zestful and captivating best, and "Il faut partir" is done with touching simplicity. "Salut à la France!" shows some dubious intonation, but with its infectious patriotic zeal and daredevil embroideries, it recalls the excitement of the wartime years.

According to Bill Park's detailed discography, Lily Pons recorded 123 sides in the 78 rpm format for Columbia between 1941 and 1954. They contain souvenirs of her remaining operatic roles: two arias from Bellini's *La sonnambula*, one from Donizetti's *Linda di Chamounix*, and a new version of Titania's lively Polonaise from *Mignon*, not noticeably different from the earlier one. Eventually, the time came to re-record Lakmé's Bell Song (in November 1944), Gilda's two arias ("Caro nome" in November 1944 and "Tutte le feste" in April 1949), and Rosina's aria (December 1947), all triumphant mementos of her early years. The introduction of the Bell Song offers a great downward staccato scale, and the E-natural is firmly placed. A few smudged passages aside, the new version holds up well.

With Donizetti's *Lucia* as Pons's paramount operatic vehicle, it was understandable that Columbia paid special attention to that role during her tenure with the company. "Regnava nel silenzio" was recorded by her for the first time ever in 1942: tastefully but not excessively ornamented, with decent but unspectacular trills. The Mad Scene appeared first in its complete form on four 78 rpm sides in 1944. The key is transposed upward, with the high F in place. Without evoking the Callas intensity and the Sutherland virtuosity, Pons gives a decent performance in which the recitative passages are meaningfully projected, the rhythms are elastic, and the cabaletta is fearlessly executed. Her re-recording of Gilda's "Caro nome" is on the facile side, lacking interpretive nuance, and the later "Tutte le feste," alas, is spoiled by marginal flatting. She also recorded two arias from Bellini's *La sonnambula* in 1949, to complete the recorded documentation of all her stage roles; both arias were decently done but without meeting the level attained by later bel canto specialists.

Although not a stage role for Pons, Elvira's "Son vergin vezzosa" from *I puritani* was accomplished in April 1949—and effectively too, though with somewhat excessive embellishments. An interesting Columbia addition was Violetta's scene from *La traviata*'s first act. Pons knew the role but sang it on stage only in San Francisco in 1952. Her 1946 recording interpolates an E-flat in the opening section and, some dubious intonation aside, is a tastefully executed addition to her legacy. Her 1947 revisiting of an old favorite, Olympia's "Doll Song," resulted in some playful accelerandos, while Rosina's "Una voce poco fa" from the same session, still boasting her trademark fluent staccatos, fails to equal the exactitude of her earlier versions.

André Kostelanetz was Pons's conductor at most of her Columbia sessions, but on 11 May 1942 she recorded a handful of Mozart arias under Bruno Walter. She did Cherubino's and Blondchen's arias in French, Constanze's "Ach, ich liebte" in Italian (she never recorded anything in German!), the violin-obbligatoed "L'amerò, sarò costante" from *Il re pastore* (something of a rarity in those days), and the Alleluia from Exultate Jubilate (K. 165). Guided by Walter's experienced hand, she was stylistically assured, neat, and precise in all instances, naturally rejoicing in the Queen of the Night's fearsome high staccatos in "Der Hölle Rache," which was also sung in French.

It was probably Kostelanetz, however, who introduced Pons to some appropriate Russian material. Queen Shemakhan's "Hymne au soleil" was revisited in 1947, but newly recorded were Rimsky-Korsakov's "Song of India" from *Sadko* in 1941 and the romance "The Nightingale and the Rose," also 1947. All these were done with tasteful coloratura flourishes; even Alabiev's showy "The Nightingale," in English this time, stayed well to this side of excess. She recorded two more Rachmaninoff songs in May 1950. "Oh, Cease Thy Singing, Maiden Fair" (Op. 4, No. 4) gets a tender, well-modulated treatment, while "Here Beauty Dwells" (Op. 21, No. 7), with its high tessitura, could have been written for her. In both songs, her intonation is more dependable than is evidenced in the earlier "Vocalise" (Op. 34, No. 14), recorded in 1947.

Toward the end of her recording career, Lily Pons participated in two complete recordings with the Metropolitan Opera ensemble. The first was *Die Fledermaus*, recorded in late 1950 and early 1951, more or less coinciding with Rudolf Bing's new production of the Johann Strauss classic. To put it mildly, that production's Broadway-oriented lyrics have not stood the test of time. A younger Pons could have been a delightful Adele—a French Adele, at any rate—but in this context she sounds uncomfortable. The second complete work, done in early 1954, was *Lucia di Lammermoor*, a signature role to the end—the role of her 1931 debut and the one she chose for her farewell 27 years later. Her singing provides fleeting moments of excitement, but the totality is disappointing.

In 1950, Pons recorded an LP of eleven Debussy songs (Columbia ML-2135). I can do no better than to echo the comments of a senior colleague, the late Philip L. Miller, in that period. He wrote: "Pons is sincere and earnest in her effort, and she deserves thanks for the unusual repertoire." Thanks to the CD explosion, the repertoire cited is no longer unusual, and Maggie Teyte and Gérard Souzay have given us superior renditions in this particular field. Lily Pons was not, essentially, a song recitalist; her concentration and special gifts lay elsewhere. Nonetheless, she did estimable work in this area (including pieces by Fauré, Duparc, and others), and the incredibly prolific Darius Milhaud apparently wrote four *Chansons de Ronsard* especially for her—"A cupidon," "A une fontaine," "Dieu vous garde," and "Tais-toi, babillarde," recorded in April 1947. They are exhibitionistic pieces in tribute to her shining top register. This period also featured a recording of one of her specialties, "Chère nuit" by Bachelet, with its delicately floated, sustained long phrases. It was one of the encores of her final "comeback" concert at Avery Fisher Hall.

The remainder of the Pons legacy is devoted to a variety of encore pieces like the bravura "Theme and Variations" of Proch (1944) and "Charmant oiseau" from David's *La perle du Brésil*, which was favored by the legendary divas of earlier generations; for her part, Pons combines playful ease and infectious charm in her 1945 recording of the piece. The charm quotient is even higher in "Les filles de Cadiz" from 1947, while Johann Strauss's "Le beau Danube bleu" loses precious little in translation. "Kiss Me Again" and "The Last Rose of Summer" take their place among her sure-fire American audience pleasers, alongside "Pretty Mocking Bird" and other aviary specialties.

Lily Pons was a phenomenon in a different—perhaps more innocent and optimistic—era. Her glory years were spent in America, and since she rarely came into contact with British musical life, she has been treated with condescension by British critics. She was not a perfect vocalist, but for this observer, who was lucky enough to enjoy her charm and vivacity onstage, she left an image forever engraved in memory.

A Lily Pons Discography

Compiled by Bill Park

THE LILY PONS DISCOGRAPHY is divided into three parts: records made for French Odeon (1928–29), American Victor/English and French H.M.V. (1930–40), and American Columbia (1941–54). This discography is a revised version of one that appeared in *The Record Collector* in April 1961.

The first numbers listed under "Catalog Number" are the original 78 rpm numbers (except for a few of the late Columbia recordings, which were issued on 33⅓ and 45 rpm only). The 45 rpm catalog numbers are marked with an asterisk (*) and the 33⅓ rpm with a dagger (†). Titles of selections are cited as they appeared on the original record labels.

Many of Pons's recordings have been issued on compact disc. The numbers given for compact discs refer to the CD collections listed at the end of the discography.

There are several people whom I wish to thank for their assistance in the compiling of this discography: John Pfeiffer and Bernadette Moore of BMG Records, Martine McCarthy and Jerry Thomas of Sony, Paul Gruber of the Metropolitan Opera, Tony Mobbs of EMI archives, Jim Cartwright, James A. Drake, Lawrence F. Holdridge, Raymond Horneman, Josh Leventhal, Kristin Beall Ludecke, William R. Moran, Ronald Seeliger, and certainly William Seward. Finally, I must express my appreciation to the lady who inspired the initial work in 1961 and who took a keen interest in it—Lily Pons. I have so many wonderful memories of Lily, first as the "superstar" who read and answered her fan mail, and later as a valued family friend.

Part One: The Odeon Recordings (1928–29)

Pressings from the Odeon masters were issued in America first on Columbia (C) and later on Decca (D). English issues from these masters were available on the Parlophone label.

Title	Composer	Date Recorded	Matrix Number	French Odeon Catalog No.	American Catalog No.	English Catalog No.	Compact Discs
1. *Le barbier de Séville*: Air de Rosine (Part 1)	Rossini	21 March 1929	KI-2278-1, -**2**	188.646 ORX-108†	(D) 20521	RO-20301	MET 213 VAIA 1125
2. *Le barbier de Séville*: Air de Rosine (Part 2)	Rossini	21 March 1929	KI-2279-1, -**2**	188.646 ORX-108†	(D) 20521	RO-20301	MET 213 VAIA 1125
3. *La bohème*: Entrée de Mimì (with di Mazzei)	Puccini	19 December 1928	XXP-6771-**1**	123.598	(D) PG-25854		MET 213 VAIA 1125
4. *La bohème*: O douce jeune fille (with di Mazzei)	Puccini	19 December 1928	XXP-6772-1, -**2**	123.598 ORX-112†	(D) PG-25854		VAIA 1125
5. *La bohème*: On m'appelle Mimì	Puccini	26 February 1929	XXP-6830-1, -2, -**3**	123.623	(C) G-9047-M	RO-20204	MET 213 VAIA 1125
6. *Les contes d'Hoffmann*: Les oiseaux dans la charmille	Offenbach	20 February 1929	KI-2221-1, -2, -**3**	188.642 OD-1013†	(D) 23016 (C) G-4054-M	RO-20255	GEMM CD 9415 MNA 38 MET 213 VA 1114 VAIA 1125
7. *L'enlèvement au Serail*: Air de Blondine	Mozart	6 July 1929	XXP-6925-1, -**2**	123.624 ORX-122†	(D) 29005	RO-20163	VAIA 1125
8. *La flûte enchantée*: Air de la Reine de la Nuit	Mozart	26 February 1929	KI-2229-**1**	188.644 OD-1013† ORX-122†	(D) PG-20522 (C) G-4054-M	RO-20153	VAIA 1125
9. *La flûte enchantée*: Air de Pamina	Mozart	26 February 1929	XXP-6831-1, -**2**	123.624		RO-20163	VAIA 1125

10. *Lakmé*: Pourquoi dans les grands bois?	Delibes	21 February 1929	KI-2204-1, -2, -**3**	188.640 OD-1013† ORX-111†	(D) 23014 (D) DL-4024† (D) ED-3513*	RO-20169	MET 213 VAIA 1125
11. *Lakmé*: Air des clochettes (Part 1)	Delibes	21 February 1929	KI-2205-**1**	188.641 OD-1013†	(D) 23015 (D) DL-4024† (D) ED-3513* (C) G-4056-M	RO-20280	MET 213 VAIA 1125
12. *Lakmé*: Air des clochettes (Part 2)	Delibes	21 February 1929	KI-2205-**1**, -**2**	188.641 OD-1013†	(D) 23015 (D) DL-4024† (D) ED-3513* (C) G-4056-M	RO-20280	MET 213 VAIA 1125
13. *Lakmé*: Dans la forêt près de nous	Delibes	21 February 1929	KI-2207-1, -**2**	188.640 OD-1013†	(D) 23014 (D) DL-4024† (D) ED-3513*	RO-20169	MET 213 VAIA 1125
14. *Mireille*: O légère hirondelle	Gounod	20 February 1929	KI-2199-1, -2, -**3**	188.642	(D) 23016 OD-1013† ORX-107†	RO-20255	GEMM CD 9415 MNA 38 MM 30446 VA 1114 VAIA 1125
15. *Les noces de Figaro*: Mon coeur soupire	Mozart	6 July 1929	KI-2480-1, -2, -**3**	188.644	PG-20522	RO-20153	MET 213 VAIA 1125
16. *Parysatis*: Le rossignol et la rose	Saint-Saëns	26 February 1929	KI-2276-1, -**2**	188.645	(D) 23017 (C) G-4074-M	RO-20187	GEMM CD 9415 MNA 38 MET 213 MM 30446 VA 1114 VAIA 1125
17. *Rigoletto*: T'amo! (with di Mazzei)	Verdi	19 December 1928	XXP-6769-1, -**2**	123.597	(D) PG-25853	RO-20342 PXO-1036	GEMM CD 9415 MNA 38 VA 1114 VAIA 1125

Title	Composer	Date Recorded	Matrix Number	French Odeon Catalog No.	American Catalog No.	English Catalog No.	Compact Discs
18. *Rigoletto*: Addio, addio (with di Mazzei)	Verdi	19 December 1928	XXP-6770-1, -<u>2</u>	123.597	(D) PG-25853	RO-20342 PXO-1036	GEMM CD 9415 MNA 38 VA 1114 VAIA 1125
19. *Rigoletto*: Air de Gilda	Verdi	26 February 1929	XXP-6832-1, -<u>2</u>	123.623 OD-1013†	(D) 29005 (C) G-9047-M	RO-20204	VAIA 1125
20. Les Variations de Proch	Proch	26 February 1929	KI-2277-<u>1</u>	188.645	(D) 23017 (C) G-4074-M	RO-20187	GEMM CD 9415 MNA 38 VA 1114 VAIA 1125

Part Two: Victor/English and French H.M.V. (1930–40)

Several recordings for the American Victor Company were issued in England on H.M.V. Four sides (*La flûte enchantée*/"Lo! Here the Gentle Lark" and "Una voce poco fa" from *Il barbiere di Siviglia*) were recorded by English H.M.V. Five titles were recorded by French H.M.V. but were never released commercially (although one is now available on CD).

For Pons's recordings of "Ardon gl'incensi" and "Spargi d'amaro pianto" from *Lucia* and "Caro nome" and "Tutte le feste" from *Rigoletto*, two different takes were published for prewar and postwar 78 rpm pressings: similarly, different takes appear on the various CD releases of these works.

Title	Composer	Conductor or Accompanist	Date Recorded	Matrix Number	American Catalog No.	English Catalog No.	Compact Discs
1. A des oiseaux	Huë	LaForge (pf)	26 September 1938	BS-027224-<u>1</u>, -2, -3	1918 (in M-599) CBL-101†		

	Composer	Performers	Date	Matrix	78 rpm	Reissues
2. *Alessandro*: Lusinghe più care	Handel	with Renaissance Quintet	9 March 1940	BS-047793-**1**, -2	2151 (in M-756) DA-1800 CBL-101† VIC-1473†	
3. *Il barbiere di Siviglia*: Una voce poco fa (Part 1)	Rossini	Barbirolli (orch.)	25 May 1935	2-EA-1492-1	8870 DB-2501	GEMM CD 9415 09026-61411-2 MNA 38 MM 30446 VA 1114
4. *Il barbiere di Siviglia*: Una voce poco fa (Part 2, "Io sono docile")	Rossini	Barbirolli (orch.)	25 May 1935	2-EA-1493-2	8870 DB-2501	GEMM CD 9415 09026-61411-28 MNA 3 MM 30446 VA 1114
5. *Il barbiere di Siviglia*: Dunque io son	Rossini	with de Luca; Pelletier (orch.)	22 March 1940	CS-048405-**1**	17233 (in M-702) CBL-101†	GEMM CD 9415 MNA 38 MM 30446 VA 1114
6. Le beau Danube bleu	J. Strauss, arr. LaForge	F. Blaisdell (fl), Kostelanetz (orch.)	7 March 1939	CS-032923-**1**	15610 (in M-599) DB-3939	GEMM CD 9415 MNA 38 VA 1114
7. Bird Song	LaForge	LaForge (pf)	11 April 1939	BS-027237-1, -**2**, -3	1913	09026-61411-2
8. La capinera	Benedict	F. Blaisdell (fl), Kostelanetz (orch.)	7 March 1939	BS-032920-**1**, -2	1905 (in M-599)	09026-61411-2
9. Chanson de Marie Antoinette	Jacobson	LaForge (pf)	11 April 1939	BS-027238-**1**, -2	1913	09026-61411-2
10. Comment disaient-ils?	Liszt, arr. Ambruster	LaForge (pf)	26 September 1938	BS-027222-1, -**2**	1918 (in M-599) CBL-101†	
11. *Le coq d'or*: Hymne au soleil	Rimsky-Korsakov	Kostelanetz (orch.)	7 March 1940	CS-047778-1, -**2**	17232 (in M-702) CBL-101† VIC-1473†	09026-61411-2 MM 30446

Title	Composer	Conductor or Accompanist	Date Recorded	Matrix Number	American Catalog No.	English Catalog No.	Compact Discs
12. Cupid Captive	LaForge	LaForge (pf)	3 June 1940	BS-051218-**1**	2137		09026-61411-2
13. *Dinorah*: Ombre légère (Part 1)	Meyerbeer	Kostelanetz (orch.)	7 March 1940	CS-047779-**1**, -2	11-8225 CBL-101† VIC-1473†		09026-61411-2 MM 30446
14. *Dinorah*: Ombre légère (Part 2)	Meyerbeer	Kostelanetz (orch.)	7 March 1940	CS-047780-**1**, -2	11-8225 CBL-101† VIC-1473†		09026-61411-2 MM 30446
15. Echo Song (Part 1)	Bishop, arr. LaForge	with Renaissance Quintet, H. Bove (fl)	9 March 1940	BS-047794-1, -**2**	2150 (in M-756) CBL-101†		09026-61411-2
16. Echo Song (Part 2)	Bishop, arr. LaForge	with Renaissance Quintet, H. Bove (fl)	9 March 1940	BS-047795-**1**, -2	2150 (in M-756) CBL-101†		09026-61411-2
17. *L'enlèvement au Serail*: Avec de la tendresse	Mozart	Kostelanetz (orch.)	7 March 1940	BS-047776-**1**	2110 (in M-702) CBL-101† VIC-1473†		MM 30446
18. Estrellita	Ponce	Kostelanetz (orch.)	7 March 1940	BS-047777-**1**	2137 CBL-101†		
19. Les filles de Cadiz	Delibes	LaForge (pf)	28 September 1938	BS-027236-1, -**2**	1997 (in M-599) CBL-101†		
20. *Floridante*: Alma mia	Handel	with Renaissance Quintet	8 March 1940	BS-047789-**1**, -2	2151 (in M-756) CBL-101† VIC-1473†	DA-1800	09026-61411-2
21. *La flûte enchantée*: Ah! je le sais	Mozart	Barbirolli (orch.)	25 May 1935	2-EA-1495-2	8733	DB-2502	GEMM CD 9415 MNA 38 VA 1114

	Composer	Accompaniment	Date	Matrix			Reissues
22. Green (*Aquarelle No. 5, from Ariettes oubliées*)	Debussy	LaForge (pf)	26 September 1938	BS-027223-**1**	1905 (in M-599) CBL-101†		09026-61411-2
23. I Dream Too Much (from *I Dream Too Much*)	Kern	Kostelanetz (orch.)	2 December 1935	BS-98186-1, -**2**	4304	DA-1456	
24. I'm the Echo (from *I Dream Too Much*)	Kern	Kostelanetz (orch.)	2 December 1935	BS-98187-**1**, -2	4304	DA-1456	
25. *Lakmé:* Où va la jeune Hindoue	Delibes	Bourdon (orch.)	26 March 1930 (takes 1–3) and 8 December 1930 (takes 4 & 5)	BVE-59725-1, -2, -3, -**4**, -5	1502 CBL-101† 17-0183* VIC-1473†	DA-1190	GEMM CD 9415 09026-61411-2 MNA 38 MM 30446 VA 1114
26. *Lakmé:* Là-bas, dans la forêt	Delibes	Bourdon (orch.)	26 March 1930 (takes 1 & 2) and 8 December 1930 (takes 3 & 4)	BVE-59726-1, -2, -3, -**4**	1502 CBL-101† LM-1786† LCT-6701† 17-0183* VIC-1473†	DA-1190 CSLP-503†	GEMM CD 9415 09026-61411-2 MNA 38 MM 30446 VA 1114
27. The Last Rose of Summer	Moore	Kostelanetz (orch.)	7 March 1940	CS-047781-**1**, -2	17231 (in M-702)		MET 213
28. Lo! Here the Gentle Lark	Bishop, arr. LaForge	G. Walker (fl), Barbirolli (orch.)	25 May 1935	2-EA-1494-2	8733	DB-2502	GEMM CD 9415 MNA 38 VA 1114
29. *Lucia di Lammermoor:* Ardon gl'incensi	Donizetti	G. Possell (fl), Bourdon (orch.)	8 December 1930	CVE-64393-1, -**2**, -**3**	7369 CBL-101† 17-0190* VIC-1473†	DB-1504	GEMM CD 9415 09026-61411-2 MNA 38 MET 213 MM 30446 VA 1114

Title	Composer	Conductor or Accompanist	Date Recorded	Matrix Number	American Catalog No.	English Catalog No.	Compact Discs
30. *Lucia di Lammermoor:* Spargi d'amaro pianto	Donizetti	Bourdon (orch.)	8 December 1930	CVE-64399-**1**, -**2**	7369 CBL-101† 17-0190* VIC-1473†	DB-1504	GEMM CD 9415 09026-61411-2 MNA 38 MET 213 MM 30446 VA 1114
31. Mandoline	Debussy	LaForge (pf)	26 September 1938	BS-027223-**1**	1905 (in M-599) CBL-101†		09026-61411-2
32. *Mignon:* Je suis Titania	Thomas	Kostelanetz (orch.)	7 March 1940	CS-047782-**1**	17232 (in M-702) CBL-101† VIC-1473†		MET 213 MM 30446
33. Les papillons	Chausson	LaForge (pf)	11 April 1939	BS-027238-**1**, -2	1913		
34. Pastorale (in English)	LaForge	LaForge (pf)	11 April 1939	BS-027237-1, -**2**, -3	1913		
35. *Phoebus et Pan:* Air de Momus	Bach	with Renaissance Quintet	8 March 1940	BS-047788-**1**	2152 (in M-756) CBL-101†		MM 30446
36. Pretty Mocking Bird	Bishop, arr. LaForge	F. Blaisdell (fl), Kostelanetz (orch.)	7 March 1939	CS-032922-1, -**2**	17231 (in M-702)		09026-61411-2
37. Quel ruscelletto	Paradies	with Renaissance Quintet	9 March 1940	BS-047792-**1**, -2	2110 (in M-702)		MM 30446
38. *Rigoletto:* Caro nome	Verdi	Bourdon (orch.)	19 February 1931	CVE-67459-**1**, -**2**, -3	7383 14203 (in M-329) CBL-101† VIC-1473†	DB-1597	GEMM CD 9415 09026-61411-2 MNA 38 MM 30446 VA 1114

	Composer	Accompaniment	Date	Matrix			
39. *Rigoletto*: Tutte le feste	Verdi	Bourdon (orch.)	19 February 1931	CVE-67460-**1**, -2, -**3**	7383 / CBL-101† / VIC-1473†	DB-1597	GEMM CD 9415 / 09026-61411-2 / MNA 38 / MET 213 / MM 30446 / VA 1114
40. *Rigoletto*: Il nome vostro ditemi	Verdi	with de Luca; Pelletier (orch.)	22 March 1940	CS-048199-**1**, -2	17233 (in M-702)		GEMM CD 9415 / 09026-61411-2 / MNA 38 / VA 1114
41. Les roses d'Ispahan	Fauré	LaForge (pf)	28 September 1938	BS-027235-1	1997 (in M-599) / CBL-101†		09026-61411-2
42. Se tu m'ami	Pergolesi	with Renaissance Quintet	8 March 1940	BS-047787-**1**, -2	2152 (in M-756) / CBL-101† / VIC-1473†		MM 30446
43. Une tabatière à musique	Liadoff	LaForge (pf)	26 September 1938	BS-027224-**1**, -2, -3	1918 (in M-599) / CBL-101†		
44. Villanelle	Dell' Acqua	F. Blaisdell (fl), Kostelanetz (orch.)	7 March 1939	CS-032921-1, -**2**	15610 (in M-599) / CBL-101†	DB-3939	GEMM CD 9415 / MNA 38 / VA 1114
45. *Zémire et Azor*: La fauvette avec ses petits (Part 1)	Grétry, arr. LaForge	with Renaissance Quintet, H. Bove (fl)	8 March 1940	BS-047790-**1**	2149 (in M-756) / CBL-101† / VIC-1473†		MM 30446
46. *Zémire et Azor*: La fauvette avec ses petits (Part 2)	Grétry, arr. LaForge	with Renaissance Quintet, H. Bove (fl)	8 March 1940	BS-047791-1, -**2**	2149 (in M-756) / CBL-101† / VIC-1473†		MM 30446

Unpublished Victors

	Composer	Accompaniment	Date	Matrix			
47. *Il barbiere di Siviglia*: Una voce poco fa (Part 1)	Rossini	Bourdon (orch.)	2 March 1931	BVE-67481-1, -2, -3	Unissued		

Title	Composer	Conductor or Accompanist	Date Recorded	Matrix Number	American Catalog No.	English Catalog No.	Compact Discs
48. *Il barbiere di Siviglia:* Una voce poco fa (Part 2, "Il sono docile")	Rossini	Bourdon (orch.)	2 March 1931	BVE-67482-1, -2, -3	Unissued		
49. Come Unto These Yellow Sands	LaForge	LaForge (pf)	3 June 1940	BS-051219-1, -2	Unissued		
50. Dites, que faut-il faire?	anonymous	LaForge (pf)	3 June 1940	BS-051217-1, -2	Unissued		
51. *L'enfant et les sortilèges:* Toi, le coeur de la rose	Ravel	LaForge (pf)	3 June 1940	BS-051215-1	Unissued		
52. Fantoches (*Fêtes galantes* No. 1)	Debussy	LaForge (pf)	3 June 1940	BS-051215-1	Unissued		MET 213
53. *La flûte enchantée:* Air de la reine de la nuit	Mozart	Bourdon (orch.)	26 March 1930	BVE-59727-1	Unissued		
54. I Got Love (from *I Dream Too Much*)	Kern	Kostelanetz (orch.)	2 December 1935	BS-98188-1, -2	Unissued		
55. I Hit a New High (from *Hitting a New High*)	McHugh	Kostelanetz (orch.)	1937	CS-09726-1, -2	Unissued		MET 213
56. Il pleure dans mon coeur (*Ariettes oubliées* No. 2)	Debussy	LaForge (pf)	3 June 1940	BS-051214-1	Unissued		09026-61411-2
57. The Jockey on the Carousel (from *I Dream Too Much*)	Kern	Kostelanetz (orch.)	2 December 1935	BS-98185-1, -2	Unissued		
58. *Lucia di Lammermoor:* Mad Scene	Donizetti	C. Barone (flute)	12 March 1930	CVE-59807-1	Unissued; Pons's "test" record for Victor		

59. La pastorella delle alpi	Rossini, arr. LaForge	LaForge (pf)	26 September 1938	BS-027221-1, -2	Unissued	
60. La promessa	Rossini, arr. LaForge	LaForge (pf)	26 September 1938	BS-027220-1, -2, -3	Unissued	MET 213
61. Villanelle des petits canards	Chabrier	LaForge (pf)	3 June 1940	BS-051216-1	Unissued	

Unpublished French H.M.V.

62. Alleluja	Mozart	LaForge (pf)	3 June 1935	OLA-545-1	Unissued	
63. La capinera	Benedict	LaForge (pf)	3 June 1935	2LA-547-1	Unissued	
64. Gavotte	Popper	LaForge (pf)	3 June 1935	OLA-544-1	Unissued	
65. La rossignol et l'empereur	Longas	LaForge (pf)	3 June 1935	2LA-546-1	Unissued	MM 30446
66. Une tabatière à musique	Liadoff	LaForge (pf)	3 June 1935	OLA-544-1	Unissued	

Part Three: The Columbia Recordings (1941–54)

The American Columbias were released in England on English Columbia (C) and later on Philips (P) and Sony.

A majority of the Columbia recordings were released in the United States in both "manual" and "automatic" sequence. The manual number is listed first in the American catalog-number column since the records were also available as singles in this coupling.

Beginning in 1939, Columbia made all master recordings on 16-inch lacquer discs, at 33⅓ rpm. (Columbia had actually been planning LPs long before they were finally introduced, no doubt delayed by the war.) Of the selections that were recorded, if more than one take was made, one was chosen for production. The approved take was then dubbed onto a 78 master disc, stampers were made, and the records were pressed. Master numbers were assigned only for the 78 pressings of the published take.

Title	Composer	Conductor or Accompanist	Date Recorded	Matrix Number	American Catalog No.	English Catalog No.	Compact Discs
1. A Cupidon (*Chansons de Ronsard*)	Milhaud	Kostelanetz (orch.)	2 April 1947	XCO-37581	72049-D (in M-689) 72053-D (in MM-689) ML-4300† D3M34294	(C) LX-1256	MH2K 60655
2. A des oiseaux	Huë	Kostelanetz (orch.)	1 May 1950	XCO-43394	7644-M (in MM-942) ML-2138† 4-7664-M* (in A-942)	(C) LX-1539	
3. L'amour s'envole	French trad., arr. Weckerlin	Kay (orch.)	14 September 1953	LP-30404	AL-53†		
4. L'amour, toujours l'amour (in English)	Friml	Abravanel (orch.)	21 June 1945	XCO-35028	71698-D ML-2181† 4-73254-D* (in A-1006)		MET 213
5. Apparition	Debussy	LaForge (pf)	25 April 1950	XCO-43357	73035-D (in MM-927) ML-2135†		
6. Après un rêve	Fauré	Abravanel (orch.)	19 September 1946	XCO-36853	72050-D (in M-689) 72051-D (in MM-689) ML-4300† ML-5073†		MM 30446 MPK 45694
7. April in Paris	Duke	Kostelanetz (orch.)	8 May 1946	XCO-36250	71832-D (in M-638) 71835-D (in MM-638) ML-2020† 4-71835-D* (in A-638)		
8. A une fontaine (*Chansons de Ronsard*)	Milhaud	Kostelanetz (orch.)	2 April 1947	XCO-37580	72049-D (in M-689) 72053-D (in MM-689) ML-4300† D3M34294	(C) LX-1256	MH2K 60655

	Composer	Performer	Date	Matrix	Issues		
9. Ave Maria	Bach, arr. Gounod	Cimara (orch.)	30 November 1944	CO-33913	17376-D ML-2181† 4-73251-D* (in A-1006)		
10. Ay, Ay, Ay	Freiere	Kostelanetz (orch.)	20 September 1947	XCO-39104	72462-D (in M-720) 72397-D (in MM-720) ML-4087† 4-72397-D* (in A-720)		
11. *Il barbiere di Siviglia*: Una voce poco fa (Part 1)	Rossini	Kostelanetz (orch.)	11 December 1947	XCO-39602	72519-D (in M-740) 72522-D (ir MM-740) ML-4300† ML-5073† A-1510*	(C) LX-1233 (P) ABE-10133*	MPK 45694
12. *Il barbiere di Siviglia*: Una voce poco fa (Part 2, "Il sono docile")	Rossini	Kostelanetz (orch.)	11 December 1947	XCO-39603	72519-D (ir M-740) 72523-D (ir MM-740) ML-4300† ML-5073† A-1510*	(C) LX-1233 (P) ABE-10133*	MPK 45694
13. Le beau Danube bleu	J. Strauss	J. Baker (fl), Kostelanetz (orch.)	15 September 1947	XCO-39097	72460-D (ir M-720) 72395-D (ir MM-720) ML-4087† ML-5073† 4-72395-D* (in A-720)	(C) LX-1170	MPK 45694
14. Bergère légère	French trad., arr. Weckerlin	Kay (orch.)	14 September 1953	LP-30404	AL-53† A-1884*		
15. Bird Song	LaForge	Kostelanetz (orch.)	27 April 1950	XCO-43380	7663-M (in MM-942) 4-7663-M* in A-942) ML-2138†		
16. Chanson de Marie Antoinette	Jacobson	Kostelanetz (orch.)	8 May 1946	XCO-36252	71833-D (in M-638) 71837-D (in MM-638) ML-2020† 4-71837-D* (in A-638) D3M34294		

Title	Composer	Conductor or Accompanist	Date Recorded	Matrix Number	American Catalog No.	English Catalog No.	Compact Discs
17. Chantons les amours de Jean	French trad., arr. Weckerlin	Kay (orch.)	14 September 1953	LP-30405	AL-53† A-1884*		
18. Chère nuit	Bachelet	Abravanel (orch.)	19 September 1946	XCO-36852	72048-D (in M-689) 72051-D (in MM-689) ML-4300† ML-5073† D3M34294		MPK 45694
19. Clair de lune (*Fêtes galantes* No. 1)	Debussy	LaForge (pf)	21 April 1950	XCO-43352	73035-D (in MM-927) ML-2135†		MH2K 60655
20. *Les contes d'Hoffmann*: Les oiseaux dans la charmille	Offenbach	Kostelanetz (orch.)	11 December 1947	XCO-39604	72520-D (in M-740) 72524-D (in MM-740) ML-4300† D3M34294	(C) LX-1122	MH2K 60655
21. *Conversation Piece* (complete musical play)	Coward	with Coward, Nesbitt, Griffies, Howard, Burton, Evans, Turner, Johnson, Nadell, Faull, and Children's Chorus; Engel (orch.)	22, 25, 26 January 1951	XLP-7368/71	SL-163†		
22. *Le coq d'or*: Hymne au soleil	Rimsky-Korsakov	Kostelanetz (orch.)	11 December 1947	XCO-39605	72520-D (in M-740) 72524-D (in MM-740) ML-4300† D3M34294	(C) LX-1122	MH2K 60655
23. Dancing Doll (in French)	Poldini, arr. LaForge	Kostelanetz (orch.)	31 July 1941	XCO-31323	71307-D (in M-484) ML-4069† 4-71970-D* (in A-484) A-1534*		

	Composer	Conductor	Date	Matrix	Issues		
24. Dieu vous garde (Chansons de Ronsard)	Milhaud	Kostelanetz (orch.)	2 April 1947	XCO-37580	72049-D (in M-689) 72053-D (in MM-689) ML-4300† D3M34294	(C) LX-1256	MH2K 60655
25. Dinorah: Ombre légère (Part 1)	Meyerbeer	Cimara (orch.)	29 January 1942	CO-32381	17315-D (in M-505) 17317-D (in MM-505) ML-4057† ML-5073† D3M34294		MH2K 60655 MPK 45694
26. Dinorah: Ombre légère (Part 2)	Meyerbeer	Cimara (orch.)	29 January 1942	CO-32382	17315-D (in M-505) 17316-D (in MM-505) ML-4057† ML-5073† D3M34294		MH2K 60655 MPK 45694
27. Die Entführung aus dem Serail: Welche Wonne (in French)	Mozart	Walter (orch.)	11 May 1942	CO-32802	17347-D (in M-518) 17349-D (in MM-518) ML-4217† Y31152		
28. Die Entführung aus dem Serail: Ach, ich liebte (in Italian) (Part 1)	Mozart	Walter (orch.)	11 May 1942	CO-32805	17346-D (in M-518) 17350-D (in MM-518) ML-4217† Y31152		
29. Die Entführung aus dem Serail: Ach, ich liebte (in Italian) (Part 2)	Mozart	Walter (orch.)	11 May 1942	CO-32806	17346-D (in M-518) 17350-D (in MM-518) ML-4217† Y31152		
30. Estrellita	Ponce	Kostelaretz (orch.)	15 September 1947	XCO-39098	72460-D (in M-720) 72396-D (in MM-720) ML-4087† ML-5073† 4-72396-D* (in A-720) A-1534*		MPK 45694

Title	Composer	Conductor or Accompanist	Date Recorded	Matrix Number	American Catalog No.	English Catalog No.	Compact Discs
31. Exultate Jubilate: Alleluia	Mozart	Walter (orch.)	11 May 1942	CO-32807	17347-D (in M-518) 17348-D (in MM-518) ML-4217† Y31152		
32. Fantoches (*Fêtes galantes* No. 1)	Debussy	LaForge (pf)	21 April 1950	XCO-43352	73035-D (in MM-927) ML-2135†		MH2K 60655
33. *La fille du régiment:* Chacun le sait	Donizetti	Cimara (orch.)	14 July 1941	XCO-30934	71248-D (in X-206)		MET 213 MH2K 60655
34. *La fille du régiment:* Il faut partir	Donizetti	Cimara (orch.)	14 July 1941	XCO-30935	71248-D (in X-206) D3M34294 (alt. take)		MET 213 MH2K 60655
35. *La fille du régiment:* Et mon coeur va changer	Donizetti	Cimara (orch.)	14 July 1941	XCO-30936	71249-D (in X-206)		MH2K 60655
36. *La fille du régiment:* Salut à la France!	Donizetti	A. Lora (fl), Cimara (orch.)	14 July 1941	XCO-30937	71249-D (in X-206)		MH2K 60655
37. Les filles de Cadiz	Delibes	Kostelanetz (orch.)	15 September 1947	XCO-39100	72463-D (in M-720) 72395-D (in MM-720) ML-4087† ML-5073† 4-72395-D* (in A-720)	(C) LX-1170	MPK 45694
38. *Die Fledermaus* (complete opera; English version by Diatz/Kanin)	J. Strauss	with Weltich, Tucker, Kullman, Lipton, Brownlee, and Metropolitan Opera Chorus; Ormandy (orch.)	24 December 1950– 7 January 1951	XLP-4627/ 30	MOP-32 MOP-4-32* SL-108†		

	Composer	Performer	Date	Matrix	Issue numbers		
39. Fledermaus Fantasy (in French) (Part 1)	J. Strauss, arr. LaForge	Abravanel (orch.)	3 October 1945	XCO-35255	71733-D (in M-606) 71738-D (in MM-606) ML-4061† 4-71738-Dˣ (in A-606)	(C) LX-968	MH2K 60655
40. Fledermaus Fantasy (in French) (Part 2)	J. Strauss, arr. LaForge	J. Baker (fl), Abravanel (orch.)	3 October 1945	XCO-35256	71733-D (in M-606) 71737-D (in MM-606) ML-4061† 4-71737-Dˣ (in A-606)	(C) LX-968	MH2K 60655
41. Green (*Aquarelle* No. 5, from *Ariettes oubliées*)	Debussy	LaForge (pf)	25 April 1950	XCO-43355	73037-D (in MM-927) ML-2135†		
42. Here Beauty Dwells (in Russian)	Rachmaninoff	Kostelanetz	1 May 1950 (orch.)	XCO-43394	7664-M (in MM-942) ML-2138† 4-7664-M* (in A-942) D3M34294	(C) LX-1539	
43. Home Sweet Home	Bishop	Kostelanetz (orch.)	31 July 1941	XCO-31324	71307-D (in M-484) ML-4069† 4-71969-Dˣ (in A-484) D3M34294		MH2K 60655
44. I'll Follow My Secret Heart (from *Conversation Piece*)	Coward	Abravanel (orch.)	3 October 1945	XCO-35254	71732-D (in M-606) 71738-D (in MM-606) ML-4061† 4-71738-Dˣ (in A-606)		
45. I'll See You Again (from *Bittersweet*)	Coward	Kostelanetz (orch.)	5 January 1946	XCO-35594	71732-D (in M-606) 71737-D (in MM-606) ML-4061† 4-71737-Dˣ (in A-606)		
46. L'Invitation au voyage	Duparc	Kostelanetz (orch.)	2 April 1947	XCO-37582	72050-D (in M-689) 72052-D (in MM-689) ML-4300† D3M34294	(C) LX-1209	MH2K 60655

Title	Composer	Conductor or Accompanist	Date Recorded	Matrix Number	American Catalog No.	English Catalog No.	Compact Discs
47. J'attendrai	Poterat	Kostelanetz (orch.)	8 May 1946	XCO-36251	71832-D (in M-638), 71836-D (in MM-638), ML-2020†, 4-71836-D* (in A-638)		
48. Je connais un berger discret	French trad., arr. Weckerlin	Kay (orch.)	14 September 1953	LP-30405	AL-53†, A-1884*		
49. Jeunes fillettes	French trad., arr. Weckerlin	Kay (orch.)	14 September 1953	LP-30405	AL-53†, A-1884*		
50. The Jockey on the Carousel (from *I Dream Too Much*)	Kern	Abravanel (orch.)	21 June 1945	XCO-35027	71698-D, ML-2181†, 4-73252-D* (in A-1006), A-1534*		
51. Kiss Me Again (from *Mlle. Modiste*)	Herbert	Abravanel (orch.)	3 October 1945	XCO-35257	71731-D (in M-606), 71735-D (in MM-606), ML-4061†, 4-71735-D* (in A-606)		MET 213
52. *Lakmé*: Pourquoi dans les grands bois? (Part 1)	Delibes	Cimara (orch.)	29 January 1942	CO-32379	17314-D (in M-505), 17318-D (in MM-505), ML-4057†, D3M34294		MH2K 60655
53. *Lakmé*: Pourquoi dans les grands bois? (Part 2)	Delibes	Cimara (orch.)	29 January 1942	CO-32380	17314-D (in M-505), 17318-D (in MM-505), ML-4057†		MH2K 60655
54. *Lakmé*: Où va la jeune Hindoue (Bell Song, Part 1)	Delibes	Cimara (orch.)	30 November 1944	XCO-33915	71640-D (in M-561), 71973-D (in M-676), 71643-D (in MM-561), 71976-D (in MM-676)	(C) LX-940 (P) ABE-10133*	MH2K 60655, MPK 45694

	Composer	Performers	Date	Matrix	Issues		
55. *Lakmé*: L'étranger la regarde (Bell Song, Part 2)	Delibes	Cimara (orch.)	30 November 1944	XCO-33916	ML-2113† ML-4057† ML-5073† 4-71976-D* (in A-676) A-1510* D3M34294	(C) LX-940 (P) ABE-10133*	MH2K 60655 MPK 45694
56. The Last Rose of Summer	Moore	Kostelanetz (orch.)	15 September 1947	XCO-39099	72463-D (in M-720) 72396-D (in MM-720) ML-4087† 4-72396-D* (in A-720) D3M34294		
57. *Linda di Chamounix*: O luce di quest'arima	Donizetti	Kostelanetz (orch.)	6 October 1949	XCO-41485	72893-D (in MM-876) ML-2084†	(C) LX-1418	MH2K 60655
58. Lisette	French trad., arr. Weckerlin	Kay (orch.)	14 September 1953	LP-30404	AL-53†		
59. Lo! Here the Gentle Lark	Bishop, arr. LaForge	F. Versaci (fl), Kostelanetz (orch.)	21 November 1947	XCO-39392	72752-D ML-2181† 4-73251-D* (in A-1006) D3M34294	(C) LX-1195	
60. Le Loup, La Biche, et le Chevalier	Salvadore	with Norman Paris Trio	2 September 1953	CO-49993	40176-D 4-40176-D*		

Title	Composer	Conductor or Accompanist	Date Recorded	Matrix Number	American Catalog No.	English Catalog No.	Compact Discs
61. *Lucia di Lammermoor* (complete opera)	Donizetti	with Tucker, Guarrera, Votipka, Hayward, McCracken, Scott, and the Metropolitan Opera Chorus; Cleva (orch.)	20–26 January 1954, 1 February 1954	XLP-31730/3	SL-127†	(P) 01161/2†	
62. *Lucia di Lammermoor*: Regnava nel silenzio	Donizetti	Cimara (orch.)	29 January 1942	CO-32377[1]	17313-D (in M-505) 17316-D (in MM-505) ML-4057† D3M34294		MH2K 60655
63. *Lucia di Lammermoor*: Quando rapito in estasi	Donizetti	Cimara (orch.)	29 January 1942	CO-32378	17313-D (in M-505) 17317-D (in MM-505) ML-4057† D3M34294		MH2K 60655
64. *Lucia di Lammermoor*: Il dolce suono	Donizetti	Cimara (orch.)	30 November 1944	XCO-33917	71641-D (in M-561) 71645-D (in MM-561) ML-4057† D3M34294		MH2K 60655
65. *Lucia di Lammermoor*: Sparsa e di rose!	Donizetti	Cimara (orch.)	30 November 1944	XCO-33918	71641-D (in M-561) 71645-D (in MM-561) ML-4057† D3M34294		MM 30446 MH2K 60655
66. *Lucia di Lammermoor*: Del ciel clemente	Donizetti	F. Versaci (fl), Cimara (orch.)	30 November 1944	XCO-33919	71642-D (in M-561) 71644-D (in MM-561) ML-4057† D3M34294		MH2K 60655

[1] A test pressing of take number 2 exists for this recording of "Regnava nel silenzio" from *Lucia*, on which Pons wrote "No, no. Kill."

	Composer	Performer	Date	Matrix	Issue numbers	
67. *Lucia di Lammermoor*: Spargi d'amaro pianto	Donizetti	Cimara (orch.)	30 November 1944	XCO-33920	71642-D (in M-561) / 71643-D (in MM-561) / ML-4057† / D3M34294	MH2K 60655
68. Mamar dites-moi	French trad., arr. Weckerlin	Kay (orch.)	14 September 1953	LP-30404	AL-53† / A-1884*	
69. Mandoline	Debussy	LaForge (pf)	21 April 1950	XCO-43354	73037-D (in MM-927) / ML-2135†	
70. La Marseillaise	De L'Isle	Kostelanetz (orch.)	8 May 1946	XCO-36251	71832-D (in M-638) / 71836-D (in MM-638) / ML-2020† / 4-71836-D* (in A-638) / Y31152	
71. Menuet d'exaudet	French trad., arr. Weckerlin	Kay (orch.)	14 September 1953	LP-30405	AL-53† / A-1884*	
72. *Mignon*: Je suis Titania	Thomas	Kostelanetz (orch.)	23 April 1949	XCO-41200	72892-D (in MM-876) / ML-2084† / ML-5073†	(C) LX-1514 / (P) SBF-198 / MH2K 60655 / MPK 45694
73. Mimosa	Plante-Giraud	with Norman Paris Trio	2 September 1953	CO-49991	40176-D / 4-40176-D*	
74. *Mireille*: O légère hirondelle	Gounod	Kostelanetz (orch.)	5 January 1946	XCO-35596	71734-D (in M-606) / 71735-D (in MM-606) / ML-4061† / 4-71735-D* (in A-606)	(C) LX-1067 / MH2K 60655
75. Non, je ne crois pas	French trad., arr. Weckerlin	Kay (orch.)	14 September 1953	LP-30405	AL-53†	
76. Non, je n'irai plus au bois	French trad., arr. Weckerlin	Kay (orch.)	14 September 1953	LP-30404	AL-53† / A-1884*	

Title	Composer	Conductor or Accompanist	Date Recorded	Matrix Number	American Catalog No.	English Catalog No.	Compact Discs
77. *Le nozze di Figaro*: Voi che sapete (in French)	Mozart	Walter (orch.)	11 May 1942	CO-32803	17345-D (in M-518) 17349-D (in MM-518) ML-4217† Y31152		
78. Nuit d'Etoiles	Debussy	LaForge (pf)	21 April 1950	XCO-43353	73036-D (in MM-927) ML-2135†		
79. Oh, Cease Thy Singing, Maiden Fair (in French)	Rachmaninoff	B. Greenhouse (cello), Kostelanetz (orch.)	1 May 1950	XCO-43396	7665-M (in MM-942) ML-2138† ML-5073† 4-7665-M* (in A-942) D3M34294		MPK 45694
80. Parlez-moi d'amour	Lenoir	Kostelanetz (orch.)	15 May 1946	XCO-36601	71833-D (in M-638) 71837-D (in MM-638) ML-2020† 4-71837-D* (in A-638)		
81. La pastorella delle alpi	Rossini	Kostelanetz (orch.)	27 April 1950	XCO-43380	7663-M (in MM-942) ML-2138† 4-7663-M* (in A-942)		
82. *La perle du Brésil*: Charmant oiseau (Part 1)	David	J. Baker (fl), Abravanel (orch.)	21 June 1945	CO-35014	17372-D (in M-582) 17374-D (in MM-582) ML-4217† AAL-14† D3M34294		
83. *La perle du Brésil*: Charmant oiseau (Part 2)	David	J. Baker (fl), Abravanel (orch.)	21 June 1945	CO-35015	17372-D (in M-582) 17373-D (in MM-582) ML-4217† AAL-14† D3M34294		
84. Pierrot	Debussy	LaForge (pf)	25 April 1950	XCO-43356	73036-D (in MM-927) ML-2135†		

	Composer	Performer	Date	Matrix	Catalog	Release
85. Pizzicato Ballerina	Delibes, arr. LaForge	Kostelanetz (orch.)	8 May 1946	XCO-36252	71833-D (in M-638) 71837-D (in MM-638) ML-2020† 4-71837-D* (in A-638) A-1534*	(C) LX-1539 MH2K 60655
86. Plaisir d'amour	Martini	Kostelanetz (orch.)	1 May 1950	XCO-43395	7664-M (in MM-942) ML-2138† 4-7664-M* (in A-942)	
87. Il pleure dans mon coeur (*Ariettes oubliées* No. 2)	Debussy	LaForge (pf)	21 April 1950	XCO-43354	73037-D (in MM-927) ML-2135†	
88. *Porgy and Bess*: Summertime	Gershwin	Kostelanetz (orch.)	31 July 1941	XCO-31326	71491-D	MH2K 60655
89. Pretty Mocking Bird	Bishop, arr. LaForge	Kostelanetz (orch.)	27 April 1950	XCO-43379	7665-M (in MM-942) ML-2138† 4-7665-M* (in A-942) D3M34294	
90. *I puritani*: Son vergin vezzosa	Bellini	Kostelanetz (orch.)	23 April 1949	XCO-41202	72894-D (in MM-876) ML-2084† ML-5073†	(C) LX-1514 MH2K 60655 MPK 45694
91. *Il re pastore*: L'amerò, sarò costante (Part 1)	Mozart	H. Piastro (vl), Walter (orch.)	11 May 1942	XCO-32808	71696-D ML-4217† Y31152	
92. *Il re pastore*: L'amerò, sarò costante (Part 2)	Mozart	H. Piastro (vl), Walter (orch.)	11 May 1942	XCO-32809	71696-D ML-4217† Y31152	
93. *Rigoletto*: Caro nome (Part 1)	Verdi	Cimara (orch.)	30 November 1944	CO-33909	17370-D (in M-582) 17373-D (in MM-582) ML-2084†	MH2K 60655
94. *Rigoletto*: Caro nome (Part 2)	Verdi	Cimara (orch.)	30 November 1944	CO-33910	17370-D (in M-582) 17374-D (in MM-582) ML-2084†	MH2K 60655

Title	Composer	Conductor or Accompanist	Date Recorded	Matrix Number	American Catalog No.	English Catalog No.	Compact Discs
95. *Rigoletto*: Tutte le feste al tempio	Verdi	Kostelanetz (orch.)	23 April 1949	XCO-41201	72894-D (in MM-876) ML-2084† ML-5073† D3M34294	(C) LX-1418 (P) SBF-198*	MPK 45694
96. Romance	Debussy	LaForge (pf)	21 April 1950	XCO-43353	73036-D (in MM-927) ML-2135†		
97. *Roméo et Juliette*: Je veux vivre dans ce rêve (Valse)	Gounod	Kostelanetz (orch.)	5 January 1946	XCO-35597	71734-D (in M-606) 71736-D (in MM-606) ML-4061† 4-71736-D* (in A-606)	(C) LX-1067	MH2K 60655
98. Rondel Chinois	Debussy	LaForge (pf)	21 April 1950	XCO-43356	73036-D (in MM-927) ML-2135†		
99. The Rose and the Nightingale, Op. 2, No. 2 (in Russian)	Rimsky-Korsakov	Kostelanetz (orch.)	21 November 1947	XCO-39394	72753-D ML-2181† 4-73254-D* (in A-1006) D3M34294		
100. Les roses d'Ispahan	Fauré	Abravanel (orch.)	19 September 1946	XCO-36854	72048-D (in M-689) 72052-D (in MM-689) ML-4300† D3M34294		MH2K 60655
101. The Russian Nightingale	Alabiev, arr. LaForge	Kostelanetz (orch.)	31 July 1941	XCO-31327	71305-D (in M-484) ML-4069† 4-71972-D* (in A-484)		MH2K 60655
102. *Sadko*: Song of India (in French)	Rimsky-Korsakov	Kostelanetz (orch.)	31 July 1941	XCO-31325	71305-D (in M-484) ML-4069† 4-71971-D* (in A-484) D3M34294		MH2K 60655
103. *La sonnambula*: Ah, non credea mirarti	Bellini	Kostelanetz (orch.)	6 October 1949	XCO-41486	72893-D (in MM-876) ML-2084†	(C) LX-1259	MH2K 60655

104. *La sonnambula*: Ah, non giunge	Bellini	Kostelanetz (orch.)	6 October 1949	XCO-41487	72892-D (in MM-876) ML-2084†	(C) LX-1259	MH2K 60655
105. *Tais-toi, babillarde* (*Chansons de Ronsard*)	Milhaud (orch.)		2 April 1947	XCO-37581	72049-D (in M-689) 72053-D (in MM-689) ML-4300† D3M34294	(C) LX-1256	MH2K 60655
106. Tales from the Vienna Woods (in Italian)	J. Strauss, arr. LaForge	Kostelanetz (orch.)	27 April 1950	XCO-43378	7663-M (in MM-942) ML-2138† 4-7663-M* (in A-942)	(C) LX-1462	
107. Tell Me That You Love Me Tonight	Bixio	Kostelanetz (orch.)	5 January 1946	XCO-35595	71731-D (in M-606) 71736-D (in MM-606) ML-4061† 4-71736-D* (in A-606)		
108. Theme and Variations (in Italian) (Part 1)	Proch	F. Versaci (fl), Cimara (orch.)	30 November 1944	CO-33911	17371-D (in M-582) 17375-D (in MM-582) AAL-14† ML-4217† D3M34294		
109. Theme and Variations (in Italian) (Part 2)	Proch	F. Versaci (fl), Cimara (orch.)	30 November 1944	CO-33912	17371-D (in M-582) 17375-D (in MM-582) AAL-14† ML-4217† D3M34294		
110. Think on Me	Scott	Cimara (orch.)	30 November 1944	CO-33914	17376-D ML-2181† 4-73253-D* (in A-1006)		
111. *Timbre d'argent*: Le bonheur est une chose légère	Saint-Saëns	Kostelanetz (orch.)	20 September 1947	XCO-39103	72462-D (in M-720) 72398-D (in MM-720) ML-4087† 4-72398-D* (in A-720) D3M34294		

Title	Composer	Conductor or Accompanist	Date Recorded	Matrix Number	American Catalog No.	English Catalog No.	Compact Discs
112. *La traviata*: Ah, fors'è lui	Verdi	Kostelanetz (orch.)	15 May 1946	XCO-36302	71834-D (in M-638) 71836-D (in MM-638) ML-2020† 4-71836-D* (in A-638) D3M34294	(C) LX-1017	MH2K 60655
113. *La traviata*: Sempre libera	Verdi	Kostelanetz (orch.)	15 May 1946	XCO-36303	71834-D (in M-638) 71835-D (in MM-638) ML-2020† 4-71835-D* (in A-638) D3M34294	(C) LX-1017	MH2K 60655
114. Variations on "Ah vous dirai-je maman" (Part 1)	Mozart, arr. LaForge	Kostelanetz (orch.)	19 December 1947	XCO-39689	72754-D ML-4217† Y31152		
115. Variations on "Ah vous dirai-je maman" (Part 2)	Mozart, arr. LaForge	Kostelanetz (orch.)	19 December 1947	XCO-39690	72754-D ML-4217† Y31152		
116. Villanelle	Dell' Acqua	Kostelanetz (orch.)	21 November 1947	XCO-39391	72752-D ML-2181† 4-73252-D* (in A-1006) D3M34294	(C) LX-1195	
117. Vocalise, Op. 34, No. 14	Rachmaninoff	Kostelanetz (orch.)	21 November 1947	XCO-39393	72753-D ML-2181† 4-73253-D* (in A-1006) D3M34294	(C) LX-1209	
118. Voce di primavera, Op. 410 (in French) (Part 1)	J. Strauss	Kostelanetz (orch.)	20 September 1947	XCO-39101	72461-D (in M-720) 72397-D (in MM-720) ML-4087† 4-72397-D* (in A-720)	(C) LX-1087	

119. Voce di primavera. Op. 410 (in French) (Part 2)	J. Strauss	J. Baker (fl), Kostelanetz (orch.)	20 September 1947	XCO-39102	72461-D (in M-720) 72398-D (in MM-720) ML-4087† 4-72398-D* (in A-720)	(C) LX-1087
120. Voici que le printemps	Debussy	LaForge (pf)	21 April 1950	XCO-43355	73037-D (in MM-927) ML-2135†	
121. Die Zauberflöte: Der Hölle Rache (in French)	Mozart	Walter (orch.)	11 May 1942	CO-32804	17345-D (in M-518) 17348-D (in MM-518) ML-4217†	
122. Zémire et Azor: La fauvette avec ses petits (Part 1)	Grétry, arr. LaForge	F. Versaci (fl), Kostelanetz (orch.)	19 December 1947	XCO-39687	72521-D (in M-740) 72523-D (in MM-740) ML-4300† D3M34294	(C) LX-1152 MH2K 60655
123. Zémire et Azor: La fauvette avec ses petits (Part 2)	Grétry, arr. LaForge	F. Versaci (fl), Kostelanetz (orch.)	19 December 1947	XCO-39688	72521-D (in M-740) 72522-D (in MM-740) ML-4300† D3M34294	(C) LX-1152 MH2K 60655

Lily Pons on Compact Disc

Lily Pons, Pearl/Pavilion Records Ltd. (GEMM CD 9415)

Lily Pons: Donizetti - Verdi - Debussy - Rossini - Delibes, RCA Victor/BMG Classics (09026-61411-1)

Lily Pons: Greatest Hits on Records (1928–1939), Minerva (MNA 38)

Lily Pons: Portraits in Memory, Metropolitan Opera Guild (MET 213)

Lily Pons: Reine du contre-fa, Music Memoria (MM 30446)

Lily Pons: The HMV, Parlophone and Argentine Victor Recordings, 1928–1939, Enterprise Vocal Archives (VA 1114)

Lily Pons: The Odeon Recordings, 1928–1929, VAI Audio (VAIA 1125)

A Lily Pons Recital, Sony Classical (MH2K 60655)

Recital Lily Pons, Sony/CBS (MPK 45694)

Several of Pons's opera performances were recorded from radio broadcasts and are available on compact disc, including the following:

La fille du régiment, Metropolitan Opera, 28 December 1940, with Baccaloni, Jobin, and Petina, conducted by Papi. (Naxos Historical 8.110018-9)

Lakmé, Metropolitan Opera, 6 January 1940, with Tokatyan, Petina, Pinza, Cehanovsky, Massue, Dickey, Browning, and Olheim, conducted by Pelletier. (Walhall WHL 17)

Lucia di Lammermoor, Metropolitan Opera, 27 February 1937, with Jagel, Brownlee, Votipka, and Pinza, conducted by Papi. (The Forties FT 1511-12)

Lucia di Lammermoor, Metropolitan Opera, 8 January 1944, with Melton, Warren, Moscona, and Votipka, conducted by Sodero. (The Forties Radio FTO 323-324)

Lucia di Lammermoor (abridged), Mexico City, 22 June 1947, with Tagliavini, Petroff, Silva, and Feuss, plus chorus and orchestra, conducted by Cellini. (Grand Tier ENGT-CD-#6/94)

Rigoletto, Metropolitan Opera, 28 December 1935, with Tibbett, Jagel, Lazzari, and Olheim, conducted by Panizza. (Naxos Historical 8.110020-1)

Rigoletto, Metropolitan Opera, 11 March 1939, with Kiepura, Tibbett, Lazzari, Olheim, and Cordon, conducted by Papi. Also included on the disc are "filler" arias and duets from the 14 January 1956 Met production of *Lucia di Lammermoor* (with Peerce and Votipka, and Cleva conducting): "Regnava nel silenzio," "Quando rapito in estasi," "Sulla tomba che rinserra," "Qui di sposa eterna fede," "Verrano a te sull'aure," "Il dolce suono," "Ardon gl'incesi," and "Spargi d'amaro pianto." (MYTO 2 MCD 921.56)

Index

The entry "Lily Pons" does not appear in this index. Contributing authors are listed only where referenced in other sources.